Nuns

Disappearing Suns

Travel tales of adventure, humour and discovery

by

Sue Mowforth and Jeannette Ellwood

Cover artists: Annette Miller & Joss Mowforth

ISBN 978-1-78792-080-4

Book production management by Into Print
www.intoprint.net
+44 (0)1604 832149

Authors' Note

Our tales are taken from photos, notes and memories of real happenings, real people in real settings. They all sprang into glorious colour as we relived and wrote about our adventures in various parts of the world. We hope we'll be forgiven for any dramatic enhancement or errors of memory we made in the retelling. They are entirely our responsibility – please put them down to the imperfect recollections of our senior years.

Sue Mowforth and Jeannette Ellwood
Summer 2024, England

Contents

Sue's Stories

Jeannette's Stories

Introduction

We are two ordinary English women who were recently introduced to each other by one of Jeannette's ex-colleagues from their teaching days at an asylum for the mentally challenged. We discovered we had a shared love for unusual wanderings.

During our often unorthodox travels around the world we've enjoyed some rollicking experiences, some amusing, some scary.

For today's traveller the planet has changed drastically since we first set out on our adventures. Places we once freely explored are now engulfed in war, tourists now lounge on sunbeds where we found hotbeds of conflict, and where those at home thought we must be fearless or just plain 'mad' to venture, we found unexpected knowledge and lasting friendships.

Ours is a wonderful world to explore. You don't need oodles of money, a travel company's itinerary, or the security of travelling companions. With a bit of common sense the world is waiting for you.

This book recounts the stories of some of our exploits. We hope you enjoy reading them, and that our tales inspire you to plunge into some adventures of your own.

Sue Mowforth and Jeannette Ellwood.

Sue's Stories

Sue's Introduction

Over the Hill

A small girl is trudging up a stony, heather-clad hillside. She is seven or eight. Tendrils of mousy-coloured hair escape from the clasp her mother had attempted to pin it back with earlier that day. She pushes the annoying strands out of her eyes which are fixed on the top of the hill, and rushes up the last few yards to the summit.

Only it isn't the summit. Open moorland stretches into the windswept distance, while the track climbs up to the next rise.

Disappointed, she trudges on, eyes focused on where the track disappears over the top of the next hill, which she is convinced will be the real summit.

That little girl was me.

Every Sunday, when I was young, our parents would pack the rucksack with sandwiches and macs, and with my two brothers we'd catch the bus or train out of Sheffield and head for the moors. No matter what the weather.

Oh, how I loved the feeling of space up there.

Huge horizons, fresh air and a track that disappeared over the hill. That's where I always wanted to be – a bit further on, just over the next hill...

And I've been lucky in that throughout my whole life I've been able to wander pretty much wherever I wanted. You can't beat having a British passport. Couple that with a robust constitution, the ability to speak English, and a smile, and you would be welcomed almost anywhere.

I first dipped my toes abroad in the 1960s on camping trips to France and the Alps with family and school. Then at university I became a bit braver – a potholing expedition to Greece, followed by a mega hitchhike to Kathmandu.

Wow, travel was cheap if you were prepared to sleep rough and go hungry!

My first proper job was teaching in Sudan; knowing my urge to explore the world, my family didn't comment.

But then came the wanderlust constraints of marriage, children and a demanding career as an air traffic controller. Opportunities to travel were limited during those years.

On retiring, I found myself with no pressing responsibilities. I was free. The travel bug had never left me, but where and how was I to start?

By accepting a range of opportunities I've found ways to do a great deal of wandering. One trip has often led to another.

Experiencing life in different countries has brought me intense happiness as well as heartache, and I'd like to pass some of these experiences on to family, friends and anyone who is interested in how an ordinary traveller like me can roam around the world. And the sort of experiences they might encounter.

Although my shelves now contain notebooks full of hastily scribbled travelogues, I've been faced with a dilemma. How was I to select which stories to tell for a book like this? The scary ones, the happy ones, the ones which taught me most about life or the ones which made me spitting angry?

This selection mainly contains tales from the Middle East, Africa and India.

They are all quite different.

Hitch-hike to the Gods

1968

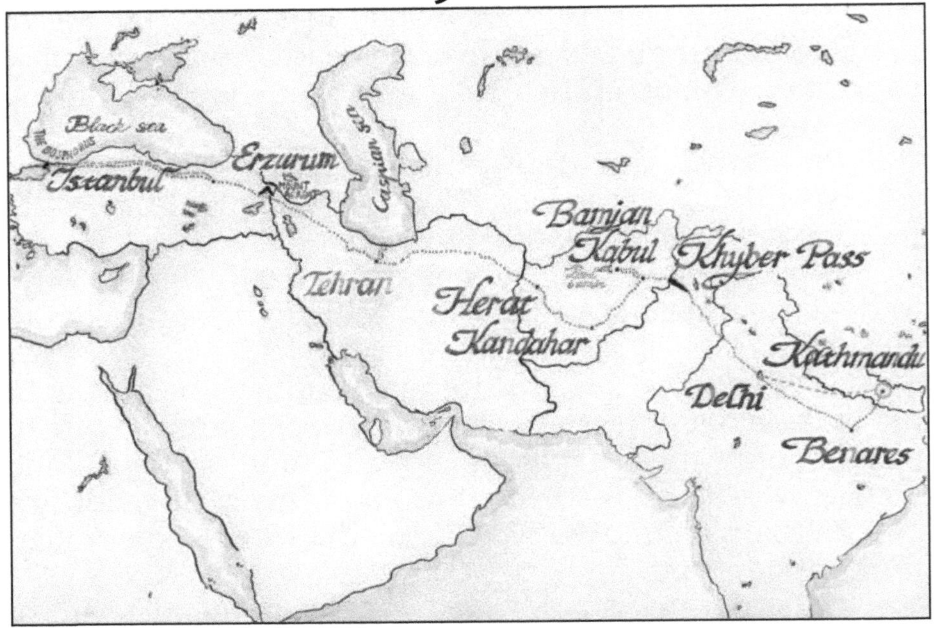

A map showing the Hippie Trail.

Myself, Kemal and Suleyman beside their wool lorry, Turkey.

Contemplating the beauty of Band-e-Amir in Afghanistan.

With a water buffalo in Delhi.

In 1968, aged just twenty, I hitch-hiked to Kathmandu and back. I didn't intend to – it just sort of happened.

Studying for a degree in Geography was as close as I could get to exploring the world. But learning about foreign places isn't the same as going there, which is what I really wanted to do.

During my first year at university I joined a potholing expedition to Greece solely for the purpose of travelling as far as possible during the long summer vacation. But the following summer there were absolutely no expeditions going anywhere interesting. So, in desperation, I asked a fellow student, Gerry, to accompany me to Istanbul.

Hitch-hiking in the 1960s was a fairly normal way for students to travel. It wasn't thought of as particularly risky or difficult in the way that it is today. I often used to hitchhike on my own from our family home just outside Reading, to university in London and back. I met some kind and really interesting people that way.

My dad, bless him, lent me £100 to get to Istanbul and back. Though thinking back, I'm not sure I ever repaid him... Anyway, armed with Dad's old rucksack and sleeping bag, I set off from home on July 6th, met up in London with Gerry, and was soon clambering aboard the Ostend ferry. Gerry was a short, wiry young man with sandy hair, who treated me like an annoying younger sister. He assumed the role of leadership, and I was quite content to let him take care of our money and negotiate the lifts.

It took us a week to hitch down through Europe to Istanbul. We were caught in a cloudburst in Germany and got ever so slightly drenched to the skin. Gerry never quite recovered from this exposure to the elements, and was still coughing and snuffling when we returned three months later.

Crossing the barrier of the Austrian Alps, the sun began to beat hotter and hotter. We were lucky with lifts and were soon bouncing and jogging our way through Yugoslavia and Bulgaria between fields of golden sunflowers and ripening maize, past farmers toiling in the fields in faded blue overalls. In Bulgaria we were given a lift by a man who spoke a few words of English. He insisted on taking us to meet his family in Plovdiv and they invited us to stay the night.

Bulgaria was under tight communist rule, so his family bombarded us with questions about life in the West. I hadn't realised how they were starved of information and promised to post them a bundle of magazines when I returned home. But I don't think the papers and magazines ever arrived because I never heard back from him.

An air-conditioned coach stopped for us the next day. It was on its way to pick up tourists in Istanbul. We sprawled out on the luxurious rear seats as we swept across the arid wastes of Turkey and were deposited at a swish seaside resort some distance outside Istanbul. The driver and his wife disappeared into a five-star hotel. We unrolled our sleeping bags on the pebbly beach. Next morning, another lift, and we were soon soaring through the massive outer walls and into the jumble and confusion of the city. I remember feeling a tingle of excitement and exhilaration.

I had made it to Istanbul – gateway to the Orient!

We booked in at a tiny 'hole in the wall'. The poster outside advertised all facilities – clean linen, flush toilets, showers and washbasins on every landing. Unfortunately they omitted to mention that they didn't supply the water as well, and my 'clean linen sheets' turned out to be a very small tablecloth. Still, for the equivalent of a few pence a night I suppose we couldn't complain. In order to wash we took to swimming in the Bosphorus, skillfully negotiating a passage between the garbage floating out to sea and the harbour ooze floating in.

I stood on the foreshore gazing across the stretch of water to the far side. There was no bridge in those days. Asia was just a short ferry ride away.

'Right, this is where we part company,' said Gerry adamantly. 'I want to go a bit further but you're going back home now. I only said I'd accompany you to Istanbul.'

I feigned disbelief. 'But Gerry, you can't possibly leave me here. If you're going on, then so am I.'

'Nope. No way. It's too dangerous. I'm not taking responsibility for you to go any further!' and he stomped off.

But, with Asia just on the far side of the Bosphorus, there was no way I was going to turn back. Begrudgingly, he eventually agreed to let me go with him, which is perhaps just as well, because the first lift we hitched on the Asian side turned out to be going the wrong way.

'Er, I think this lorry is heading north,' I ventured after a couple of hours. 'Get the map out and ask the driver again.' So our first day in Asia was wasted as we retraced our steps.

'See, I can be quite useful,' I teased Gerry, who just grunted.

Eventually we were picked up by two men in an exceedingly ancient lorry carrying sacks of wool. Kemal was the driver, a large Turk with a nasty temper who bossed his rather weedy assistant called Suleyman unmercifully, slapping him round the head with every other instruction. It was hugely embarrassing. We spent three gruelling days and two nights with them as the lorry crawled its way over the mountains of central Turkey.

On the third day – a good day for miracles in this part of the world – Suleyman was refuelling the lorry at a filling station. Kemal had wandered off to a café to eat his lunch and I was sitting on a rock in the garage forecourt when three Land Rovers swept into the petrol station.

English accents! I rose from the dust and asked sweetly if they were heading towards Tehran.

Surprised eyes swivelled in my direction. They turned out to be a group of British Grenadier Guards heading for the Trucial States. Gerry and I were invited to join them, and we sped away from the wool lorry rejoicing in our good luck.

The Guards looked after me as if I was royalty, bringing me a morning cup of tea as I emerged from my sleeping bag, and inviting us to their meals. We were really sorry when our routes diverged; they were heading south and we continued eastwards out of Turkey to the Iranian border.

A few miles further on, two German ex-police wagons stopped to pick us up. On board was a group of young men who were towing a generator which they hoped to sell in India, thereby paying for their trip. One of the main drivers was called Klaus. Although still in his twenties, he was a mountain of a man with a hearty laugh that erupted periodically like a rolling thunderclap. He let me sit in the passenger seat whenever he was driving, attempting to chat by bellowing in broken English above the grind of the engine. They were a really cheerful, well-organised bunch of Germans, the only downside to travelling with them was the pall of diesel fumes which accompanied each vehicle.

But I was impressed by their laundry arrangements – a big milk churn attached by springs to the rear of one of the vehicles. Dirty clothes, water and washing powder went in each morning, and having bounced around all day, cleaned clothes came out in the evening to be rinsed and dried overnight. Magic!

'Zat is Mount Ararat!' roared Klaus, pointing to a distant cone-shaped mountain.

'Wow! Really?' I exclaimed. For a geography student I was woefully ignorant of the landscape we were travelling through. 'Gosh. Amazing. I had no idea Mount Ararat was round here.'

We spent a couple of hours at the Turkish-Iranian border post, waiting for documents to be read and stamped, then continued on towards Tehran. The Germans knew of a campsite in the outskirts of Tehran which had the unbelievable luxury of sit-down toilets and a swimming pool.

It was necessary to get visas in order to enter Afghanistan, so a small group of us went into town to various embassies. A crowd of angry people were holding a protest outside the British Embassy gates, and the security guards advised us to disappear and return discreetly to collect the visas a few days later. I'm not sure what the protest was about but it was obvious that the crowd didn't like the British. I felt quite intimidated and was glad to get back to the campsite.

'You vant come vis us to see ze Caspian?' asked Klaus when we were back at the campsite. 'Might as vell while you vait for visas.' So Gerry and I accompanied the Germans north over the mountains, past a huge hydro-electric dam and reservoir to the edge of the Caspian Sea. Here I saw acres of irrigated cotton fields – the first time I'd ever seen cotton growing – with the blue-grey haze of the inland sea shimmering in the distance.

We returned to the Embassy, and armed with passports safely stamped with new visas, were invited to continue in the police wagons eastwards through Iran towards Mashhad. Here the road was unmetalled, mile after mile of compacted dust and gravel. Unless a vehicle slows to a walking pace it's impossible to avoid the bone-shaking vibration of driving over these corrugated surfaces. So, we bumped and shook our way along the dusty desert roads, breathing in the beauty of the scenery through a fog of diesel fumes.

Sitting in the open front of the wagon, my face, hair and clothes were soon covered in a black greasy veneer. But, who cared! I was bowling along, further and further east, through deserts and hills, past people and landscapes I'd only ever seen before in the pages of the *National Geographic.*

I was in heaven!

The land was bone dry. The road seemed to follow a wide, flat-bottomed valley with steep hillsides barely visible in the distance. Occasionally a few trees and a splash of green indicated a watercourse and a village, but otherwise the landscape was grey and gritty.

The border post between Iran and Afghanistan took us a whole day to pass through. Getting out of Iran was easy enough, then there were several miles of no man's land before arriving at the desperately lonely cluster of concrete huts that represented the Afghan border. I wondered what terrible misdemeanours the officials had done to get posted out here!

But there was no one there.

We knocked on the locked door. No answer. We tried to peer in through the dusty window. Total blackness. There was no question of just ignoring the border post as we knew we wouldn't be able to leave Afghanistan without an entry stamp in our passports, so we prepared for a long wait.

After several hours a man turned up. I've no idea where he appeared from as I was asleep. He collected our passports and disappeared. We waited again. The Germans were getting worried by the delay, as it was a long drive to the nearest town and they wanted to be there before night fell.

Eventually, with passports stamped by a grumpy official, we were speeding along the corrugated track of a road again as the sun set behind us. The night was pitch black, with only the pinpricks of stars providing any light.

Suddenly the leading wagon jammed its brakes on and came to a dusty stop. It was the first of a series of local tolls. Men from the nearby village, its high mud-brick walls preventing any flicker of light escaping, had placed long poles across the road. Lanterns and rifles swinging, they demanded payment for crossing their land. The Germans were quite unprepared for this, and a lengthy argument started. Eventually it was decided to pay part of what was demanded, and we were waved on.

A few miles further on, the same thing happened again.

At the third toll the Germans decided on a different course of action. Instead of stopping, they accelerated straight through the barrier. There were yells of anger as we passed, but no shots were fired. Gerry and I rolled into Herat later that evening and stayed just long enough to wolf down bowls of yoghurt and some greasy mutton, and to drool over the fox, deer, tiger and leopard skins that were brought to our tables. Klaus bought a stylish fox-skin hat for his girlfriend back home. As the night air was chilly in the open-topped wagons, he insisted I wear it to keep my ears warm. Nice man!

The direct route from Herat to Kabul lay east, through the mountains. However, there was no proper road, and as well as the probability of getting lost, there were dangers of rockfalls, bandits and wild animals. We were strongly advised to head in a big loop to the south via Kandahar. Somewhere along the route we pulled up in a broken-down sort of village. It was difficult to tell if it was abandoned or just in a bad state of repair. The map was consulted and compared with the mileometers and then it was announced that this was the village.

'What village?' I asked.

'Zat tower!' said one of the Germans, pointing to a tall, round, minaret-like structure. 'It vas built to contain ze heads of ze defeated. Zere are many such skull towers in zis country,' and he proceeded to give us a potted history of the waves of armies that had swept back and forth over Central Asia. These towers, filled with the heads of the defeated and the massacred, must have been intended as a deterrent against rebellion, but what an awful fate for the losing side!

It all sounded very gruesome.

In Kandahar I lost my ring. Before I left home, someone had advised me to wear a simple ring on my right hand to pretend I was married. Apparently, no respectable single woman could travel without her husband or father in places such as Istanbul (and beyond). My 'status' had been questioned a number of times, especially in Turkey, and the ring had helped convince curious Turks that I was 'of good repute'. Unfortunately, in Kandahar we had been invited into a house to look at some semi-precious stones spread out on a cloth on the floor. There were also some items of jewellery and I was persuaded to try on a few of the rings. Suddenly I heard Klaus out in the street yelling,

'Snell, snell. Quick, we go!' and, leaving the pretty stones, I scrambled to my feet and rushed back to the wagons. It was only later that day, and many miles further along the dusty road to Kabul, that I realised I'd left my ring behind.

I wonder who is wearing it today...?

A week after leaving Tehran we roared into Kabul, drawing up outside one of the last strongholds of British Imperialism – The Khyber Restaurant. After correlating the price-list with our diminishing resources, we settled for ice cream, commonly known in Kabul as 'deep frozen dysentery' though miraculously Gerry and I managed to avoid any mishaps.

We all sat and relaxed for a while, relieved to be in an illusion of western civilisation. Most men wore traditional loose outfits, but some were in suits. Women wandered past in heels and western-style clothing. If you didn't look too closely it could have been Europe.

But Kabul was a strange city, half colonial, half shanty. The Khyber River (really a euphemism for Khyber Sewer) slid its way through the centre. The stench was unbelievable; but what amazed me most was the way the local children splashed and bathed in it. No wonder cholera was king in Kabul. What I found more upsetting were the beggars. I hadn't come across the sort of professional beggars who disfigure their childrens' limbs. The way the little childrens' arms and legs had been deliberately broken to increase their begging appeal was something I'll never forget.

It was heartbreaking.

We found somewhere to camp on the edge of the city. Then Klaus announced that they were going up into the mountains to a place called Bamiyan to see the largest stone-carved Buddhas in the world. Would I like to come?

'Try and stop me!' I squeaked in excitement, and raced off to stuff still-damp laundry into my rucksack.

The dirt road twisted up through the mountains for mile after mile. Skillfully constructed water channels snaked around the contours delivering precious water to patches of fields and orchards, small villages with apricots drying on the flat-roofed houses, people waving at us and selling fruit and vegetables. Lorries decorated with every colour under the sun, full of people and overladen with sacks – occasionally overheating as they struggled over the passes. The drivers would stop, lift the bonnet and throw a bucket of water onto the overheated engine which would crack and bang alarmingly.

The road wound up and up.

Eventually we reached the Bamiyan Valley and parked the wagons outside a string of low houses alongside the river. This had once been an important junction on the Silk Road between China and the West, and Bamiyan was one of the oldest cities in Central Asia. But drought, invasions and population exodus had left the valley with just a line of simple dwellings and a thin strip of green along the riverbank.

The cliff face above the houses was pockmarked with caves, but the most staggering feature was the huge standing Buddha, carved out of the natural rock inside a protective archway. It must have been nearly two hundred feet tall. Apparently the image was carved almost two thousand years ago and had originally been covered in gold, jewels and colourful tiles. But now it was badly scarred, having been attacked over the centuries by various political and religious hoodlums.

Even so, its huge presence loomed over the valley. A little way to the right was another slightly smaller Buddha. I got out of the wagon and stood gawping at the carvings.

Of course, none of us knew then how lucky we were to see these statues before the recent Taliban's attacks reduced them to piles of rubble.

Parked on a natural terrace at the feet of the Buddha were a couple of large white vehicles and a queue of local people. Curiosity, as ever, got the better of me and I went to investigate. 'Médecins sans Frontières', who I'd never heard of before, were performing eye and cataract operations. I was unbelievably impressed that these doctors had come to such a remote spot to perform these wonderful life-changing operations.

I still have the image of that queue of people waiting patiently for the miracles performed in that big white vehicle. In fact, just recently I received a newsletter from MSF, who I've supported for many years, and on the front cover was an image I instantly recognised.

MSF vehicles parked at Bamiyan.

A combination of the best and worst in humanity – the positive generosity of the MSF staff underneath the destructive brutality of the Taliban together in the same picture. I felt quite uplifted that MSF still goes there to perform their miracles after all these years.

The next day we continued further along the track into the mountains. I had no idea where we were going, just excited to be driven through some of the most starkly beautiful mountains I had ever seen. Everywhere were rolling vistas of peachy pink and ochre grey, with razor-edged mountains in the distance.

When we suddenly rounded the corner at the top of a pass I was unprepared for the colour spread out below.

A flat-bottomed valley, with a series of lakes stepping down through the levels. Each lake was a different shade of vivid blue. There was no sign of humans, buildings or vegetation, just splashes of iridescent peacock, indigo, azure, and lapiz blue contrasting vividly against the peachy grey background.

We all got out of the wagons and stood on the edge of the road gasping at the technicolour spectacle.

We spent the night camped beside one of the lakes and I was able to explore. The water there must be extremely alkaline, for as it trickles slowly out of each lake to the one below it deposits a few minerals of calcium on the waterfall. Over hundreds of years the dam walls grow higher, the lake behind becomes a little bit deeper. So each lake varies in depth, creating a different shade of blue from its neighbours.

A few years later I was saddened to learn that the US army had used this jewel of a place – it was called Band-e-Amir – for recreation. However, I'm overjoyed to read that since 2009 the area has become Afghanistan's first national park, ensuring that it remains the pristine ecological wonder I was so astounded by in 1968.

As the sun began to set behind the mountains, a small boy turned up, gazing with frank curiosity at our simple pieces of camping equipment. In height he looked to be aged about five or six, but his face was that of an old man. His skin was burned leathery brown by the strong sun at that 10,000 foot altitude, yet he had what looked like frostbite on his cheeks. I handed him a couple of hard-boiled sweets. He popped one into his mouth, cellophane wrapping and all, so I had to show him how to undo it. Gleefully grabbing a handful of the sweets he raced away.

Gerry and I had no plans for going further than Kabul until we looked at a map. With India only three and a half inches away, who could resist?

We couldn't. So we went.

The Germans took us over the infamous Khyber Pass and down into Pakistan where we bid them thanks and farewell. We'd decided to get our fifty per cent student reduction and continue by train. The station master sat in his office in Peshawar dwarfed by piles of dusty paper and files. We shook hands. He produced a wad of forms and a squeaky pen. We filled in the details of our lives and passports, parents and education. The information was copied out in duplicate, signed and stamped, taken away, signed and stamped again. A ticket was produced, and the procedure was then repeated.

When eventually the ticket was handed over, amid beams and handshakes all round, it proved to be merely the entitlement to a student reduction. The purchasing of the ticket was yet another story.

We rattled into Delhi the next afternoon. It is a fascinating, sad and beautiful city, split into two halves – the old and the new. New Delhi was clean and spacious, a city of boulevards, embassies and American cars. Old Delhi was a tangle of bicycles, carts and cows, wooden shacks and slums; of people, people and more people.

Skeletal bodies, stark naked or in filthy rags, lay in rows outside the station. It was necessary to step over them to move along the pavement. I was initially shocked at the sight of these unfortunate Indians but what I found more shocking was the way I soon found myself stepping over these people, almost without seeing them, in the same way as did everyone else. Life and death were all jumbled together here – glossy Sikhs and women in gaily coloured saris, children selling individual cigarettes or little packets of biscuits, beggars, street hawkers with tanks of drinking water on their backs, rattling their metal cups, market traders pushing handcarts of fruit and tomatoes along the road.

In Delhi the two faces of India were brought together. I wondered which would prevail.

Wandering across an open space, I had the misfortune to graze my shin as I stepped over a rusting piece of metal. The next day my leg had ballooned with infection. I decided it needed serious treatment, so headed to a hospital. The grounds and entrance area were full of Indians in various states of medical distress, all sitting, lying, leaning, hobbling... waiting for attention.

An attendant noticed me and waved me in through a door. He beckoned me to follow him along a corridor. Stepping over groaning bodies, I was ushered straight into a waiting room, where the doctor saw me immediately.

He was a pleasant young doctor who had just qualified and explained he was doing his 'bit' working in India for a couple of years before escaping to America. He seemed to want a chat, so we quizzed each other for quite a while. I could well understand why a local doctor would prefer the salary and conditions in the West, yet considering the queues of untreated people outside, it didn't seem right. It also didn't seem right that I was given such speedy treatment, presumably for being a westerner and someone the young doctor could chat to. Of course, I was grateful for the penicillin he prescribed at a tiny cost (which cured the infection), but it made me feel uncomfortable.

From Delhi we continued eastwards with our third-class railway tickets. As there was no such thing as 'full up' on the trains, it was every man for himself on boarding. Having elbowed our way with everyone else into a carriage, I took to leaping onto the luggage rack, by far the least uncomfortable place to stretch out.

Thus for the next few days I became intimately acquainted with the ceilings of third-class railway compartments, but alas, saw little of Northern India. My limbs grew stiff and aching, and on a diet of bananas and tea passed in through the open windows for a few rupees, I grew hungrier and hungrier.

I was woken in the middle of the night by someone shouting, 'We're here, quick, get off!' We emerged onto a dark platform and slunk off into a cluster of half-built houses to find somewhere to sleep.

Next morning, I awoke slowly and painfully, gazing around bleary-eyed at the plastered walls and cold concrete floor on which we were lying. Where were we this morning... Tehran... Kabul?

Gradually the last few days swam into focus and I crashed into consciousness – Nepal; yes, we were actually in Nepal!!

It's a physical impossibility to leap out of a sleeping bag, so I crawled out, then flung wide the door to greet my first Nepalese morning.

All a bit disappointing really. Southern Nepal is the same as Northern India – flat, marshy mosquito country covered in paddy fields, mud villages and thin, ragged peasants. Not a hippy or a Maharishi in sight.

After breakfast of fried rice and curried potatoes, Gerry and I fought our way onto the local bone shaker which was to take us up over the foothills and into the Valley of Kathmandu. With a fearful blast from the horn the bus juddered into action. It splashed its way through the puddles and potholes, honking loudly at anything that moved within a hundred yards of the road, and swerving with cool accuracy and a two-inch clearance around buffalo carts, donkeys, children and bicycles.

Halfway up, it stopped to pick up two peasant boys who squatted in the gangway next to me and proceeded to be regularly and prodigiously travel sick for the rest of the journey. Demurely I lifted up my feet and concentrated desperately on the window. It didn't take much effort, for the scenery was beautiful. Tiny flowers glittered like jewels among the ferns and grasses, while higher up, huge misshapen trees floated silently out of the mists – sylvan monsters marching through an arboreal dreamscape. Between the clouds, far, far below lay a long line of turquoise – the Indian Plain.

It was dark on arrival in Kathmandu and it was raining – big fat warm drops which melted their way through to my skin. We were peddled off into the night by two grubby rickshaw boys who dumped us outside a rather dubious-looking café and demanded five rupees apiece. Hardened by past experience and diminishing resources, we halved this to allow for their doubling and cautiously pushed open the door of the 'Blue Tibetan' to be greeted by the proprietor – a young Tibetan refugee – who said we could doss down in his attic for a rupee a night. And thus we were installed in Kathmandu.

Next morning, we tottered out to explore the town. Wandering around in dazed confusion the magic began to work on me – bewildered, bedazzled and bewitched, I gradually lost my heart to this tiny capital of Nepal.

Kathmandu was not so much a city for the people as a home for the gods. Life, merchandise and architecture revolved about the little gods whose aura of magic, mystery, gaiety and wisdom pervaded every aspect of living – watching every movement, hearing every inner thought.

The city was a jumbled, colourful patchwork of shrines, temples and sanctuaries, with little painted gods peeping mischievously from every corner. Each square inch of woodwork was carved into exotic and intricate designs of men and idols, birds, flowers, leaves, strange symbolic patterns and prayers to the ever open ears of the gods. Wreaths, chains and bouquets of flowers were festooned from every available nail, draped over shop windows and doorways, wound lovingly around idol necks.

The local women, like colourful butterflies, fluttered between the shrines carrying baskets laden with presents for the gods – milk, cakes, fruit, flowers, rice, coins. On the steps of a small temple at the gates of the old palace sat three barbers. Steps and street were inches deep in a mat of black tufts of hair that had accumulated over the years. A tiny god gazed out at them with quiet benevolence through the gilded doors.

We wandered north and through the backstreets where the delicate smells of joss-sticks and incense gave way to the nauseous aroma of excrement and rotting flesh. This was the butchers' quarter. We reached the river just after a slaughter.

Three butchers, the remains of a buffalo, and an exceedingly ancient wheelbarrow were grouped on the bank. Two men were attacking the carcass with great vigour, hatchets raised above heads and descending into the mottled redness with a sickening scrunch. Aided and abetted by a pack of scavenging hounds, blood, bone and skin were flying in all directions. The third butcher, a young urchin, was sitting cross-legged in the mud methodically squeezing out the coils of glistening intestines. As he finished, he noticed me watching him with a mixture of curiosity and horror. He dragged the intestines down to the water's edge and sloshed them in. Then, hygiene attended to, he grinned happily at me, dragged the wriggling coils back up the muddy slope and heaved them into the barrow.

Remembering the buffalo rice eaten for breakfast... I quaked.

I was determined to seek out and find Rudyard Kipling's *'one-eyed yellow idol to the north of Kathmandu'*, so braved the trembling bridge across the river and set out to look. The track led up through a tiny village to the hill of the monkey temple – a wooded slope rising out of the valley floor which was a paradise for the monkeys that swung through the trees, ran up and down the steps, and sat in the laps of the numerous statues.

I examined each shrine and buddha with meticulous care; some were yellow, some were green-eyed, some one-eyed, but nowhere could I find that legendary one-eyed yellow idol to the north of Kathmandu. Perhaps he never existed...

Perhaps he was hiding alone in some forgotten glade, gazing out with his one good eye through the trees, over the river and past the butchers, still guarding with ferocious tenacity the thriving, colourful, sacred city of Kathmandu below. Behind me was a little temple and inside, monstrous as a giant orchid, sat a golden god. Through the open door drifted the sound of chanting – beautifully sad – accompanied by the lone steady pulsing of a drum. The beating seeped into my every fibre; the trees, the valley, the hills echoed the call until the whole landscape throbbed and trembled with the headiness.

Suddenly a cymbal clashed, the chanting stopped – the spell was broken. For a long time I sat enveloped in the heavy silence, until the saffron sun disappeared behind the western cloud-banks hiding the Himalayan peaks from view. Then I wandered back down to the flickering town.

In the evenings we would sit sipping tea in the 'Blue Tibetan'. Other travellers and also friends we had last seen in Istanbul, Tehran, Kabul or Delhi would suddenly turn up.

They were a strange crowd. There was 'Swede', a Swedish boy who had absconded from school and was trying to reach Australia, the young French couple who had exchanged their last rupees for a sitar, an American Peace Corps worker patiently making a chip basket out of chicken wire, and a group of gourmet Austrians who had gorged their way across Europe and the Middle East.

We would sit and talk and swap tales of our adventures, of bazaar-haggling and the black market, of record hitch-hikes and scrapes with death, disease and dysentery, of smuggling hashish and lapis lazuli, of what to see and where to go, and how much to pay for it all. We would talk and joke and laugh deep into the night. The proprietor would let some sleep on the tables downstairs. The rest of us would squeeze up through a hole in the ceiling to the attic above. We were next to the kitchen so were not surprised to find ourselves sharing the room with several large rats, a pigeon, also a collection of smaller guests inside the mattresses.

It was decided to exterminate the latter, so Gerry squirted everywhere and everything with some garden DDT he had brought in case of fleas. A few days later I noticed small spots on my arm.

'Just the fleas,' said Gerry, squirting DDT over me with renewed vigour. Next morning, I was covered with boils which erupted in fiery bursts all over my arms, back and legs.

'Fleas?' I queried, gazing with deep suspicion at the now-empty packet of DDT. If faced with the choice between fleas and DDT poisoning again I think I'll choose the fleas!

We were surprised to find no hippies in Kathmandu. Apparently a few days before we arrived the authorities had begun a massive hippy clean-up and exodus. A few pseudo-intellectuals were gathered at 'The Camp' where they would sit for hours discussing the length of their hair and the aesthetic merits of Shintoism. And then of course, there were the tourists who came by aeroplane, kitted themselves out in local dress, bought a few flowers and beads and wandered around feeling thoroughly integrated.

Somehow we felt superior to the tourists who had flown in, as if struggling through all our discomforts had made us more authentic. Travelling more slowly than flying, and watching the landscapes, people and cultures gradually unfold had certainly given me a sense of perspective on where we were. When I'd set out I'd dreamt of reaching somewhere beyond western civilisation. I really hoped that I'd find that in Kathmandu.

And mostly I had. But already there were signs in the city of westernisation. A modern concrete bridge had been built over the river and tall neon lights illuminated the main dirt road. A new post office and hospital decorated one of the main streets, ugly transformers and telephone wires juxtaposed uncomfortably between the shrines and tilting roofs.

Of course, mass communication, medicine and a thriving tourist industry should be welcomed in these underdeveloped corners of our world. But we had travelled such a long way in order to find what life was like beyond the reaches of westernisation.

It made me sad to realise we were witnessing the passing of a unique era, a character and a culture.

Time drifted.

We had been in Kathmandu for over two weeks when Gerry (in charge of the money) informed me that we had only £7 each to get us home... £7 each for one month and six and a half thousand miles. Still, I comforted myself, at least I'm £7 better off than many people in Kathmandu.

We decided to have a sale. So we informed the proprietor and spread out the contents of our rucksacks on the floor. Within a few minutes the room was crowded with shouting, excited Nepalese outbidding each other for holey socks, sweaters unwashed since Tehran, and trying on shoes, vests and jeans. Hastily I rescued my sleeping bag and knife, then joined in the fray. Nobody wanted my western-style clothes, but poor Gerry was cleaned out save for what he was wearing and one clean shirt for the Dover customs.

We went out for one last wander around the town. I trundled heartbroken through the twisting streets, between the higgledy houses and past the golden shrines. Gazed covetously at the carved hubble-bubble pipes and inlaid knives, the bright carpets and fabrics which I couldn't take home.

I whispered 'au-revoir' to the little idols, and turned the prayer wheels for the last time. Early next morning we hurried down to catch the daily fleet of lorries for the Indian border. Then turning our backs to the rising sun, began the long trek home.

For travellers like ourselves with precious little money and thereby few monetary scruples, it was easy to hitch free lifts on the Indian trains. We had to wait a day in Benares, now called Varanasi, for the Delhi express and were intrigued and slightly horrified at the lines of bodies waiting their turn to be cremated on the steps of the sacred Ganges. While there, we were taken to see the 'Temple of Love'. A tiny wizened priest with an expression of infinite boredom led us round the carvings outside, pointing out a variety of highly improbable Kama Sutra positions.

We raced on through Delhi but in Lahore Gerry had the misfortune to be relieved of half of our precious rupees by a skilful pickpocket. (That's what he told me at the time, though I later learned he had actually used the money to buy some semi-precious stones for his girlfriend. I was SO naive!) Fortunately we had some tea and dried food bars (ugh!) to keep us going, although many people offered us hospitality and meals. Over the last couple of months I'd really noticed the generosity of people who had very little. It was quite humbling.

With hardly a stop we were into Afghanistan and through Kabul.

The desert can be beautiful, but it can also be awfully lonely when you're dumped in the middle with not a house, village or camel in sight.

Yes, we got stuck, right bang in the middle. We sizzled by the roadside in the blistering heat for a whole day, and then froze under the stars, trying to snatch some sleep on the uneven gravel. Our water bottles were empty and I was beginning to think the end was nigh when some kind, generous, bountiful Afghani brought his lorry to a rattling halt and we clambered aboard once again. We passed an overturned lorry that had been carrying dried apricots, stopping to offer solace to the driver and to replenish our diminishing food stocks. Soaked in water overnight, the apricots made a delicious breakfast.

Gerry calculated that we could just afford to take the train in Iran from Mashad to Tehran, and then if we hitched into Turkey, the train from Erzurum to Istanbul.

On the Iranian-Turkish border we met up once again with our German friends with their two ancient police wagons. They hadn't washed since Tehran and were as black as soot with diesel fumes. They offered us a lift to Erzurum. Unfortunately, during the last few weeks I had acquired the nickname of 'jinx'. Even when Gerry and I were travelling in different wagons in a convoy, something always seemed to happen to the vehicle I rode in. In the middle of the night the wagon I was in died, so we finished the journey under tow. The poor Germans were then informed that they couldn't dump it or sell it, but must tow it back the one hundred and sixty-odd miles to the border to get it struck off their passports. With a sigh of resignation they unloaded their dried peas and beans upon us, and turned back.

Wishing them well and thanking them for all their hospitality, we waved Klaus and his friends farewell for the last time.

We bought our student-reduced tickets and boarded the train but the journey turned into a nightmare for me. The Turkish men kept trying to touch me and pull at my clothes. They would not leave me alone and any interference on Gerry's part threatened to escalate into a fight. Active retaliation on my part became my only defence. I got off the train in Istanbul shaking with anger, but the sight of Europe on the far shore of the Bosphorus soon banished all thoughts from my mind, save those of home.

On the ferry across to the European side Gerry wandered off – he was always wandering off – and came back with a garbled tale of how he'd helped to save a young German girl from the wrath of a nightclub owner. In return we were invited to a nightclub that evening, a meal and free accommodation in a hotel. I never quite believed Gerry's stories – but I wasn't going to complain. We went to see some Turkish belly dancers – not a bit like the Turkish Delight adverts, which in those days advertised exotically flavoured chocolates accompanied by slim, graceful dancers in Turkish attire. I couldn't help laughing at the three enormous women lumbering about the stage.

Next morning we hurried on.

By now my mind was full of thoughts of my mother's cooking, roast chicken, green beans, and of home, sweet home. We travelled non-stop through Greece and Yugoslavia, three days and two nights without sleep. Then up into the green mountains of Austria, where we were invited to spend the night in the birthplace of that infamous Nazi, Goering, just over the border, in Germany.

Once we hit the autobahns we were well away. Munich, Stuttgart, Frankfurt flashed by unnoticed. I was counting the hours now to striding up my road and pushing open the back door...

Ostend, a rough night crossing, and we were greeted by a pale watery dawn over Dover. I left Gerry in London and continued alone. As I hitched up through Caversham, the car driver glanced at my torn and travel-stained rucksack.

'Where are you hitching from,' he asked with mild curiosity, 'London?'

'Kathmandu,' I replied nonchalantly, wondering if he'd believe me.

He obviously didn't.

'Oh yes?' he came back with a twinkle. 'And my name's King Soloman. What's yours?'

Headlines

1969 – 1971

Just before the accident... and after the accident!

I'd enjoyed three glorious years at university, but like all good things, the fun had to stop at some stage. I spent the summer of '69 lolling about at home and going for long cycle rides on my own around Oxfordshire. Dad had tried to tackle me about my future, but apart from a restless desire to roam the world, I didn't have a clue. One day he came back from work, beaming.

'I've got you a place at Oxford!' he announced. 'Term starts in two weeks. Department of Education.' Dad was a teacher, with numerous contacts in the Oxfordshire Department of Education through his work for the National Union of Teachers.

The shock jolted me out of my daydreaming. 'But, but I don't want to be a teacher...' I protested.

'Well, you've got to do something,' he replied. 'I've had a word, and you've got all the qualifications. The Department of Education is so oversubscribed this year that one more student won't make any difference. You'll never be short of a job if you're a teacher... and you'd be able to work anywhere in the world!' he added slyly.

And that's how I finished up with a teaching qualification that I didn't want, but which – as my Dad predicted – came in useful from time to time.

Its first use came immediately. Just after I qualified.

I still have the scar. It stretches from my left ear, across my forehead and through the hair to the back of my skull. A memento of my first job.

While finishing my year learning how to be a teacher, an opportunity had arisen to teach in Sudan. So I packed a small bag, climbed on board an ancient SudanAir aircraft at Heathrow and landed, completely unprepared for what was to come, in Khartoum.

The school I was to work in was a girls' secondary school set in a concrete compound where the town of Omdurman ended and the desert sands began. The school had been established by a remarkable Sudanese intellectual called Babikr Bedri who had been a pioneer of modern education. His tomb was right outside my doorway. The school later became a jewel in the crown of Sudanese education – Ahfad University for Women – but although the school's ambitions were first rate, the facilities in 1971 were basic.

The heat scorched me to a crisp. The mosquitoes feasted on me morning and night. With no aircon in the concrete oven where I lived, sleep was impossible. The girls I was teaching were curious about me and life in the West, but had no interest in learning English and anyway, there were no textbooks or syllabus. I winged it for the first term.

I also bought my first car. It was a sky-blue Triumph Mayflower sold to me for twenty Sudanese pounds by a retiring SudanAir pilot. It was a delight to drive. I loved bowling around the dusty streets of Omdurman and Khartoum with a cooling wind blowing in through the open windows. It's only trouble was starting up. Something to do with a mismatch between the flywheel and starter motor, apparently. It could be coaxed into life with a good push, but the local boys and men seemed to disappear whenever I ventured out. So, in the end I had to abandon it behind a friend's house. Metal doesn't rust in the desert. It's probably still there.

A small group of Europeans socialised at the Sudan Club over the White Nile bridge in the centre of Khartoum, a couple of miles away. The Club had a swimming pool and a bar so I took to escaping there in my spare time. I overheard talk of an expedition to visit some Voluntary Service Overseas teachers during the Muslim holiday which follows Ramadan, and I expressed an interest. Someone organised two UN Land Rovers which we packed with spare food and a few goodies not available outside the capital. It was strongly suggested that we all take out insurance, which fortunately I did – a decision which changed my life – but more of that later!

The small group of us set off east across the desert for Kassala, on the Ethiopian border.

* * *

On the way back from Kassala a young English volunteer called John was driving. The road was just a dirt track which wound through scrub and rocks, across wadis and round small hills. He was driving fast round a tight bend when the wheels became ensnared in some deep ruts. The Land Rover swayed right, then left, then rolled over and bounced to a standstill on its side. As we climbed out through the side window I couldn't understand where the wet was coming from. I put my hand to my head and felt a deep dent.

With a sickening jolt I assumed that my skull was cracked open – I reasoned that I would probably start with having fits, lose consciousness and then die.

Someone helped me lie down under a thorn bush and a sheet was draped above me for shade. Although the vehicle was a twisted write-off, fortunately no one else seemed to be injured. While I waited to slide into unconsciousness I tried to take my last look at the world through half an eye, as the other eye was stuck shut with drying blood. There wasn't any traffic on this desert track so all we could do was wait, wait for help, wait to die.

After an hour or two I heard voices and squinted up. Staring down at me was a nomad perched atop a tall camel. I remember noticing he was a Hadendowa tribesman, with a halo of what Rudyard Kipling referred to as 'fuzzy-wuzzy' hair stuck through with sticks and bones. He gazed down at me and shook his head before turning the camel and riding slowly away.

I think I slept.

I heard it first, as my head was close to the ground – the intermittent rumble of an engine. The others thought I was hallucinating. Then they heard the engine too. Eventually a lorry came round the bend and stopped. I was lifted up into the back which was already crammed with locals, bulging sacks and some smelly sheep. John climbed in with me and the lorry bumped, rocked and swayed for what seemed hours to a small town.

Instead of taking me straight to hospital the driver stopped at the police station. John said later that he had lost his temper when confronted with a requirement to start filling in forms. Someone in uniform climbed up the side of the lorry; I remember seeing his look of horror as he stared at me before he quickly waved us on. The lorry stopped at the hospital gates and a huge black man gently lifted me down and carried me into a waiting room. A surgeon appeared in green scrubs and started asking me questions – my name, what day it was and how long I'd been in Sudan. Not realising he was trying to see if I was concussed I sobbed at him to fix my skull which I was convinced was broken open.

'No, it's not broken,' he replied calmly.

Pathetically I whined, 'How do you know?'

'Because I can see it,' he said.

A man appeared with a razor and a bucket which he put down between my legs. He indicated for me to put my head over the bucket. I was confused and absolutely terrified. Slowly he started scraping the razor across my skull and lumps of bloody hair fell into the bucket. I must have been screaming hysterically because John said everyone in the town seemed to turn up to watch.

There followed blurred memories of being wheeled into an operating theatre and the surgeon poking and prodding at my head as he stitched the scalp together.

I awoke on a badly stained mattress in a small '2nd class female' ward which was my home for the next week. John stayed with me while the rest of the group returned (somehow) to Khartoum. There was no food in the hospital as the locals cooked for family members beside the patient's bed, so John had to find what he could in the market. My diet consisted of bread and raw eggs in milk.

Eventually, I was put on a train back to Khartoum where I began a slow and erratic recovery filled with panic attacks and mood swings. Fortunately there had been a long postal strike in the UK so presumably my parents weren't surprised by my lack of letters. I had been offered the use of the 'diplomatic bag' to let them know what had happened to me, but not wishing to alarm them, I waited until my hair started to grow back and I was looking less like Frankenstein's monster. Then I had a passport photo taken which I sent with an explanatory letter.

While I was slowly recovering and returning to work, the political situation in Khartoum deteriorated. President Nimeiri suddenly decreed that he was going to scrap the last vestiges of Sudan's colonial past and apply Sharia Law throughout the country, with amputations, floggings and a complete overhaul of the university syllabus. This caused an uproar in the capital. The university, where I was working part-time, shut down as students barricaded themselves into the building. I watched with growing concern as tanks, their huge guns festooned with gun belts, rumbled through the streets.

I decided it would be prudent to leave. My parents sounded relieved.

Although my head injury had been serious, it wasn't the only incident of note during the year I spent in Sudan.

A few weeks after my return home to England my ears pricked up when I heard a name mentioned on the radio – Michael Hinchcliffe, a diplomatic aide at the British Embassy in Khartoum. We had known each other. He was a tall, rangy chap with a predilection for the stage (like me) and we'd both taken part in a few theatrical productions at the Sudan Theatre Club.

It had been the Queen's birthday, an occasion at which all the British expats were invited to a party at the Embassy. I turned up on the back of a friend's motorbike dressed in as much finery as I could assemble. Mike Hinchcliffe was at the front gate welcoming the guests, but much to my chagrin, on seeing me informed me that I wasn't invited. I remonstrated, and was told it was because I was 'unpatriotic', having taken part in a minor demonstration outside the visa office. I was a child of the sixties, after all, and had felt the need to show my opposition to the British

Government's decision to restart the sale of arms to South Africa during apartheid.

As I recognised Mike Hinchcliffe's name on the radio broadcast in the kitchen at home I couldn't help laughing. Mike, now back in the UK, had just been convicted at Bow Street Magistrates' Court of spying! A somewhat more unpatriotic offence than mine!

My year in Sudan taught me a great deal about myself – not all of it very complimentary. It was a wake-up call that began the process of turning me from a spoiled, self-centred, overprivileged child into the beginnings of an adult. And when I returned home I was able to use the £240 awarded me by the Sudanese insurance company (for 'reduced marriage value') to start flying lessons. It struck me at the time as rather funny, though it's actually sad that a woman's value was calculated in terms of her worth as an attractive bride. The scar across my forehead looked horrendous for a time, but has since faded, and, I'm pleased to say, no one has ever suggested that it devalued me as a bride or anything else.

I eventually gained my private pilot's licence and a fascination with aviation that steered me away from teaching into a completely different career – that of an air traffic controller.

Supersonic Sue

1990

With the captain on Concorde's wing at Washington Airport.

Mid-Atlantic with me at Concorde's controls!

I learned to fly at Wycombe Air Park near High Wycombe, bolstering my £240 insurance money with every spare penny of my salary as a supply teacher in order to gain my licence. I'd had almost no previous experience of leaving the ground, so gazing down at the landscape from a little single-engined Piper or Cessna was novel and exhilarating.

As well as flitting around the UK, the Flying Club often arranged flying trips to other clubs in Europe. A few of us would sometimes share the cost and fly to places such as the Channel Islands, Geneva, and Bordeaux.

My mother tragically died prematurely of cancer in 1972, and I felt the need to focus on something completely different. That something turned out to be aviation.

While immersed in this new hobby, I was introduced to air traffic control and discovered it was a much more enjoyable career than that of teaching. Pilots tended to do as they were instructed, unlike the totally undisciplined and unpredictable monkeys I was faced with in a classroom. Fortunately I was still young enough to change careers.

Wycombe Air Park was the home of the British Airways Flying Club, so I found myself mingling socially with some highly qualified BA aviators, some of whom I kept in touch with after I'd stopped flying and had my two sons.

I was in my early career, and enduring a particularly traumatic domestic period. Word of my circumstances must have got around, though I was quite surprised when a kindly Concorde captain, I'll call him Uncle Adam for the purposes of this book, contacted me out of the blue and offered me a ticket to the States with him on Concorde.

I was overwhelmed!

As air traffic controllers we were encouraged to fly in the cockpit of commercial airliners in order to exchange professional experience. I had already taken as much advantage as I could of this scheme, flying to Iceland and Portugal and many airports in between. Although there was an arrangement for controllers like myself to experience Concorde, the number of tickets was strictly limited and I was down at the bottom of the pecking order. I would never be selected for such a privileged flight.

'Just go through check-in and get on board with the normal passengers,' said Uncle Adam, handing me my Concorde tickets. 'Turn left into the cockpit instead of right and I'll see you on board.'

The cockpit was long, with an engineer's seat and panel on the right, and my 'supernumerary' crew seat on the left, behind the captain. Uncle Adam introduced me to the first officer and engineer. I took my seat and gazed around at the dials and panels. Most of the flying instruments were familiar to me, but I was surprised that the cockpit looked so antiquated. This was not one of the modern 'fly by wire' computerised cockpits that were just starting to be introduced. Although she was sleek and beautiful on the outside, Concorde's inner workings seemed to be held together with rivets and screws – a bit like an elderly matron in a tightly contoured corset. And the windscreen was tiny – even with the pointy nose lowered for taxying.

I donned my headset and tightened the straps of my safety harness. The take-off acceleration was a kick in the back that I'd never experienced before or since. This was no elderly matron!

With the nose now raised we climbed through the layers of cloud into sunshine over the River Severn Estuary, and I waited to hear the familiar words in my headset that we were cleared to accelerate and climb. Up, up through layers of whispery ice-clouds until we were far above the other aircraft. Concorde slowly climbed to ten miles high as she burnt fuel during her three-hour dart across the Atlantic. The sky above was black, and the visible curvature of the earth gave me the impression that I was floating in outer space.

I couldn't quite believe where I was.

At one point Uncle Adam pointed out the distant dot of the opposite direction Concorde. One quick glance and she was gone.

The stewardess appeared and mentioned to Uncle Adam that a passenger was insisting on visiting the cockpit. Visiting the cockpit was fairly common in the more relaxed days before 9/11. A man pushed his way past her and peered around.

'I want to sit up front,' he stated in a rather abrupt way, glancing dismissively at me occupying the only spare seat. He had no idea who I was and I was wearing what would pass for a uniform. Uncle Adam politely murmured that there were no spare seats. The man snorted and looked pointedly at me again.

This time Uncle Adam said quite firmly, 'We have extra crew today. There are no spare seats. I'm sorry.' The man gazed at me in disbelief, muttered something under his breath and left.

On approaching US airspace, Uncle Adam suggested I made the initial radio call. What an experience! I don't think the American controller had heard a female voice announcing that Concorde was entering US airspace before. He certainly sounded surprised. We landed at Washington where Uncle Adam showed me round the outside of the aircraft, and we had our photo taken standing on the wing. We flew subsonically (because of noise restrictions) south to Miami, where, amazingly, some of my Wycombe Air Club friends were waiting for us, and we all went out for a meal.

Next morning, we took the crew bus from the hotel back to the airport. At first, the flight north to Washington went according to plan. We were on the approach path and putting the gear down when the sequence of amber, red and green lights indicated a failure of the undercarriage system. The flight engineer sprang into action, pushing my knees out of the way and pumping the gear down. I could feel the tension in the cockpit as we neared the threshold, landed safely and taxied in.

I waited with the other passengers in a windowless, airless underground room for several hours while the problem was diagnosed and fixed. Nobody came to tell us what the problem was, nobody offered us refreshments, and nobody could tell us what alternative arrangements could be made to get to London. I saw one man catch a passing uniformed woman and grab her by the lapels of her jacket, shouting into her face in his rude desperation. I sat quietly in a corner watching the tempers fraying and the rumours spreading. It was mortifying that British Airways or Washington Airport didn't have better procedures to deal with our delay. A terrible advertisement.

But eventually, an announcement was made and we reboarded. The crew did their best not to show annoyance as I related to Uncle Adam how we had been treated in Washington, but he made a mental note to pass my experience back to BA. We took off again, quickly reaching Mach 2 as we headed out across the Atlantic.

Then the most amazing thing happened.

Uncle Adam turned around in his seat and said, 'Would you like a go at flying?'

The first officer grinned at me and climbed out of his place at the controls. I buckled myself into his seat and Uncle Adam provided me with a few hints about the handling. The fuel was continuously being pumped around between different tanks which affected the trim so it was important to feel the changes in pressure on the control stick and keep the aircraft straight and level. Then he uncoupled the autopilot, and for a magical few minutes I was actually flying Concorde.

I concentrated hard. Yes, I could feel the trim alter and gently kept the artificial horizon level. I scanned the other instruments as I'd been taught to do, but Uncle Adam was obviously keeping a watchful eye on everything. There was no real need for anyone to feel nervous that I, little ol' me, was flying Concorde manually with a full crew and a cabin-load of passengers.

I felt, indeed I was, on top of the world!

If I sometimes mention to people who wished they had had the chance to travel in Concorde that I've actually flown her, of course, they don't believe me. And I don't blame them. Sometimes I don't believe it myself. But then I look at the photos that the flight engineer took, and I remember how good it felt.

An ordinary woman like me at the controls of Concorde? Whatever next!

Well, it wasn't the last of my adventures, but it was certainly the fastest.

Dogs, Deaths and a Wedding

2004 – 2005

The old Boma Hotel in Mikindana
and some local children with their swimming certificates.

Mr Thomas in the tree nursery, Yvonne (temp hotel manager) and Becki.

Years passed with few opportunities for real adventure. As I neared retirement, and with both my sons independent of me, it became easier to take longer breaks. I spent several weeks touring around Namibia with friends, I bounced around in a yacht in the English Channel to watch the 1999 total eclipse, and journeyed across Asia and China, marvelling at the wonders along the fabled Silk Route.

My job had changed from controlling aircraft to helping to create the new air traffic control centre on the south coast. It was a mammoth project which took thirteen hugely satisfying years to complete. When the new centre eventually went 'live' I asked for early retirement. There was so much more I wanted to see and explore.

Then, almost immediately, life conspired to dump a binload of stressful events on me. In 2004 I retired, divorced, moved house and lost my father all in the space of a few months. So, as the dust settled I decided to turn my back on the legals, logistics, financials and emotions, and escape.

'Hampshire-based charity
are looking for an
Education Supervisor
in Southern Tanzania.'

I stared in amazement at the advert in the local paper – my dream had just come true. I was on the phone to the charity in the blink of an eye.

My duties would involve supervising the work and well-being of a rotation of young UK students who would come to help with the charity's various projects in the East African village of Mikindani. It sounded idyllic.

And in many ways it was!

Mikindani is a long way from any tourist hotspots but is visually brochure-perfect on the edge of a near circular bay looking out across the azure blue of the Indian Ocean. Once an important trading port, the village is now a jumble of dilapidated coral-built houses and mud huts that stretch along the coastal road and inland up a long valley. Most of the locals are subsistence fishermen and farmers, trading what little surplus they can scrape together.

Sitting incongruously on a rise above the village is what was once an old German fort, or *boma*. Volunteers with our charity had renovated the ruin into a rather lovely, if somewhat lonely, hotel – The Old Boma. The 'Boss Man' told me that the charity's aim was to provide training and local employment at the hotel and eventually, if possible, to hand it over to the village.

When I applied for the post Boss Man told me, 'For the first two weeks you'll be expected to live with a local family to gain cultural experience.'

That didn't sound too bad.

Later I wrote home:

I'm staying with a local family. The house they live in is actually a ruin. There's no electricity or running water, kitchen or bathroom. The ceiling has fallen in – there's a heap of rubble taking up most of the floor space in the main room. The house belongs to the local 'street chairman' who lives up the road with wife number one. I'm staying with wife number two, sisters, daughters and grandchildren. I've been allocated the 'master bedroom', a curtained-off corner with nothing but a worm-ridden four-poster bed with a really hard, lumpy straw mattress and a dusty mosquito net peppered with holes. Every evening at just after 7pm the owner bids us goodnight, closes and bolts the front door, and we're left in darkness except for one kerosene lamp. Until we're unlocked the next morning there's nothing but infants wailing and rats running across the rafters. I can't even chat to the women in the house cos they don't speak any English and I can't speak Kiswahili. It's grim!

After two weeks of excruciatingly uncomfortable boredom I moved into a renovated coral house. I'll never take electric lights, running water and SIT-DOWN TOILETS for granted again!

My predecessor, Becky, was to stay on in the village, ostensibly to teach me Kiswahili. Becky was a happy hippy with a permanently slurred grin – she appeared to be stoned most of the time, but pleasantly so. I think the real reason for her agreeing to stay on was that she'd fallen temporarily in lust with a local lad.

Unfortunately, there was no hotel manager when I arrived and so there were things that needed doing everywhere I looked. With no students for me to take care of, the hotel became my priority. Every task was made harder by the sweaty heat. My room and office desk were in a building at the bottom of the slope, and the Old Boma Hotel was at the top. I lost count of the number of times I toiled up and down those steep steps every day.

My year in Mikindani involved fending off a relentless stream of instructions from back in the UK. Unless you have actually lived and tried to work in a remote and underdeveloped corner of the planet, it's impossible to know how difficult it is to achieve even the simplest project.

Instructions from HQ back in Hampshire: *'Sort out the Information Room – it needs proper display boards, maybe a big map of the local area...'* Mental note: whitewash, brushes, floor covering, painter, tape-measure, wooden rails, nails, saw, carpenter, big map, tables, display stands, information, money??? The nearest town was several miles away and the only shops in the village were a couple of small kiosks selling cigarette lighters, little bags of dried food and sweets.

HQ: *'We've had complaints that the meals take too long to arrive. Can you sort that?'* Training, menus, kitchen staff, waiting staff, shopping, money?

HQ: *'Make sure we get a proper paper trail for all outgoings. We want to computerise the accounting system.'*

How do you do that in a society that only uses cash? How do you get a receipt for goods haggled over in the market?

A few weeks after my arrival the charity found a new hotel manager. Yvonne was a striking-looking young woman who had travelled widely. Being Dutch she towered above the locals. When she smiled, which was often, her face radiated with good humour so she had a real knack of getting her own way. She was a terrific asset to the hotel. Everyone loved her. But her presence didn't relieve me of the endless series of requests.

HQ: *'We've heard about flea-ridden dogs running round the hotel. Keep them out!'* Dog-gates, carpenter, wood, receipts?

HQ: *'There's another Land Rover being shipped over. Just pop to Dar and get it imported correctly. It's full of kids' books and other bits. Make sure nothing gets stolen!'* Dar es Salaam was an expensive flight or a gruelling four hundred mile drive away. It took me three weeks of serious queueing to get the Land Rover through the legal paperwork, and a nasty confrontation with a gang of robbers masquerading as officials to get it out of the port – intact!

HQ: *'You'll need to get a driving licence. Make sure the Land Rover is ONLY used for hotel business. There's to be NO taxi service for the locals!!'* A driving licence! That sounds like more wasted hours of queueing in a government office. However, as luck would have it, Yvonne also needed a Tanzanian driving licence. She used her winning smile and an embarrassingly low-cut blouse to great effect the morning we went to get our licences. We got them after a long rambling interview, but no queueing.

Then, Becky, still hanging around the village, dropped a bombshell.

'I've arranged a rock concert for the village,' she informed HQ.

HQ went apoplectic. *'You absolutely can't. They're not used to things like that. Where is the band staying? Definitely NOT in the hotel, they'll all get drunk and run amok . It'll be total mayhem.'*

But Becky was cheerfully persistent.

Later HQ admitted a hysterical defeat. *'If you promise it's not a band, just one man, he can stay for one night maximum. But you must treat this like a military operation. Keep the Land Rover engine running through the performance and as soon as he's finished you must whisk him away into the hotel, push the big wooden front doors shut and bolt them. Have all the staff ready to repel anyone trying to get in,'* screamed the instructions from HQ.

So Becky got her way.

The sounds of sawing, banging and hammering were heard from down in the village. I went to take a look.

Becky had somehow found the money for some wood, and a raised stage was being built. A tangle of wires at the back was for a sound system. It all looked quite impressive. I wondered who the rock star was.

On the morning of the show Dudu Baya (Bad Insect) flew in from Dar. Becky persuaded Yvonne to drive to the airport and pick him up. He was a huge, handsome young man with the confident air of a megastar. He took up position on a sun lounger under a parasol by the pool and proceeded to drink. Serious alcohol in Tanzania is sold in triangular plastic pouches. Dudu didn't move a muscle all day other than to bite open the corner of another pouch and empty the contents down his throat.

Yvonne and I watched with growing concern. At this rate he'd be unconscious by the evening. Becky arrived to suggest he have something to eat and soak up the alcohol.

'No way,' he slurred. 'I'm not doin' it.'

'Not doing it? The gig? But, but you must!' Becky wheedled. 'You've come all this way, and the whole village wants to hear you. You're a big star. The best. Come on, man, let me get you something to eat.'

'No, I'm not goin' to do it,' Dudu repeated.

This went on for several hours. It got dark.

I think that's when Yvonne, leaning tantalisingly across the sun lounger, had a private word with him.

The next thing I knew was that Dudu had agreed to sing one number. He was poured into the Land Rover and driven down to the village square before he could change his mind.

Considering his condition, he gave an impressive performance. He belted out song after song for nearly an hour. Becky was in heaven, though I don't think the audience knew what to make of it. Unused to his style of house music, I didn't either.

I watched the crowd. The children stared wide-eyed and open-mouthed. The young women giggled in small groups showing off their best blouses and most colourful kangas (rectangular cotton shawls) and the young men strutted around eyeing up the girls. It was the sort of show where the audience is supposed to sing along and join in the chorus from time to time. But they didn't know they were supposed to do that so Dudu was left to make as much noise as he could on his own. He showed amazing stamina, and we whizzed him back up the hill to the hotel as soon as he finished.

He didn't fly back to Dar straight away and I didn't cotton on for a while. But eventually I realised that Dudu and Yvonne had become 'an item'.

'Sue, dear,' Yvonne asked me sweetly one day, 'Can you get curtains put up in my bathroom? Apparently the staff have been seen peeping in!'

Measurements, wood, design for curtain rails, talk to carpenter, curtain hooks, material, someone to sew them.

I usually walked around part of the village every day. I occasionally needed to ask the street chairman about something. He was responsible for most things that happened in his part of the village such as whose turn it was to sweep the street and burn the rubbish and I needed his approval for activities like clearing overgrown bushes at the back of the hotel. Sometimes I'd have a neighbourly wander to say 'hello' to the children and the women sitting outside their front doors, weaving palm-leaf mats, or selling a few tomatoes or mangos, or to watch the women pounding cassava roots – a hideously vigorous chore – to make the starchy gruel which was the locals' staple food.

Occasionally I walked up the paths through the coconut groves to where the houses were more spread out and various garden patches had been cut out of the undergrowth. At first, I found it difficult to tell the difference between wild scrub and a garden, as fruit and vegetables were grown almost individually amongst the wild vegetation. It's a really natural way of growing food which avoids concentrations of pests and diseases.

Sometimes I was accompanied by the dogs, or a little band of skinny, scruffy children who picked and tasted wild fruit and leaves as they raced around. I noticed how their energy levels improved when the mangos were in season. They get so little to eat normally.

I had also had a daily excursion to Becky's Kiswahili lessons. However, these didn't last long. Shortly after the Dudu Baya show she made a hasty exit from the village having 'dumped' her boyfriend. Her rejection hadn't gone down well with the young man who became increasingly violent towards her. She wisely left Mikindani before she got seriously hurt.

The requests from HQ kept coming. *'We need a report every week, and a charity newsletter every month. Try and make it sound upbeat!'* PC problems, internet availability, intermittent electricity supply?

HQ: *'Don't forget to walk the dogs every day. And de-flea them.'*

I didn't need telling to walk the dogs. Walking the dogs was my welcome escape every evening. And I'd happily sort out the fleas if HQ would send me the flea collars I kept asking for...

HQ: *'Your temporary resident's visa expires soon. You need to get it extended.'* Another trip to Dar. More queueing...

Yvonne was spending more and more time in Dar, officially 'marketing' the hotel. On the odd occasion I needed to go to the big city, we would meet up, often with

Dudu in attendance. I have memories of being driven slowly through the bustling crowds of Kariokor Market in the back of Dudu's blacked-out souped-up mean machine with his music on full blast while crowds pressed their faces up to the windows trying to see which stars he was driving around.

Sorry. No pop stars, just Yvonne and little ol' me!

HQ: *'We need furniture for the new lounge. Can you order some?'* Order? IKEA doesn't deliver this far. Maybe I could combine that with the visa trip to Dar?

I couldn't find any shop in Dar selling the kind of club furniture we needed for the hotel, but I'd spotted some rattan-covered furniture for sale at the side of a busy street. Pointing to the photos outside the salesman's booth, I asked if they could make what we needed.

'Yeh, no problem, lady,' the young salesman drawled. 'Okay, yeh, but I need to go get the special grass for the rattan. I need money to go get the grass. Then we start making it. All ready in a month.'

It sounded too good to be true.

'That's great,' I replied. He seemed so positive and genuine that I gave him the Tanzanian equivalent of sixty dollars, but not before I'd wisely taken his photo 'because you're so good-looking!' I'd laughingly explained. It was a good job I did, because, after I'd not seen him for three weeks, I showed his photo to the police. They recognised him straight away as a well-known druggy and con man.

'Come back to the police station tomorrow,' they said confidently.

At the police station the next day the policeman calmly peeled the money I was owed from a thick wad of notes in his top pocket. I'm not sure how that worked out for the con man, but I was relieved to get the charity's money back.

But I still needed to get hold of some hotel furniture.

I kept asking around until one day someone said he had heard they made furniture at Dar es Salaam prison.

And it was true – the prisoners did make furniture. They agreed to make what I ordered.

A couple of months later in Mikindani, I received an email to say the bulky consignment of rattan club armchairs and sofas was ready for collection. The hotel's temperamental Bedford lorry was inspected and declared fit and I accompanied the driver on the sweaty four-hundred-mile drive north to Dar es Salaam. A few days later we piled the furniture into the back of the lorry...

After a few hours driving we stopped for a break at a small truck-stop and I noticed one of the front wheels was glowing orange with heat. It needed a special part that was only available back in Dar. I stayed at the truck-stop with the lorry while the driver hitched a lift back. I was stranded there for four days. The only place to stay was riddled with fleas, which inevitably I brought back to Mikindani.

Fleas are tenacious little beasts! As well as scrubbing and washing when I got back to Mikindani I looked suspiciously at my bed. What if a few of the little blighters had escaped into the mattress where I'd thrown myself, exhausted, the previous night? I found myself itching and scratching at the thought. The mattress had to go.

I consulted Mtipa, the helpful man who looked after the building. He was short in stature and was permanently dressed in a pair of dark-blue shorts which ended mid-calf. Could he get rid of it for me? Mtipa's wrinkled face lit up into a wide smile.

'No problem, Bibbi Sue!' (Bibbi is the Kiswahili word for 'Aunty'.)

'But, Mtipa – it has fleas – nasty dudus that bite. Itch, itch.' I emphasised by scratching my arms.

'No problem, Bibbi Sue,' Mtipa replied. 'Thank you, thank you,' and the mattress disappeared, to be replaced by a brand new piece of foam.

'Bibbi Sue, Bibbi Sue!' came an anguished cry from the hotel kitchen a few days later. 'There's no water!' Because someone has left a tap running and emptied the hotel tank (again). I sighed with frustration. Sorting out another extortionate bill from the water authority was added to my list.

'Bibbi Sue, man from the dive school asks if any vet students with you now?'

No, I didn't have any vet students. (In fact, I only had three helpful and enthusiastic but short-term students the whole year I was there.) So, I wandered down the beach road to see what the problem was. The couple who ran a little dive school had bought a pair of Dobermans which needed castrating. A vet had been flown in from Dar, but he needed an assistant.

'I need someone who is not emotionally involved with the dogs,' explained the vet, glancing over his shoulder at the owners who were looking tense and edgy. He looked me up and down. 'You have any experience of vet work?'

'Oh, yes. I've done courses in animal health and anatomy,' I bluffed, silently wondering if A-level zoology counted. He nodded, seemingly reassured.

Scrubbed and gowned, I helped him deal with the female dog laid out on a trestle table on the veranda. We exchanged the patient for the male dog. Standing on the veranda gazing through the palm fronds at the dazzling Indian ocean while holding a dog's warm, slippery gonads in my gloved hands, I mused on the serendipity of life.

'Bibbi Sue, Bibbi Sue, the swimming club are waiting for you to give out their swimming certificates. They need balloons and sweets.' Certificates – do we have any, how many, why did no one pre-note me?

'Bibbi Sue, Bibbi Sue. Bin Kubwa very sick. She gone to the witch doctor.' Was I supposed to intervene or wait to see if our hotel cleaner recovered? And on a more practical level, would we need extra help to clean the rooms?

Mr Thomas, a smartly dressed elder with military posture in charge of our charity-sponsored tree nursery, presented himself at my desk with a bundle of receipts. 'Good morning, Bibbi Sue. I have just returned from a conference on reforestation in my home town. Here are my expenses, please.' Nobody had told me about any conference. Home town – there's a coincidence! Head Office won't sanction these expenses! How do I tell Mr Thomas without him getting exceedingly upset?

'Bibbi Sue, Bibbi Sue, come quick, the Uhuru Torch is coming.' The Uhuru Torch is a swanky gold-coloured ceremonial gas burner which was doing the rounds of Southern Tanzania. The Old Boma was being blessed with its fleeting presence in recognition of the work done by our tree nursery project. It arrived on the back of a truck, accompanied by soldiers and shrieking schoolchildren.

I stood with the hotel staff and a crowd of inquisitive villagers in respectful silence while a series of dignitaries delivered congratulatory but endlessly long speeches. Mr Thomas had already told me he had several pages of a speech prepared along the lines of 'we need more money'! He was wearing an immaculately pressed suit.

The time came for him to deliver his speech.

He took a few steps forward and had barely opened his mouth when he was cut short. The dignitaries jumped back into their vehicles and the Uhuru Torch was bundled back onto the lorry. Mr Thomas was left gazing at the departing dust cloud with a look of resignation.

His work is actually very important. I did feel sorry for him.

HQ: *'We need more activities for guests. Go to Lake Kitere and see if it's suitable for boat excursions.'*

I looked at the new map in the information room. Lake Kitere is at least two or three hours' drive up a rough track off the main road. I didn't trust the Land Rover – it was always breaking down – I needed to take a mechanic. This had the makings of quite an exciting adventure! Later, I reported back on the swamps, thick reed-beds, mosquitos, bilharzia and other nasties in the water, and that the only boats available were damp mouldy log canoes. A disaster if anyone fell in. Though I couldn't personally recognise the difference between a swamp hen and an ostrich, I had noticed the fantastic variety of birdlife. Recommended for extreme twitchers only!

HQ: *'We should have a big Christmas celebration, traditional xmas lunch and all that. Invite all the local bigwigs!'* Oh, surely not! Who wants a big roast lunch in this heat! Where can I find a turkey? I did eventually find someone who agreed to sell us one for an exorbitant price. I was grateful that they offered to wring its neck for us. No one seemed to have a clue how to dress a turkey, so I volunteered. Although I'd dressed dozens of chickens in my time, and had stuffed plenty of christmas turkeys, this bird was nothing like any turkey I'd dealt with before. It had tough, muscular thighs and absolutely no breast meat. How on earth was it going to feed the fifty guests who had inexplicably booked a traditional Christmas dinner? Amazingly, by eking out the meat to a few slivers each, we managed. And bamboozled by the Chinese crackers, copious bottles of wine, balloons and loud piped carols, no one complained.

After another long spell in Dar, Yvonne resigned from her job at the Old Boma. Eventually a new manager arrived. Something about his manner gave me the creeps. He kept asking for a private bungalow to be built behind the hotel for his use. He turned out to be a paedophile and was swiftly sent back to the UK where the police were waiting to interview him. Another manager arrived, but he didn't last very long either.

'Bibbi Sue, Bibbi Sue. The rains have made deep ruts in the road up to the school.' We need to organise a working party. Plant more bamboo and trees. Talk to the children.

HQ: *'There's a school party from Oxfordshire arriving sometime. They're going to be building a toilet block for the local school. Apparently they're completely self-contained so they won't bother you. You probably won't even notice they're there.'* I was woken up at eleven o'clock one night by a pounding on the door. It was nineteen teenage girls from Banbury expecting accommodation, and unfortunately needing guidance on how to dress and behave appropriately in this traditional Muslim village.

The next afternoon one young girl in very short shorts (!) complained to me loudly of being raped. On investigation it turned out that she had been getting friendly with one of the village youths who had mistaken her relaxed western ways for a more serious invitation. Some fumbling had ensued. She'd screamed. He'd run away. No harm done, fortunately, but I had a serious talk with her.

'Bibbi Sue, Bibbi Sue. Hotel guest wants to walk round to the end of the bay. Needs a guide.' Great. I could do with a walk. Unfortunately he got attacked by a swarm of wild bees and blamed me for not advising him to wear protection. I tried to tell him life here is full of adventure.

After one particularly busy day I drove back into the village. In the headlights I saw the distinctive silhouette of Mtipa in his calf-length shorts waving me down.

'Bibbi Sue. My daughter very ill. She needs hospital. Please!' Mtipa's very pregnant daughter was sitting outside the door of his house. With the stern instruction 'Absolutely NO taxi service for the locals!!' echoing in my head, I bundled Mtipa, his daughter and two concerned aunts into the Land Rover and drove them to the awful local hospital a few miles up the road and waited. She had to stay in, but nobody had thought to pack any food or overnight bag. I drove Mtipa back home where he had to light a fire, cook some maize porridge in the dark, and pack a small bag before I took him back to the hospital.

The next morning he glumly announced that she'd given birth to two boys. I smiled my congratulations, but he continued to look gloomy.

Later that day I had to go into the local town and bought two knitted baby gowns. When I returned I gave them to Mtipa, but by that time the first baby was already dead. The second one died the next day. Giving birth where medical facilities are only basic is a risky procedure. Although pregnancies with twins are not uncommon in Africa, infant mortality among twins is much higher than for single births. I visited the mother a few days later, but she was still very weak and utterly depressed. Poor woman.

HQ: *'Great news! You've got a very special wedding to organise. A couple who stayed at the hotel last year have decided to get married at The Old Boma. Isn't that romantic? Such a privilege!'* Fantastic! Ummm... has this ever been done before? Who officiates? How do we get a licence? What language? What sort of ceremony and what words do we use? There followed hours and hours of form-filling, sitting outside offices to get permissions and licences, translating and adapting wedding vows.

The entire staff pulled together to prepare the ceremony, decorate the gardens with wreaths of palm fronds and flowers, prepare the wedding breakfast and welcome the guests. A troop of schoolchildren arrived and entertained us with singing and dancing.

After the ceremony, packets of money were handed out, and the local officials and children left. We collapsed onto some cushions on the sunset terrace and watched the day end in a blaze of pink and purple clouds. I'd been exhausted by the nervous stress of trying to anticipate what might go wrong.

But nothing had.

Maybe I was trying too hard. Maybe we all were. Perhaps that's where voluntary organisations and charities go so wrong in places like Mikindani. During my year-long stay there I'd met Europeans returning to view the enduring legacy of the church, school or hospital they had spent their working lives establishing a generation previously. Most of them returned home disappointed, their projects dilapidated or abandoned.

I too was soon to go home. The year had been a glorious, though exhausting, adventure. I'd learned loads, laughed, cried and swapped tales with people from all over the world. And though I'd helped out in small ways, I don't think I had made much overall difference to the lives of the people who call Mikindani their home.

Looking recently at pictures of Mikindani on the internet, nothing much seems to have changed. The village looks much as it did when I arrived in 2004.

Life in rural Tanzania is messy and uncomfortable, people die who could be saved by modern medicine, and grow up not knowing all the wonders we learn about at school and beyond.

But people are incredibly resilient.

If the so-called developed world disappeared one day, the inhabitants of impoverished villages all over the world could carry on without much change in their lives. They would survive.

It's strange, but after all the money and effort thrown at places like Mikindani, and all the disappointments and lost dreams of generations of well-meaning westerners, I find a paradoxical degree of comfort in that thought.

Silks and Sewage

2005

Below: Trying to choose silk! Laundry in the river.

Above: Before and after the microfinance scheme.

I hadn't visited India since my mega hitch-hike across Northern India to Kathmandu in 1968 so when an opportunity arose to visit Southern India I jumped at the chance.

It happened like this. While I was in Tanzania in 2005 I occasionally worked with an Indian development expert called Krishnan. I helped him with his monthly reports which had to be written in English and in return he showed me how to set up and run a microfinance savings scheme for the hotel staff. We came to know and respect each other.

Then one day he said, 'Would you like to come to my house in India and see the work I am doing in my communities?'

Krishnan's invitation in his lilting Indian accent was straightforward and kind – just like he was himself. He looked like an ordinary, middle-aged family man from Southern India. I knew he'd had a long career working for various international charities in some seriously challenging parts of the world, but at that stage I had no idea that this modest man was far from 'ordinary'.

I was due some leave from the charity in Mikindani, so I accepted his invitation.

I flew from Tanzania to Chennai in Southern India and from there to a regional airport somewhere unpronounceable where, after the long, tiring journey it was a relief to be greeted by his smiling face. We, Krishnan's wife and one of his grown-up sons, together with my luggage, all piled into his ancient, but rather stylish black sedan and we set off for his town a couple of hours' drive away.

Their family home is an airy, three-storey house with running water and electricity – a real luxury after the basic facilities back in Southern Tanzania! As we drove along the noisy, congested high street of his home town of Sathyamangalam, I clocked the range of shops which clamoured for the attention of my retail-starved eyes.

On my first evening I ventured beyond the front gate to explore the dusty lane outside. A few doors along was the back of a butcher's shop where offal, chicken heads and other unmentionables were dumped into the roadside culvert to the frenzied delight of a cloud of flies. The ditch held a trickle of slimy, contaminated water which oozed down to a river where women were bashing clothes on some big rocks. I hoped Krishnan's wife got her laundry done elsewhere.

Night was falling – which it does quickly in the tropics – and lamps were being lit. Across the lane stood a row of tiny houses, their sky-blue painted walls glowed luminously as they reflected the purple and orange tones of the setting sun. From the line of houses came a rhythmic ker-clack, ker-clack, ker-clack. Curious to see what was making the noise, I peered through one of the open front doors and was greeted by smiles of welcome and an invitation to step inside.

As my eyes adjusted to the dark I could see that the room was completely filled with a wooden frame threaded with hundreds of strands of white silk. In the orange glow of a kerosene lamp an old man was seated in front of the huge loom pedalling the levers with his feet. One arm was pushing and pulling a wooden bar and the other hand was flicking the shuttle. He acknowledged me with a brief nod but didn't slacken his pace. I stood mesmerised by the pulsating pattern of the complex movements and the rhythmical beat of the sound.

I must have stood transfixed for several minutes.

Someone took my elbow, and a plastic chair and cup of hot sweet tea appeared. A young man with stumbling English was brought and he explained how the looms are operated day and night. The whole family, indeed the whole row of houses, was involved in weaving silk which was their main livelihood.

I gradually became aware that I was being watched by dozens of pairs of eyes – women, some young and others stooped with age, shyly half-hiding their faces, and barefoot, skinny youngsters gazing at me with wide-eyed curiosity. They all seemed so tiny with delicate bones like sparrows. I wondered whether the children went to school and where the family slept, as the loom seemed to take up the whole space. I made a note to ask Krishnan.

Krishnan was passionate about rural development, so in addition to his working life, he had set up a whole range of his own projects in India and was eager to show me some of them. He had a small motorbike. I would cling onto the back seat as he skillfully wove between the potholes, meandering cows and colourfully decorated, fume-belching lorries – my eyes swivelling everywhere.

First, he drove out of town into the hills where he showed me some of the small earth dams he had helped farmers build to hold back rainwater for the dry season.

Then he proudly introduced me to a community which until recently had been a slum. Now it was a village which had its own small school and some basic but modern houses – all built by the locals. He had shown the villagers how to set up and operate a similar microfinance scheme to the one he had shown me in Mikindani.

I'd already noticed as we'd whizzed around the countryside, groups of women sitting at the roadside beside huge piles of rocks. They sat all day with little hammers chipping away to reduce the rocks into road chippings – an activity based on extreme desperation by any standards. Such groups were very vulnerable to the dishonesty of the lorry drivers who charged what they liked for buying and selling the stones.

Krishnan had shown the road-chipping women in this village how to save money collectively, a few rupees each week. The system relies on keeping accurate ledgers and ensuring that the money tin was secure by having two trusted members of the group each having a separate key. The savings gradually grew until the group was able to buy their own lorry load of stones and then sell the chippings at their own price.

Using this technique on this and other schemes, they had pulled the whole village out of their previous poverty, enabling them to escape the exploitation of money lenders and organise their own small lending banks.

'It doesn't always work,' Krishnan conceded modestly. 'But it has certainly worked in this village!' I looked at this gentle, unassuming man with renewed respect.

Krishnan was very proud of a potion he and a local chemistry teacher had developed. The middle floor of his house was set up like a chemistry lab. Plastic tubs lined the walls and one room was full of large barrels of a fermenting brown liquid. Krishnan explained the magic. The potion of microbes he produced reduced sewage to dust and completely neutralised the terrible odours which were the scourge of India!

'So why isn't everyone using it? India has a terrible problem with sewage!' I gasped.

Krishnan's head wobbled in that very non-committal Indian way. 'I wish I knew. I can't give it away, it needs paying for, and you need to spray regularly,' he said with a sigh. 'And word has to get around. It's very difficult to get people to change. But we're selling some to a chicken farm not far away, and the local school. Come, I'll show you!'

We arrived at a large secondary school and I hopped off the back of the motorbike. He explained the problem had been that the sewerage system hadn't been built to cope with the growing size of the school population. Rainfall in India is in a different league to anything seen in the UK, so when it rained, raw sewage regularly emerged from the drains and overran the school grounds.

'You must see for yourself, please,' he insisted, lifting the large hatch off the sewer.

I hesitated. 'Really? You want me to go down that ladder?' I wasn't sure I was ready for this experience.

'Yes. It's okay! You'll see!' He grinned triumphantly.

As I heaved myself back out through the manhole cover, thankfully having encountered no raw sewage or gagging fumes, I found myself pondering the surprising twists of fate that had led me to a holiday inspecting the depths of a school sewerage system in rural India. Life can be wonderfully bizarre!

Another of Krishnan's passions was cow dung.

I was used to seeing cows lazily chewing plastic bags and other rubbish – cows might be seen officially as sacred but this doesn't guarantee any special treatment. Allowed to roam wherever they choose and eat whatever they wish, they regularly die painful deaths, their stomachs swollen with the litter that chokes Indian roadsides. So I was eager to see what he was going to show me.

He took me to a demonstration farm where six cows were kept mainly for their dung and urine, which are made into eight really useful products.

'See, the cows here are happy. They have good things to eat,' he explained as we walked towards the cows which were tethered under a bamboo shade on a slightly sloping concrete floor.

'The urine runs down and into this drain where we collect it,' he explained. Then we went into a shed lined with large plastic buckets. The smell was 'organic' but not unpleasant.

'We mix the urine with special leaves and twigs, and leave it a few days. This bucket is herbicide.'

Then onto the next row of buckets. 'Here, we mix with different leaves and twigs – this is plant tonic. Much better than expensive fertiliser!'

The next row of buckets was being fermented to produce a pesticide.

'So,' he continued, 'we can use the dung as compost to help plants grow, or we can do this with it!' and he pointed like a magician to the top of a bunker half buried in the ground.

'See, the dung goes inside through this door, and the gas...' he said, pointing to a pressure gauge and pipe coming out of the side of the bunker, 'leads into the kitchen. We can cook with it!' He took me into the kitchen where the pipe had been connected to a small gas ring. He was beaming with pleasure at the ingenuity of it all.

'See this floor!' he continued, tapping his foot on the hard brown floor in the demonstration house. 'Mix the dung with water and spread it down. This is very hard, lasts for years, and is antibacterial!' he added with a flourish.

On the way back through the garden I pointed to some drying discs of cow dung.

'Is that dung used for fuel?' I asked tentatively, as I'd seen similar lumps of dung being dried by the roadsides.

'Yes, it can be, or to store seeds inside. They keep better that way,' he added.

So, there it was! Eight different uses for cow dung and urine. I was impressed, and could now understand Krishnan's frustration at the way Tanzanians just tipped their cow dung into the river!

Krishnan's next-door neighbour was a silk wholesaler and was keen for me to visit them. I was invited round for a cup of tea and ushered into a warehouse filled from floor to ceiling with bolts of silk in every hue and colour.

The housewife was in charge. She was a large lady, wrapped in a magnificent pink saree, her greying hair beautifully oiled and plaited down her back. From her 'throne' of an ornately carved armchair she waved her arms and snapped orders at two thin young men who rushed hither and thither pulling out silks as ordered. I was offered a cushion to sit on while the shimmering fabrics were waved in front of me. Any that I gasped at were unrolled in a waving flourish across the floor until the room was awash in a psychedelic blaze of azure blues, emerald greens, bright pinks, purples and bright acid gold.

Silk is bought in saree lengths so, of course I bought a few. I had no expectation of ever wearing a saree, but the colours were irresistible, as was the sales technique!

All too soon it was time to return to Tanzania. Opportunities for retail therapy are sadly lacking in Southern Tanzania so I had overindulged in delicate hand-woven rugs and rich silks, not only from the next-door neighbour, but from elsewhere too. I gazed at the results of my shopping expeditions and decided I needed to post the fabrics back home to England.

Krishnan found a strong bag into which it all fitted. I tied it up, labelled it and we took it to the local post office.

'Ummm...' There was a lot of head-scratching and consulting of the Book of Rules. I was told that they couldn't accept an international parcel at the local post office. It had to go to a main post office in a bigger town. I'd planned my return to Chennai Airport via a night-sleeper train which left from a city two hours' drive away, so having packed and said my thank-yous and goodbyes, Krishnan drove me, luggage and parcel to the city post office and main railway station.

Mercifully we arrived in the city centre in one piece thanks to Krishnan's lightning-fast reactions in the traffic. He parked near the post office.

'You can't send a parcel in a bag,' they said. 'Parcels have to be wrapped in cotton cloth, with the seams hand-stitched and secured with sealing wax. All addresses have to be handwritten in biro onto the cotton cover.'

By this time the post office was about to shut, but never mind, apparently there was a 24-hour parcel depot at the railway station. Feeling slightly pressured for time, we took the parcel down the high street to find some cotton cloth and a tailor. Krishnan managed to find both, as well as a shop selling sealing wax.

As I tried to pay I realised I'd left my duffle bag in the post office – my duffle bag containing my passport, money, train ticket, flight ticket... Arghhhh!

Krishnan had turned a funny colour and I thought he was about to have a heart attack.

Hearts pounding, we raced back to the post office which was just closing. Unbelievably my bag was still sitting on the chair where I'd left it.

My heart took a little while to stop pounding.

We hurried back to the tailor and collected the now correctly wrapped and stitched parcel. Krishnan borrowed a cigarette lighter to melt the sealing wax but his hands were still shaking so badly that he burnt his fingers – quite painfully. Nursing his blisters, he managed to seal the stitching and I wrote out the address. By the time we arrived at the railway station we had just a few minutes to spare before my train left.

We found the parcel depot. Once again we got the 'Mmmm...?' Yes, the parcel was wrapped correctly, but could I just pop it on the scales one more time?

'Mmmm...? Twelve kilos is an awfully big parcel, isn't it!'

'What's wrong with twelve kilos?' I asked, exasperated.

Apparently every post office is allocated a certain number of stamps each day, and the post office didn't have nearly enough stamps to cover the cost of this parcel. They looked at the Book of Rules from every angle. They offered to telephone their colleagues in other post offices, and tried hard to find a way of accepting it, but in the end it was decided that it was just not possible. Because the bag was now tightly wrapped in cloth there was no handle with which I could carry it, and the train was about to leave.

By this time Krishnan, still clutching his blistered fingers, was trembling with stress, and I would have been happy to dump my once-precious silks at the feet of the nearest beggar. I was physically and mentally exhausted.

But Krishnan is not the sort to give up. Heroically he volunteered to take it home and try and post it next time he was near a really big post office. As I waved him goodbye from the train window I believed I'd never see those silks and rugs again.

But why did I ever doubt him?

True to his word he managed to post the wretched parcel. I don't know how or where from, but weeks later it turned up in the UK.

And he can't have been too upset with me because he invited me to visit him again – but that's another story...

Land of Adventure

2005 – 2006

In the ruined palace at Kilwa and working for Coastal Travels in Tanzania.

The witch doctor with his potions and the Massai cattle market on the slopes of Mount Meru.

Tanzania is an exciting land. Not just for its wild expanses, exotic creatures and tropical islands, but for the adventurous characters who live here. I had the great fortune to meet one of Tanzania's most dynamic entrepreneurs, who took me under his wing and gave me endless opportunities.

It happened like this.

Towards the end of my first year in Tanzania, a man of Italian heritage called Nicola Colangelo visited the Old Boma Hotel in the coastal village of Mikindani where I was volunteering. He had settled in Tanzania as a young man and made this land his home. Fairly short in stature, he had an open, honest face and a way of looking people straight in the eye. He invited me to come to Dar es Salaam when I'd finished my contract in Mikindani, and work for him. It sounded fun.

So I did.

Living in Dar es Salaam was a completely different experience from the grim, rural poverty of Mikindani where I don't remember ever being physically comfortable. In Dar the local people were much more motivated, educated and energetic – which was only to be expected as there were better schools, work and food there.

I only gradually became aware of who Nicola was. He invited me to look around his business and tell him what I'd like to do – an unusual way to start a job. I knew he had an airline but had no idea then of his wealth and the extent of his business empire.

His brand name was 'Coastal'. As I had a background in aviation, I suggested I work for Coastal Aviation.

'Before you start there, I have a little job for you,' he said casually. 'You'll be staying in one of my apartments – my driver will show you. At the moment they are very basic – they need furnishing. See if you can make them all a little more welcoming.' He told me how to draw money from the accounts office, and left me to it.

Wow, I was in heaven!

I inspected the three big apartments, spoke to the odd assortment of *mzungus* (westerners) who were lodging there and set off to explore the shopping opportunities in the city. After my experiences the previous year buying furniture for the Old Boma Hotel I considered myself quite an expert on shopping in Dar. The jumble of backstreets known as Kariokor Market was the place to head for the small stuff – kitchen equipment, drinking glasses, cutlery – 'No, not the tinfoil ones from China, thank you.' Electric kettles? – 'I'll take the one without the bare wires hanging out underneath, thanks.'

Nicola turned out to be a fantastic person to work for. I was careful to be as economical as I could, but he never once queried any of my expenditures. He also had a great sense of humour.

'My wife doesn't like spending money,' he confided in me one day, and although she never interfered with what I spent, I could feel Carolina's watchful eyes on me.

Nicola continued with his mouth twitching into a smile, 'Carolina says we are a poor family. We have a little place in America where she says her gardeners are poor, her chauffeur is poor, her guards are poor, her maids are poor... we are all poor!' Nicola chuckled. He liked making jokes. 'Use my furniture factory if you like. They sew curtains there as well. It doesn't matter what they charge as I expect Carolina will take it all back when you leave.'

That's how I found out he owned a huge woodyard and a furniture factory.

I took to spending my free time at 'Slipway', the European piazza on the seafront in Oyster Bay – the posh suburb where I was living. Apparently Nicola owned and had built it all. Slipway, with its boutiques, restaurants, café and children's playground was a magnet for us *mzungus* – a place to escape from the frustrations and inconveniences of living in an African city, and it was always buzzing with life.

He and Carolina lived fairly simply, in a modest house right next door to Slipway. Occasionally he would invite me there for breakfast.

One particular morning after the safe in Slipway's admin office had been blown up and robbed, he told me, 'I don't have anything worth stealing in my house, and no security system. That way is safer.'

Apparently the robbery had all the hallmarks of an inside job. I was puzzled that he seemed so relaxed about it.

'You don't seem upset,' I ventured. 'Doesn't it make you angry knowing that it might have involved some of your staff?'

Nicola laughed. 'Not really.' He shrugged. 'It doesn't matter as long as I can make it faster than they can steal it.'

I was allocated a car. It felt wonderful to have my own set of wheels, but dicing through the traffic took nerves of steel, which I suppose I must have had. The local minibuses were an absolute legend – they sprinted in and out of gaps both on and off the road, belching out clouds of evil fumes, while their bumpers were painted with thought-provoking slogans such as 'Smoking Kills' and 'Protected by the blood of Jesus'.

As Dar was blessed with unpredictable power cuts while I was there, the traffic lights were playfully unsynchronised. I approached each junction with my eyes spinning, edging as close as possible to the vehicle in front – unless it was a petrol tanker with a swarm of young lads round the back syphoning petrol into containers and plastic bags.

My little Suzuki had a clutch problem which caused it to hop in traffic like a spring lamb. The queues were mind-numbingly long, blue with foul-smelling diesel fumes, the crunch of metal on metal and the crackle of fibreglass panels, but what I remember most was the good-humoured way that the drivers bounced off each other.

Furnishing the apartments was a long process, so while I waited for things to become available, I started work at the airport. At that time Coastal Aviation had about thirteen aircraft; portly little Cessna Caravans plus a heftier Pilatus aircraft. Cessna Caravans are single-engined utility aircraft with a baggage hold underneath and room for thirteen passengers plus the pilot.

As Coastal's new 'quality control manager' I got to fly the length and breadth of Northern Tanzania in the front seat next to the pilot.

I felt incredibly lucky to be able to fly low over the safari parks, peering down at giraffes resembling tiny stick insects and hippopotamuses wallowing like fat black slugs in the meandering rivers and lakes. We flew over volcanic craters, the Great Rift Valley, and out over the blue-green waters of the Indian Ocean to exotic islands such as Zanzibar and Pemba.

That's how I learned that Nicola also owned a number of tourist lodges and hotels. Occasionally we flew to a mine – great scars in the landscape where a variety of metals and minerals were scoured out of the rocks. However, I was glad I wasn't on board the Pilatus aircraft which was parked at one of these remote airfields while picking up a cargo of newly mined gold when it was written-off by trigger-happy bandits.

'Another inside job,' Nicola conceded. 'There was shooting, but no one got hit. The guards knew to keep out of the way.'

Sometimes Nicola just wanted me to spend time at airfields he hadn't visited in a while, to reassure the local staff that they weren't forgotten. Sometimes he wanted my opinion on a problem, but I never came up with any solutions that he hadn't already considered. The experience was fantastic, and no two days were ever the same.

But there was one big downside to life in Tanzania.

Malaria!

I'd already had this miserable illness twice the previous year (despite taking the recommended anti-malarials). Fortunately there was less chance of contracting it again in a city. However, I was often out and about in rural areas. And it worried me. Nicola was always dreaming up new schemes – that's how he'd made all his money – and one of his dreams was to make the Tanzanian islands and beaches a thriving tourist destination for middle-class *mzungus* like me. He asked my opinion.

'Ummm,' I'd replied, 'I don't think that'll happen until malaria is effectively dealt with.'

'You are right, of course,' he continued and went on to tell me about the teenage daughter of one of his Italian friends. She had come to Dar on work experience, fallen ill with cerebral malaria and died six weeks later. A sobering tale.

I was sent to Mwanza on Lake Victoria to meet the Coastal Airways staff who were based there and listen to their problems. The chief pilot invited me to stay for a few days in his house with his wife and family. They lived on the edge of the lake and showed me the remains of an Ilyushin 76 cargo plane which, a few weeks earlier, had crashed into the water shortly after take-off from Mwanza Airport. It had been carrying fifty tons of fish. Apparently industrial scale overfishing is becoming a big problem in this massive lake.

One day Nicola asked me to go to Kilwa, 350 kms south of Dar. He wanted me to set up a Coastal Aviation Ticket Agency there. I was flown south and we touched down on the short, sandy runway. I started by checking out the only decent hotel in the village, right on the beach, built in the local style of wood and coconut-leaf thatch with a big covered area for the bar, restaurant and poolside lounge.

The South African owner, a straight-talking, no-nonsense slip of a woman, sat down and chatted to me. I asked her what sort of customers came there.

'Sports fishing from South Africa mainly. There's another bunch coming next week. Big buggers. Huge appetites. They always drink far more than we can stock so they bring their own. Beats me how they can drink all night, then get up early and spend the day pitching and tossing around in a boat stinking of fish guts!'

She laughed when I suggested it must be their tough colonial genes.

'Yeh,' she continued, 'You have to be tough here! When we first took this place over, Chinese labourers from the road project just kept wandering in. They'd creep into a corner and go to sleep. Used to find them all over the place! Had to keep kicking them out. I was in the restaurant one day when I noticed one of them lying on the sofa with his finger stuffed up his nose. He snorted out this huge green bogie and flicked it onto the floor. Well, that was it! I screamed at him, "You can bloody well clear that up yourself, you disgusting, uncivilised, snot-nosed, slit-eyed peasant", threw a bucket and mop at him and stood over him while he swabbed it clean. Huh,' she sneered, 'they've not been back, thank God!'

While I was sure our pilots wouldn't behave like Chinese labourers I made a note to keep on the right side of her.

A short walk from the hotel was a tiny harbour. I'd heard that a visit to the island of Kilwa Kisiwani was not to be missed so I waited for the ferry with a group of half a dozen villagers and their baggage. A small wooden dhow sailed across the inlet towards us. We waded out into the pebbly harbour and scrambled aboard for the twenty-minute sail across to the island.

Kilwa Kisiwani is a magical place with a fascinating history, and no tourists. I wandered around the island absolutely amazed at the wealth of ruins in this overgrown and abandoned port city. One of the most complete buildings is the Great Mosque, but I also stumbled across an imposing fort and other smaller mosques and wells half hidden amongst the rambling vegetation.

Strange to think that in mediaeval times this small island was a rich and beautiful city – the biggest, most important settlement on the east coast of Africa, trading in slaves as well as gold, ivory and all manner of treasures.

Wandering across a tidal inlet of damp sand, I pushed my way through an archway of tangled bushes to the base of a truly huge and ancient baobab tree. It had a spectacular girth of smooth-skinned bark and truncated branches characteristic of what people sometimes call the 'upside-down tree'. I sat for a while in its shade alongside a jumble of ornately carved gravestones, now crumbling and crooked – there was no sound except for the twittering of birds and the sighing of long dead spirits.

The agency I was helping to create would undoubtedly bring tourists – it seemed desecration that they would disturb the peace and mystery of this magical island.

Back in Dar, Nicola and I discussed what was needed for the new agency building, and shortly afterwards work started. Upgrading the tiny concrete hut that had been used by Coastal passengers involved multiple trips for the workmen from Dar, and a huge headache for me sorting out the expenses and receipts. When it started operating, the accounting procedures for ticket sales involved the Kilwa agent giving the pilot a bag containing money and ticket stubs in multiple envelopes.

But after a few weeks the accountant in Dar told me that the invoices and money were making absolutely no sense – so would I try and work out where the sums were going wrong? The agent in Kilwa had only had a very basic education and, in common with many Tanzanians, saw his job as an opportunity to cream off a little extra. Nicola knew that pilfering was endemic, but told his staff he would turn a blind eye if they kept the pilfered sums 'small'.

'Just don't get greedy,' he told them. Sorting out what was 'small pilfering' and what was poor accounting procedures took another flight to Kilwa, but trying to make sense of the paperwork was a nightmare. There was no lazing around or exploring for me on that trip!

Nicola had a habit of collecting people. As well as those, like myself, who might be useful, he also collected people who needed help. One of these was a middle-aged lady called Maria (not her real name), originally from somewhere that had once been part of Ukraine. Nicola had offered her part-time employment in the travel office at Slipway. She was a small, outwardly fun-loving lady, always laughing, cheerful and fond of parties.

We became friends.

She had an interesting history. While still a student back in Ukraine she had set her heart on marrying a black man and against advice from family and friends she found one and married him. Life was difficult, especially with a black husband and a coffee-coloured baby, so he brought her back to Tanzania. But he was killed shortly afterwards in a car accident.

His family, as is the tradition, immediately sought possession of their fridge, furniture and all their assets, including her baby daughter. Maria had to spend all her savings (and a deal of cunning) in order to keep the baby. On marriage, Maria had officially become Tanzanian, and when she tried to return home, she found that she wasn't entitled to citizenship in her homeland which had since become part of Belarus.

So she was stuck in Tanzania. Unable to earn enough to keep her daughter safe, suitably educated and fed, she found herself in increasing amounts of debt.

She did whatever she had to in order to survive.

After a few years of degrading poverty she asked a New Zealand couple she had met for help. She begged them to adopt her daughter and take her back with them to New Zealand for the chance of a decent life. I can't begin to imagine what heartache that must have caused. By the time I met Maria her daughter was in her late teens and growing up a world away in New Zealand.

On New Year's Eve, Maria and I went to the gala party that Nicola had laid on at Slipway. I was whirling and twirling on the dance floor when I noticed Maria, unusually for her, sitting alone in a corner. She said she wasn't feeling too good, so I drove her home. Apparently she spent the next day in bed so I was concerned enough to take her to the Agha Khan (private) hospital the following day. Nicola handed me some money to cover her fees.

She died ten days later.

The speed of her deterioration shocked us all. It was only after talking to two of her closest friends that I began to build up a better picture of her. She had been incubating AIDS, TB and more recently, cancer, but had been fanatically insistent that no one knew. She obviously knew she was dying. Two days after being admitted to the Agha Khan she had a very private interview with one of the surgeons, who, the next day performed some sort of 'exploratory' operation on her.

She never regained consciousness.

All that raised huge questions in my mind, but no answers. Surgeons must sometimes be faced with impossible quandaries.

Maria was a strong, brave, independent lady. She was just forty-one.

The funeral service four days later was quite an experience for those of us more used to the sanitised procedures back home. The best substitute venue for a Russian Orthodox funeral was found. I trooped with a large party of her friends into the Greek Orthodox church where Maria's remains were brought down the aisle on an open pallet. Her body had been kept as cool as possible in the tropical heat, but even so, her exposed face was mottled black.

The priest muttered his blessings, flicking whisks of water as he walked around her. Then he called to his assistant who emerged from a side chapel with a bottle of Filippo Berio olive oil. The priest then upturned the bottle, ceremonially sprinkling the oil over Maria's body. Knowing that Maria was about to be cremated, it was like basting the turkey. The performance could have been hugely comic if it hadn't been so horribly macabre.

A crowd of her friends, including her daughter who had raced round the world to say farewell, sat quietly beside the Hindu-style funeral pyre as Maria's body was cremated. Then, in keeping with the fun-loving friend we had so recently lost, we drove back to the Russian Cultural Centre and had a huge party.

'Go to Arusha and see how they're getting on,' said Nicola. So I flew to Arusha.

At an altitude of four and a half thousand feet, the air in Arusha is noticeably cooler and more comfortable than on the coast. While there I decided to go on a 'cultural tour' to the slopes of the nearby Mount Meru. These cultural tours are a great way of enabling tourists to see something of the authentic culture, while ensuring that the proceeds of tourism go straight to the local people. For the equivalent of £12 I would get the services of an English-speaking guide who would escort me to a village, introduce me to some local characters, and provide me with tea and a typical meal.

Being the only customer that day, I had the exclusive company of Thomas, the sort of tall, imposing Maasai usually seen in travel brochures, but that day wearing a T-shirt and jeans. Thomas towered above me, taking one giant stride to ten of my hops and skips as I tried to keep up.

I trotted along behind Thomas through the side-streets of Arusha and up a dusty track to the start of the bus route. The minibus was so beaten up that I was amazed when the engine actually fired, which it did once every available seat, nook and cranny was jammed full of passengers and bags. Coughing, snorting and belching out clouds of black fumes, the minibus started its long climb up the mountain.

Halfway up, we changed buses in a little village. The more sophisticated urban passengers pushed their way off first. Then Thomas and I climbed on board an even more decrepit bus with a set of really rural characters. I had a young boy with a runny nose sitting on my lap, a skinny young woman on my left and a very dignified old man on my right.

The air inside the bus smelt vaguely familiar – if you've ever cleaned out the inside of a horse's hoof you will recognise the smell – the sweetly organic, farmyardy smell of animals, sweat, manure and hay. Not unpleasant – just distinctive.

Part-way up the mountain something started to break free underneath the chassis. The bus pulled over, people sighed with resignation and the driver and conductor climbed out. They did a bit of kicking and banging, then, all sorted, we set off again.

It was market day in the village where we were heading, and the roadside was scattered with locals half-heartedly waving for the bus to stop or just sitting on piles of sacks hoping to get a lift. Incredibly we picked up a couple more passengers and squashed them in.

As the bus crested a shoulder of the mountain the view was endless – mile upon mile of ash-coloured plain dotted with unexpected volcanic cones, bounded by distant mountains. Gathering speed, the bus bucked and swayed down a long strait before reaching the next uphill section.

A few dusty grey miles later the bus turned off the road into a market square. I was totally unprepared for the swirl of colour and activity. There were Maasai everywhere, in bright red, orange and blue checked robes, with huge silver earrings, long socks made of coiled white beads, ornately beaded necklaces, and the men carrying traditional sticks and swords.

I was getting quite used to seeing a few Maasai in towns, even dressed in traditional garb sitting next to me in an internet café, but the sight of crowds of Maasai in their spectacular costumes is an amazing sight.

Thomas was obviously pleased with my reaction. 'We go to see witch doctor?' he asked.

'Yes, I'd love to. Is it far?'

'No. Very close,' replied Thomas, and he set off at a terrifying pace while I stumbled along the trail behind him. After nearly an hour of scrambling up and down ravines, round thorn fences, and over rocky outcrops, we topped a small rise and Thomas pointed out a group of mud and thatch houses below.

Dripping with sweat and grey with dust, I leant on the doorpost of the witch doctor's hut trying to get my breath back.

I peered through the entrance, my eyes slowly adjusting to the darkness. Inside the one-roomed hut was an iron plough, a palm-leaf mat, two low stools and a string bed. The witch doctor had laid out the tools of his trade on the mat and gestured for me to sit opposite him on one of the stools. I studied his face in the dim light. In common with most older people in the dry air of this sun-scorched land, he had the wrinkled, weathered skin of a tortoise. I couldn't read his expression, and I wondered how he felt about talking with *mzungus* like me who were totally ignorant, and possibly even scathing, about his 'professional' knowledge.

While Thomas interpreted, he explained in a single-toned monologue about the various powders which he poured out of dried gourds.

'This powder, you mix with water and drink if you want baby, this powder you make cuts in your skin and rub in to cure liver problems, this powder you make into paste and rub over face if you get headache, this powder you sprinkle on food if you want to feel more like making love...'

There seemed to be a lot of powders to help women get pregnant, but he didn't show me any medicine to prevent pregnancy. This got me wondering about Maasai cultural attitudes to family size and fertility, so I asked him if the Maasai used anything for contraception. Both he and Thomas seemed bemused by the question.

The best number of babies for a woman, he confided in me, is ten.

I left two thousand shillings (about £2) on the mat, shook his hand and then Thomas and I scrambled back out into the blinding sunshine. We took a roundabout route back to the village, stopping at a rather smart shelter which had been specially constructed for cultural tourists. The lady who lived next to the shelter kept 'the books', and here

I paid for my tour, wrote my name in the visitors' book and was given an official receipt. She then offered me tea or coffee. Tourists are sometimes squeamish about genuinely local food and drink, so she offered me a Lipton's yellow label tea bag or a cup of instant coffee.

Wanting the authentic cultural experience, I asked her what she drank, and persuaded her to brew me a cup of local tea. It had much more flavour than the ubiquitous tea bag. A good choice.

By now Thomas was feeling hungry. 'You only book culture tour yesterday, so sorry, no time for special meal. But you like barbeque?' he asked hopefully.

'Oh, yes, I like barbeque,' I replied, much to his relief. I guessed it was that or nothing.

He strode – I trotted – through the market to the back of the livestock section. Thomas explained we needed to order first, to give the meat time to cook while we explored the market. He stopped at a hole in the wall of a shed. In the darkness inside I could just make out a few glistening piles of meat and offal.

'You like sheep, goat or cow?' I settled on sheep. There was a bit of haggling and Thomas selected a leg of lamb. It was whisked to the rear of the hut and onto a barbeque grill where it nestled snugly between a goat's head and some ugly-looking knuckles. We left it roasting and wandered into the livestock market.

There were hundreds of cows and bulls, some with magnificent sets of horns. Some, unfortunately, were little more than skeletons, their flanks so shrunken with starvation that I wondered they had the strength to stand. The drought in this part of Africa was everyone's concern, and the Maasai and their herds were really suffering. I wandered among the cows, the sheep and goats, exchanging greetings and as much banter as my limited Kiswahili and the men's English would allow. Everyone seemed to be in good humour.

Then we returned to the barbeque.

Passing a plump, but worried-looking sheep tied to a fence, we entered the dining sheds and found space at one of the trestle tables. Most of the customers were men, and quite a few of them were obviously a bit tipsy. There were two men sitting opposite me, gorging themselves on a huge piece of meat. The older of the two looked like a pantomime pirate. He was wearing a filthy old jacket stretched tightly over the top of his Maasai robes. His face was covered in day-old stubble and he sported long gashes in his ears – the height of Maasai fashion. His chin was greasy with sheep fat. He narrowed his eyes at me as Thomas and I sat down.

Wow, I thought. *What a wonderful face. I must get a photo.*

'I want to take a photo of that man,' I hissed at Thomas, 'but I'm fed up with people asking for money every time I get my camera out! Can you tell him he's got a great face...?'

Long John Silver across the table burst out into a roar of laughter. 'No picture! I want money!' he thundered at me.

'No money! I want picture!' I echoed back.

We sat and stared at each other while he picked up a bone, sliced off the remaining slivers of meat with his razor-sharp knife, and then proceeded to gnaw the knuckle ends.

I shrugged and looked around the room, pretending to be unimpressed by the tantalising photo opportunity across the table.

He muttered something to Thomas.

'He says you can take picture,' said Thomas.

So I sat and took dozens of photos of him while he gnawed his way through the last of the gristle. He pulled out his knife again and chopped the knuckle ends off the shanks, tipping the broken ends of the bones up in the air and sucking out the marrow with several satisfying slurps.

By this stage the table was awash with half-cooked blood and I was wondering why I'd been stupid enough to wear my white linen trousers for this outing. Long John roared at one of the young serving lads who came running with a sheet of newspaper and made some rather ineffectual sweeps across the table, chasing the blood onto the floor. Long John grabbed the newspaper, screwed it up and tried to show him how to clean the table, but all he did was spread the mess around even more.

A bowl and a jug of water came our way and we rinsed our hands. Then our leg of lamb arrived. The serving lad attacked it with a huge and very sharp knife, cutting it up neatly into little cubes which he piled onto a battered metal plate edged with salt.

Thomas and I picked our way through the mountain of meat, Thomas nudging the more tender pieces towards my side of the plate. We sat and chewed stoically for a long time. I ate as much as I could but Thomas was a serious meat eater. He just kept chewing and swallowing until all that was left was the salty paste at the bottom of the dish.

We left the bones for Long John.

Thanks to Nicola, Arusha was just one of many fascinating places I found myself in. He sent me to Maputo in Mozambique to explore options for a scheduled service. There I was entertained by a friend of his, a politician who had been a freedom fighter in the intense civil war which ended in 1992. We had some long chats about politics, life and liberty.

He sent me to Tanga in Northern Tanzania to help improve the local agency. There I watched the highly entertaining and dangerous Tanga rally – thirty-six specially prepared rally cars exploding out of the busy town centre, racing around the local area and back through the middle of the town.

They don't bother with safety barriers or marshalls. It was absolutely terrifying.

He sent me numerous times to Zanzibar where I visited the House of Wonders – the first to get electricity on the island – and the ruined house where Freddie Mercury lived as a child.

I was sent to the other Spice Island, Pemba, and to Mafia Island where I came face to beak with a fish eagle – I was snorkelling around a rocky islet and looked up to find myself staring into the yellow eyes of a huge black and white pile of beak and feathers flexing his talons on a rock just a few feet away.

And when my son, Simon, flew out from England to visit me, Nicola provided us with a land cruiser and driver to tour around the Serengeti, and then a hotel for us to stay at in Zanzibar. He never asked for any payment.

Working for Coastal Aviation was a unique and fascinating experience. So why on earth did I want to come home? It's only looking back through the notes I wrote at the time that I remember the frustrations of trying to get things done in a culture where standards and expectations were completely different from mine.

I'm too impatient to sit quietly in long queues. I get cross with people who aren't honest or who try to rip me off. I hate being kept waiting. In short, I didn't find working in Tanzania very relaxing, and I'm sure many of the things I did manage to achieve have slipped back to the way they were.

Sadly, Coastal Aviation no longer operates. Nicola died prematurely in 2017.

He was a remarkable man, admired and respected throughout Tanzania. Although I only worked for Coastal for a year, I remember him with gratitude for the wonderful opportunities he gave me and the vivid memories I shall keep forever.

By the time I left Tanzania I was nearly sixty, and I was beginning to wonder if my experiences with Coastal Aviation would be the last opportunity I'd get for adventuring.

Fortunately it wasn't.

A Disappearing Sun

2006

Roundabout flight between African countries and a trek to the centre of the eclipse.

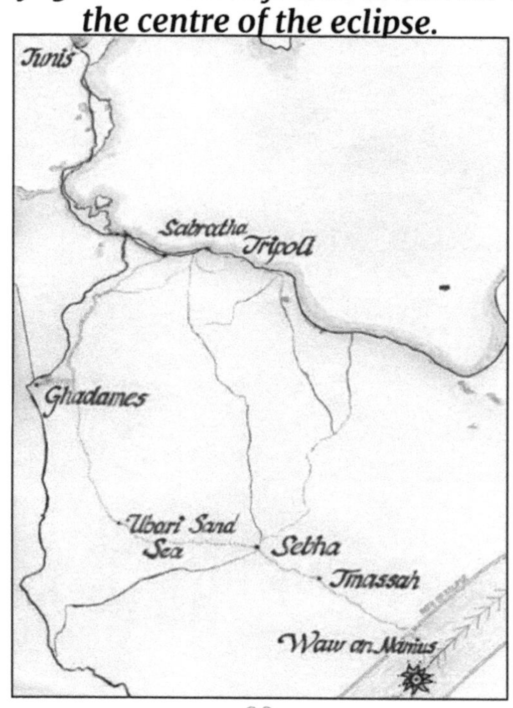

Visiting Libya's Roman ruins
and standing on the edge of the Waw an Namus crater.

In 2005 I was working in Tanzania when an email pinged onto my screen.

Are you interested in a total eclipse in the middle of the Libyan desert next March? It'll be brilliant fun!

Yes – sounds great. Count me in, I pinged back to my friends.

Total eclipses are magical experiences! I'd witnessed a number of eclipses with these friends – bobbing about in the middle of the English Channel in 1999, in Botswana, even China. This expedition into a desert that I love sounded even more intriguing.

My friends talked a company called Sahara Travel into organising the trip. The company had been reluctant – Libya being politically dodgy with a limited tourist industry in a remote and challenging part of the world. And 'Who else would possibly want to join an expedition to the back of beyond for four minutes and seven seconds' worth of total darkness?' Sahara Travel argued.

But they eventually agreed. For a price!

I glanced at a map. Southern Libya wasn't very far from Tanzania – as the crow flies. However, when I enquired about flights at the travel agency in Dar es Salaam there was a considerable amount of sucking of teeth.

Apparently, crows don't fly between Tanzania and Libya. The best that could be offered from Dar was all round East Africa via Kilimanjaro, Nairobi and Addis Ababa, then north to Rome, and south again to Tunisia. Getting into Libya itself presented impossible paperwork. Undeterred, I bought the flight tickets, and waited for March to arrive.

At Kilimanjaro Airport I, unwisely, ate a 'freshly made' sandwich. During the long wait at Nairobi Airport my stomach started making some funny noises. By the time I arrived at the brand spanking new Addis Ababa Airport in Ethiopia I was getting uncomfortable stomach cramps and spent the entire stopover in the white-marbled and up till then, unsullied, ladies' toilets.

By some miracle to do with the earth spinning, my flight arrived in Rome only shortly after it had taken off, i.e. it was still the middle of the night. Other grim-faced passengers were hunkered down into their jackets because, being March, it was cold. I started to shiver in my tropically thin cotton blouse because I hadn't packed, indeed, didn't have any warm clothes. The airport was devoid of seats so I looked around for a baggage trolley to park my bag and sit on. But as I was travelling from Africa, to Africa, and hadn't reckoned on all the shops and exchange bureaus being shut, I hadn't packed a one-euro coin for a trolley!

So I spent the next six hours alternating between the hard plastic chairs outside a closed café and frequent dashes into the ladies' loos.

My incarceration in Rome Airport was made slightly more bearable by a chance meeting with one of those unfortunate souls who made me realise that despite being bone-tired, frozen and with my stomach turning somersaults, how lucky I actually was. A middle-aged Indian with thick glasses and crutches hobbled painfully over to where I was huddled over my book and started a conversation in halting English. He had been living in Italy, working for the past seven years in Rome's waterworks department, and had just been to visit his ailing mother in India. On arriving home to Italy, the immigration officials wouldn't let him back in. He had been waiting for three days to get his entry sorted out.

'But where do you sleep?' I asked. He gestured to the hard plastic chairs.

'And what do you eat?' and as if on cue the coffee shop where I was sitting opened and one of the waiters brought him over a bottle of water and a sandwich. Nice of them!

I dug around in my money belt, pulled out some dollars and bought him a cup of coffee. He might still be sitting there for all I know. There's a book and film about a man who had been marooned for years inside Paris Airport...

And so, eventually, onwards to Tunisia, where I was to meet up with Sahara Travel. My friends were flying from Gatwick directly into Libya on special visas. Apparently I would meet up with them somewhere in the middle of Libya in a week's time. Sahara Travel had apparently found some other madcaps wanting to join the trip, though I didn't realise just how many madcaps until somewhat later! This initial group had travelled in eight various off-road vehicles from the UK through France and caught the ferry from Marseilles to Tunis. Arrangements for me to meet them were rather vague, so I was relieved to be greeted at the airport and escorted to the port where these adventurers had just disembarked from the ferry.

Wow, I thought. *Amazingly well organised! This must be the advantage of paying extra for a small, bespoke trip*.

A young man with dark hair, leather trousers and sunglasses introduced himself in a broad Irish accent as 'Frank', the tour organiser. It turned out that he was 'Sahara Travel'. Not a very big organisation then.

I was to ride in a Mercedes G-wagon driven by a tall cheerful bloke called Dave. Everyone welcomed me and I was introduced all round, though still feeling fragile, instantly forgot most people's names. Dave slung my travel-stained holdall into the back of his wagon, which was piled with camping beds, tents, jerry cans, and other wilderness essentials, plus, I couldn't help noticing, an immaculate set of luxury suitcases. I had only one fellow passenger, Rosalind, a rather sophisticated-looking lady in a floaty dress and large floppy hat, wearing conspicuous amounts of make-up. We leapt into our vehicles and the convoy roared out of town.

Rosalind hardly said a word to me the whole trip other than to tell me that she lived in the south of France and was an ex-rally driver(?). I realised quite quickly that the whole trip as well as her 'travelling companion' weren't up to the standard she thought she was paying for.

It was hardly surprising. That night my continuing stomach problems eclipsed all other thoughts.

Fortunately, our first night's accommodation was in a hotel. After a sleepless night I shuffled downstairs the next morning, my trousers stuffed with pre-emptive wadding. That day's drive passed in a distressing blur and I didn't start to take note of my surroundings until we had crossed the border into Libya (long, long queues and a night stop on a beach, knee-deep in rubbish) and were exploring the Roman ruins of Sabratha (the group explored – I slept, curled up under a shady tree). By that evening, I hadn't eaten for three days, but I was starting to feel better.

Somehow our 'small, bespoke group' had now become a convoy of eleven vehicles, one of which was the all-important chuckwagon containing two local chaps who would regularly conjure up fresh salads and buffets out of an assortment of polystyrene boxes. Our vehicle had acquired 'security' – a quiet, inoffensive man. Perhaps I should have felt comforted by the obvious gun that he kept 'hidden' under his shirt – but somehow, sitting next to him, it just worried me.

By this stage, in addition to our own on-board policeman, we were accompanied by an olive-green police van which patrolled up and down the convoy. It had darkened windows, but they drove with the front windows rolled down, waving cheerfully as they passed and repassed our line of vehicles. As our wagons had different loads and engine power, and Frank, at the front, forced a blistering pace, our vehicles became strung out along the tarmac road. We also kept losing contact with each other via the line-of-sight CB radios. Our convoy was also joined for a while by a menacing-looking police wagon. It was wider and lower than an average van with double refrigerator-type doors on the back. But it was definitely not selling ice creams.

Our strange convoy headed inland, up into the Atlas Mountains. As it was early in the year the mountain slopes were still grey, covered with scratchy clumps of last year's vegetation. I wondered what these barren-looking valleys would look like when spring carpeted them with patches of fresh crops and flowers. In one hilltop settlement where we camped for the night we were shown an ancient storehouse perched on the edge of a precipitous cliff. Used until recent times, each family had their own store room accessed via a rough scaffold of wooden steps. There was only one entrance to this edifice, fiercely guarded at all times against opportunistic bandits.

We spent another night in a campsite outside the UNESCO World Heritage site of Ghadames – a now deserted underground city where we could explore how the local Berber tribes had lived for thousands of years. Temperatures outside vary between blisteringly hot during the day and icy cold at night, but the climate underground was perfect. The city is divided into seven segments, one for each of the local tribes. Men lived on the lower floor, where underground passageways open out into market squares, while women and girls lived on the upper floors. Women could meet up with other women by skipping across the rooftops and, during some strictly observed times of day could venture downstairs and into the market squares or outside the city, unseen by other men. We were allowed into a couple of the houses, still furnished in traditional style. Comfortable, colourful and really stylish.

On the lower floor the front doors of each house told a story. If any of the family had pilgrimaged to Mecca then the door would be highly decorated with colourful paint and iron nails. I was fascinated by the intricate locks.

What a stunning souvenir a key would make, I thought as I gazed at the doors, and asked a couple of old men selling tourist bits and bobs. Each one shook his head. But our accompanying guide must have overheard me. As we were sipping cool mint tea in a café in the walls of the city, a young boy appeared and offered me two keys. I chose the one with smudges of green and blue paint on it. It has pride of place in my house today.

In the modern market outside this subterranean complex, I bought a bright-red velvet dressing gown, embellished with sequins and wildly coloured embroidery. I probably looked a bit mad but at least it was warm!

We needed to fuel up. Unfortunately the petrol station on the edge of town was without power.

'What do you expect – this is Africa!' fumed Frank, but by the time someone had found the key for the generator and all eleven wagons had fuelled up, the afternoon had slipped by. Frank, as ever, infected us with his inner stress, reminding us of the distance to go, the scary terrain ahead, and in a week's time the 'eclipse that wouldn't wait'!

Even thinking about the eclipse would send shivers down my spine. The shadow of this particular occurrence was due to touch down on Earth in eastern Brazil at 08:36 UTC. Having raced across the Atlantic, Africa and Central Asia, it would finally lift off the Earth's surface at sunset along Mongolia's northern border at 11:48 UTC. A total distance of over nine thousand miles in just over three hours. In other words, it would be travelling at an average speed of over three thousand miles an hour. Impressive!

Being on the centreline of the shadow as it raced across planet Earth was a 'must' for every serious eclipse watcher. The length of the shadow and the maximum time of complete darkness varies with every eclipse and we had chosen to aim for the one spot where this eclipse would last the longest – a full four minutes and seven seconds – which happened to be in the middle of the Libyan Sahara.

Frank was right to push us on. The eclipse wasn't going to wait.

A few miles out of town our convoy took a right turn off the tarmac road. This was it – we were now in the desert proper. We were heading for the Ubari Sand Sea – an area of huge dunes which Frank's rather overblown travel notes had described as 'The Sahara at its finest'. This add-on to the main trip had been arranged because the boys wanted to try out their off-road vehicles and sand-driving skills.

The undulating landscape became drier and more desolate. With tyre marks everywhere it wasn't possible to follow a main track. As before, Frank was driving too fast for everyone to keep up. All we could do was to follow the occasional cloud of dust and hope it was the vehicle in front. The policeman sitting next to me sucked his teeth loudly every time we completely lost sight of the others. He was right to be worried. I'd once been given instructions on how to travel in a convoy – and it wasn't like this!

The afternoon shadows were starting to lengthen as Dave raced his G-wagon out of a shallow wadi when the inevitable happened. There was a fairly obvious fork in the track but no indication of which way to go. Dave selected the right-hand fork and zoomed off at top speed.

It was the middle of the night before Frank eventually rounded up all eleven vehicles. There followed a good deal of dark muttering as everyone wanted to blame someone else, but it seemed that Frank got the message that, at the head of the convoy, he needed to slow down and keep checking to see the vehicle behind.

Next day, we were travelling across a high plain, interspersed with the remnants of an even higher plateau of strangely shaped rocky outcrops. These were shrink-wrapped by a harder capping stone which glistened in the sunlight like a crackle-glaze. Away to our right we started to see a long line of dunes. As we drove further and further south we noticed sand dunes on our left as well. We were being channelled down a funnel which could only end in more sand dunes dead ahead.

This was it. The start of the Ubari Sand Sea.

We all got out of our vehicles and gazed in awe at the height and steepness of the dunes blocking the way ahead. I'd never been through sand like this. It was truly daunting. The drivers let their tyre pressures down, and we all climbed back on board.

'Want to have the first go, Dave?' murmured Frank to our driver.

Dave revved the Mercedes engine, took a long run, and we shot up the face of a precipitous dune. I hardly had time to catch my breath when we crested the top, hung momentarily in mid-air, while the bonnet swung through the sky until it was pointing almost vertically down the other side. We bounced to a stop at the bottom.

The next wagon to try the dune was a brand-new Land Rover Discovery. It too revved up the front face of the dune, crested the top and promptly nose-dived into the soft sand at the bottom. It had to be dug out. The owner, who had been boring us with the alleged unique sand-tackling capabilities of his vehicle, was embarrassed, blaming the salesmen for the over-enthusiastic claims of their latest (and very expensive) vehicle. And himself for his gullibility in believing them. Over the next couple of weeks we had to dig his heavy vehicle out of soft sand a number of times.

Next to try was the elderly Dutch couple in their stately old Land Rover 110. It didn't even have the power to reach the top, so one of the guides in the chuckwagon showed them a gentler route round the back. A bit like scrambling up Snowdon and finding the café and road at the top, I thought.

That night, the first of four days crossing this desert, we camped in a sand valley. Rosalind, my 'ex-rally driver' travelling companion of the immaculate complexion and few words, decided she wanted a go at dune-driving. Having unsuccessfully asked Dave if she could borrow our vehicle, she persuaded a fun English couple with a Toyota Landcruiser that she was seriously experienced at this kind of driving and their vehicle would be perfectly safe in her capable, elegantly manicured hands. The wife agreed to go with her. They came back shame-faced with a battered vehicle and badly wrenched backs. Both women were in silent but serious pain for the rest of the trip, while the husband raged loudly about his bent, and only just driveable, Toyota.

Driving through the high dunes was a weird experience. It felt exhilarating as Dave was a very good driver, but it was also terrifying. The surface was like a stormy sea, with huge waves and deep dips. If any of our vehicles had slipped into the deepest holes we would never have got it out.

At the end of each day I would walk to the top of a high dune and just sit, looking out at the desert – nothing but sand dunes for mile after mile. Yet there were signs of life – the hatch-marks made by a snake, regular sets of dimples where a lizard had scampered, and occasionally I'd spot a migrating swallow flying low, its wingtips almost brushing the sand as it battled heroically northwards.

I didn't use my tent, preferring to sleep under the stars. Occasionally I would wake up and note the stately passage of the Milky Way as it rotated lazily through the deep inky blackness that extends forever, through mysteries that none of us have yet explored or understood.

Quite magical!

Each morning, accompanied by Frank's goading that 'The Eclipse won't wait', we would break camp in a mad rush – still chewing our breakfast bread and jam, leaving our campfire of rubbish still burning, and speed away to tackle more sand dunes.

Late on the fourth day, euphemistically described as a 'rest day' in Frank's travel notes, we emerged out of the sand onto a road and arrived at our next destination – the Hotel Africa in the remote town of Sebha. Frank had described the hotel facilities in glowing colours. After days of bathing in dust, I was looking forward to a shower.

I've experienced hotels of similar horror in other parts of the world – chaotic checking-in which took several hours to provide everyone with a room, and lifts, none of which worked. The concrete stairwell got filthier and filthier as I hauled my bag up to the fifth floor. The steps and walls were splattered with ominous stains. I edged around one particularly nasty-looking pile – either the remnants of a sheep slaughter or someone had given birth there! Quite disgusting.

One floor even opened out into fresh air. There was a concrete floor, ceiling and side walls, but no outside wall! Just a precipitous drop into the car park below.

My room had filthy carpets, no toilet seat, and worst of all, a shower with no functioning tap. I washed by crouching in the bath, splashing in the thin dribble of cold water from the bath taps.

I couldn't blame Frank for the state of the hotel – it was probably the best in town. But from here onwards our 'special bespoke' trip began to slide at ever increasing speed into a pantomime of comedic chaos. His refrain of 'What do you expect– this is Africa!' began to morph into 'What do you expect – this is Frank!'

The next day, my friends were supposed to be arriving – flying from Gatwick to Libya's capital, Tripoli. And from there on an internal flight to this remote southern town. Although I'd been told to expect them at lunchtime, they didn't arrive until late into the night so I met them at breakfast the following morning.

'How did it go?' I asked, 'Flight okay?' I was met by a chorus of groans. Frank had told them that their special diplomatic visas would be waiting for them at immigration in Tripoli, not realising that the airline wouldn't let them leave Gatwick without first seeing their Libyan permits. As Frank's 'small bespoke party' was filling half the plane (!), there was a tense stand-off and long flight delay while Frank's group and the officials traded 'regulations' and insults. Amazingly, bureaucracy eventually gave up and allowed them all on to the flight. As well as being weary, they were starting to get an inkling of Frank's organisational skills.

And that morning Frank was nowhere to be seen. Overnight, the hotel car park had filled up with dozens of vehicles, perplexingly many of them sporting Frank's 'Sahara Travel' stickers. It seemed that our expensive 'bespoke' trip had become just a small part of Frank's huge and expanding armada.

We were aiming for an extinct volcano called Waw an Namus, which would be almost on the centreline of the eclipse in three days' time. Dave, our driver, said we were to rendezvous later that day at the end of the tarmac road in a town called Tmassah. It was the last fuel station before we ventured out into the desert again en route for the volcano.

Various vehicles kept arriving and leaving the hotel but Dave had his eye fixed on our chuckwagon and followed it out of the car park. At midday the chuckwagon turned off the road by a scrubby patch of trees. We followed it and helped to set out some trestle tables and food. There was a constant stream of vehicles of every description racing past – eclipse watchers all heading for the filling station at Tmassah.

Seeing food, many of them turned off the road, passengers jumped out and started helping themselves. It was a free-for-all. Intimidated by the crowds and with more people arriving all the time, our cooks could do little to stop them. Unfortunately none of them were with 'Sahara Travel'.

There seemed to have been a 'Frank-style' misunderstanding – the Sahara Travel drivers had apparently been confused as to whether they should follow Frank's vehicle out of the hotel car park, or wait for a signal on the CB radios. Frank had been one of the first to race out of the car park that morning, followed by a stampede of all the other Sahara Travel vehicles. Except our savvy Dave who waited to follow the chuckwagon. So, Frank, well ahead of the chuckwagon, went blistering down the road to Tmassah pursued by his slightly confused entourage, which meant that they all missed lunch. That went down really well.

After our picnic melee, we merged back into the one-way stream of traffic and continued along the road to Tmassah.

There is a lot of money tied up in this desert. The dry stony wastes sprouted what looked like huge oil wells in the distance and the road was lined with giant electricity pylons in rows five deep. We passed a few small settlements and farms where underground water was used to grow huge irrigated circles of arable crops.

Later that afternoon we arrived in the small town of Tmassah and found the petrol station besieged. I wandered around chatting to the passengers and inhabitants of the vehicles who had come from all over the world. They were a highly entertaining crowd of misfits, fun-seekers and serious astronomy intellectuals. Their vehicles ranged from lived-in lorries from Australia, American motorhomes, converted buses and serious huge-wheeled off-road trucks, to domestic cars and even some fragile-looking local taxis.

The queues for fuel (cheaper than water in Libya) lasted all night and into the following day.

We camped that night in a hollow of scrubby palm trees just outside the town – a rubbish-strewn mosquito pit. Stumbling around the camp in the pitch dark I eventually found my friends. We sat drinking mint tea (Libya was strictly alcohol free) and chatting until supper was ready. Mint tea is ubiquitous in much of the Arab world and bunches of fresh leaves are available at most grocery stores. I've grown to really like it, though I don't ladle sugar into it the way the locals tend to. The mosquitoes in the camp were equipped with clothes-piercing pneumatic drills and our backs became peppered with vicious bites despite numerous layers of clothes.

Our little get-together fortunately meant that we didn't get involved in the heated discussion going on around the chuckwagon. Some of my original group were seriously annoyed by the problems of Frank's now huge posse. He had obviously sold tickets for the trip to whoever had made an inquiry. I had no idea how many people he was now responsible for, but it was obviously far more than he could manage single-handed. The adventurers from our original group of eight vehicles had opened up a 'this is not what we paid for' argument – 'plans and information were lacking or constantly changing', 'the party could only move at the pace of the slowest', 'meal times were impossibly long', in other words it was definitely not the sort of trip Frank had promised them. Yet again, Frank's

'What do you expect – this is Africa' was reworded into our traditional chorus, and there was serious talk of solicitors and compensation.

Personally, I felt a bit sorry for him. He had obviously been taken by surprise at the number of 'madcaps' wanting to join his trip and had decided to take money from all of them. But communication wasn't his strong point and he hadn't anticipated the numerous things that could go wrong. And we later found out that all internal Libyan flights for eclipse watchers had been provided free. Frank had apparently charged his customers for these.

Not surprisingly, whenever I did catch sight of him, which wasn't very often, he was always deep in argument with someone.

However, my friends and I were feeling sanguine. It was true that the logistics were looking increasingly disorganised, but we were where we were. And as long as we experienced the eclipse and nobody actually died, we would be quite content.

At first light, Dave led a small trio of vehicles out of camp while others were still wandering around with toothbrushes sticking out of their mouths. My friends were nowhere to be seen, scattered as they were among various vehicles. Dave found a track and shot off, but on consulting the GPS twenty minutes later, decided we were heading in entirely the wrong direction.

More teeth-sucking from 'security'!

We bounced off-road, over hillocks and more rubbish heaps until we found some sets of tyre marks that were pointing in the right direction. We were soon racing along with numerous other vehicles. The track widened out. Vehicles could be seen fanning out to the right and left, all racing into the morning sun.

The track past Waw an Namus volcano is a centuries-old camel route and is described in a number of guide books. The surface alternated between soft sand *'let the tyre pressures down'* and straight gravel sections *'pump the tyres up again'*. The guide describes landmarks along the route –

'a blue-painted barrel', *'a patch of white gypsum on a hill'*, *'over a small col marked with stone cairns'*.

Occasionally we halted at isolated huts for some sort of official scrutiny. Our policeman chatted amiably to the smartly uniformed soldiers before we were waved on.

Fortunately Dave had scrounged some bread and cheese from the chuckwagon that morning (sensible man!) and we had plenty of water on board, so we had a scratch lunch.

Bouncing through a desert landscape is my idea of heaven. I've read plenty about how the Sahara was once a rich and verdant landscape supporting vast herds of animals, and thousands of people. On previous trips into the barren mountains of Southern Algeria I've seen rocks covered with chiselled images of giraffes, deer, elephants, and all manner of animals now long gone. In the middle of the Sahara I've scrambled into ravines where crocodiles wallowed within living memory. I've seen cave paintings of hunters, found arrowheads and fish hooks, and where the desert winds have shifted the sand dunes, I've stumbled over the stone kitchenware of prehistoric homes.

I love reimagining this huge desert as it once was – with streams and lakes, tree-covered hills, and waving grasses. All gone now, apart from a few small patches where water still seeps to the surface, if you know where to look.

As the afternoon wore on I started scanning the hazy horizon for a Mount Fuji-esque cone. We were getting near to Waw an Namus but I could see nothing ahead except a row of low hills. The track wound up a slight incline and suddenly – we had arrived!

We were at the first crater.

Waw an Namus has two craters – one white and one black. I scrabbled around picking up interestingly weathered white stones while we waited for the other three vehicles to catch up, and then we continued on to the bigger, totally black cone of Waw an Namus's main volcano.

We arrived on the crater edge about an hour before sunset. It was big. The opposite crater wall was over two miles away. Down in the centre the bright greenery almost hurt my eyes. There was water down there! That's why it was on the old camel route.

We stood and feasted our senses at the sight. A small group of eclipse watchers were gathering as other vehicles arrived. People were wandering close to the edge of the crater.

Suddenly I heard the low drone of an aircraft engine. Perplexed, I scanned the skies. Someone shouted, and people started pointing.

Across the far side of the crater I could see movement, which materialised into a Chinook helicopter and a small red biplane. The two aircraft dipped down into the crater, then as they approached us, they rose up the inside wall of the volcano and passed a few feet above our heads.

We were later told that Colonel Gaddafi himself was in the helicopter. I'll never know if that was true. We were also told that several miles north near a town called Jalu (which crucially wasn't on the exact centreline of the eclipse), he had provided a free tented camp for seven thousand eclipse watchers. That definitely was true.

People kept arriving at the volcano and then driving off in various directions. Other groups were putting up tents. We hung around and waited to see if any other vehicles with 'Sahara Travel' stickers on them would turn up. We were just one of four vehicles out of our original group. We had no idea where anyone else was, and no way of contacting them. Brian, a retired ship's captain, took charge and kept trying to raise an answer on the CB radio, but all he got was a load of static.

Precious little information on the 'grand plan' had been passed down to me. All I had to do was to keep Dave in sight. As the sun set we dithered about whether we should pitch camp on the lower slopes of the volcano and wait to see if any others turned up, or drive in the dark – dodgy in the desert – to a Lat and Long coordinate that Frank had scribbled on a torn piece of paper and thrust at Brian as we had left camp. The coordinate, which should be on the exact centreline of the eclipse, indicated a spot about seventy kilometres due south of Waw an Namus – but that could have been an error. The scribble was difficult to read.

Brian made a decision. We would drive to his best guess at the almost illegible coordinates and hope that we'd find the rest of 'Sahara Travel' amid a great gathering of eclipse watchers. We set off.

It was now night-time. The desert was covered with the blackest of black grit. There was no moon. The vehicle's headlights were swallowed as if within a sea of black ink. We seemed to be driving blindly but fortunately the surface was flat – apart from some nasty little dry gullies caused by showers which passed every few years – when bounced over at sixty mph they tended to rattle the eyeballs.

After about an hour the latitude on the GPS clicked into the appointed coordinate. The vehicles slowed and stopped. In the darkness it looked no different from any other piece of dead flat desert – i.e. totally deserted. There was certainly no great gathering of other eclipse watchers.

Nothing. Nobody.

We climbed out and listened to the silence. Apart from the occasional cracking from the cooling engines, everywhere was eerily quiet, dark and totally empty.

Like being on the moon.

Equally disturbing was the fact that we had lost contact with the chuckwagon. Separated from my friends, with no idea if we were even in the right spot for tomorrow morning's eclipse, and with no prospect of any supper, I rolled out my sleeping bag and went to sleep.

* * *

Eclipse day dawned bright and sunny, as I guessed it did every morning here. I was excited, I was hungry, not convinced we were in the right place, but most of all I was dreadfully disappointed that after all our planning and anticipation, I was not going to experience the eclipse with my friends.

With barely an hour to go to the first contact of the moon with the sun, we heard the faint noise of a vehicle engine. A couple of small dots appeared on the horizon, followed by more dots, wobbling in the desert heat. The dots grew bigger. You can imagine my feelings when I realised that my friends had caught up with us. I couldn't quite believe it.

It was also Rosalind's birthday. We had asked the Hotel Africa to bake a special birthday cake (which amazingly, they had) and we'd transported it carefully across the desert sands. It was only slightly bent! A bit like her still-painful back. We all sang 'Happy Birthday', chopped the cake up into a multitude of tiny slices and handed it out. Rosalind seemed well pleased with the occasion.

Frank and the chuckwagon arrived shortly afterwards, but most of the Sahara Travel group had to watch the eclipse seventy km north of the centreline, back at the volcano. Apparently, the Libyan drivers had refused to drive any further without extra payment. However, now that my little group was together and miraculously in exactly the right spot for the longest possible four minutes and seven seconds of totality, I was on cloud nine. Barrie, one of my friends who was a professor of astronomy at the Open University, had left his big telescope on the slopes of the volcano with the other astronomers. But he seemed happy to witness the eclipse without it.

We collected our camp chairs together and sat chatting as the moon first touched the edge of the sun, and started its slow but inevitable progress across its face.

I put on my eclipse glasses and climbed onto the roof of one of the vehicles. The light faded gradually, thinning out until the desert was a silvery grey.

Glancing around at the upturned faces I noticed two of the guides had unrolled their prayer mats and were praying.

'Watch out for the shadow bands!' someone called out. And there they were, just as the final darkness passed over us – a fleeting glimpse of unworldly wriggling patterns of light and dark, squirming over the desert surface.

At totality the sky overhead was perfectly black. A faint orange glow of the shadow's rim could be seen all the way around the desert horizon.

I could gaze at the sun now, face to face with no protective glasses. It's the only time you can look straight at it without being blinded – a thin corolla of light around the edge of a pitch-black hole, and in the blackness beyond, the bright pinprick of Venus clearly visible.

People were standing around, stock still, absorbing the strangeness. They spoke in whispers, as if in church or some place of exceptional majesty.

Totality was nearing its end. Somewhere over West Africa the edge of the moon's shadow was racing towards us at unimaginable speed. It passed over us with the force of an express train.

As the first sharp rays of the sun broke the spell of the total eclipse a big cheer went up.

An unbelievably emotional moment. Light and life returning.

In times past, kings and astronomers who could predict these events must have been able to command immense power.

We broke camp quietly, still stunned by the experience, and began the long trek back.

* * *

Our return journey had its moments, like all journeys. We got hungry, lost and split up, and a number of people complained bitterly about being overcharged. But I didn't really care. I'd seen the eclipse with my friends and was quietly ecstatic – especially as I got to see the enormous Roman ruins of Leptis Magna, as well as exploring Tripoli.

We bade farewell to our 'security' – he was well pleased with his tip, and I was overjoyed that he never had to use that gun.

Back in Tunisia, I waved goodbye to the rest of the group in Tunis and spent a happy day wandering around the souq on my own before catching the first of my many flights back to Tanzania.

And remembering my food poisoning at the start of the trip I bought enough sealed and sanitised snacks in Rome to last me the journey.

* * *

The following year when I was back in England, I ran into Frank. He was advertising 'Sahara Travel' at a local country fair.

I sidled up to his stall. He obviously didn't recognise me, so I mentioned I'd been one of his 'special bespoke' group on the Libyan eclipse expedition. He visibly flinched and looked around wildly for a second. When he'd got over his shock and realised that I had no intention of haranguing him, we fell to laughing about some of the things that had happened on the trip. He admitted he still had nightmares about some of it – but he wasn't specific. There had obviously been many more problems than we were aware of.

'But, hey,' he concluded. 'That's Africa!' I had to stop myself from adding our group refrain.

I don't think it was one of his best trips. But for both of us, it was obviously one of our most memorable – though probably for quite different reasons!

Harvest of Hate

2008

Israeli army bullets fired into a Palestinian bedroom and Israeli soldiers forbidding a Palestinian from harvesting his olives.

I've found this trip intensely distressing to write about.

Palestine, or 'The West Bank' as it's often called is a conflict zone. I stayed with Palestinians and saw life from their perspective. If I had stayed with an Israeli family, no doubt I would have seen and heard a different story.

It's not my conflict, and I try hard not to take sides. What I've written about here is what I saw and heard while I was there.

You can make your own minds up.

* * *

'Can I go too?' I asked.

In 2008 I was sitting at a friend's house in the Lake District, chatting with some women when I overheard one of them talking about going to Palestine later that year to help with the olive harvest.

She turned and looked at me with a furrowed brow. She was a stocky, middle-aged lady with a mop of white hair. Her name was Josephine, Jo for short, and I hadn't met her before.

'It's not a holiday, you know!' she replied in an aggressive tone of voice.

'Yes, I gathered that, but it sounded interesting.'

'Yes, it'll certainly be that. Umm, do you know much about the situation out there?' she queried.

The other women turned back to their own conversations.

'Not much, just that Israel is illegally occupying the West Bank, and there's obviously huge tension between the two communities.'

'Yes, that's it in a nutshell,' replied Jo. 'There's an organisation in Bristol who go out there each year with a bunch of volunteers to help the Palestinians get their olive harvest in. The Israelis try to stop them picking the olives, so we go as "observers". We hope just by being there we can prevent situations turning nasty.'

'Oh, so have you been there before?' I queried. 'And what do you mean by "nasty"?'

'Well, you'd see, if you came,' she continued. 'Yes, I have been before. Just for one week, mind. That was bad enough. I think this year I want to spend a week chilling out in Jordan before coming home. Just to cool off. I got so angry.'

I was intrigued. Jo gave me the name of the organisation in Bristol – it's called 'Zaytoun' which means 'olive' in Arabic. So I made contact.

Before being accepted as part of the group, the lady from Zaytoun told me I needed to attend a training weekend. It was starting to sound a bit heavy.

The training course was seriously scary. How to enter Israel without mentioning where I was going or who I was going to be meeting. What not to take photos of. How to ensure my diaries and photos weren't seized by Israeli security. How to respond to questioning. How to react if an Israeli patrol demanded access to a Palestinian house I might be staying in. How not to compromise my Palestinian hosts... the scenarios went on and on.

I was given a potted history of the political situation. Jews and Palestinians had lived in the political entity known as Palestine for millennia. During and following Israel's creation in 1948, the State of Israel have taken more and more Palestinian land, destroyed Palestinian cities and towns and expelled thousands of locals. They have now illegally occupied most of what is called The West Bank, and encourage Jewish settlers to build on Palestinian land and disrupt the life of the remaining Palestinians. Despite all this being declared 'illegal' in international terms, it's a complicated scenario and the international community has achieved very little in sorting the situation out.

At the end of the weekend I felt prepared for (almost) anything. I knew that relations between Israelis and Palestinians were fractious, but the training started to bring home to me what living in an occupied country meant. I was beginning to understand the facts of the situation, but I was totally unprepared for the emotional side of things. That only came later.

The visit had been arranged for October. In order to avoid the hassle of Israeli airport security, Jo and I flew to Amman in Jordan, and caught a bus over the River Jordan via the Allenby Bridge into Israel. I had expected the River Jordan to be 'deep and wide' so was surprised by the swampy trickle that it had been reduced to.

The check-point was my first experience of Israeli security. There was a long, long queue for local Arabs. Being Europeans, I was surprised but pleased to be waved straight into passport control and through security. We weren't given anything like the grilling we'd been told to expect at the airport. We were outside the building and onto a waiting bus in next to no time. Big relief!

Arriving in Jerusalem, Jo and I stayed in a large and rambling, run-down hotel just inside the city walls in the Christian quarter. It looked as if it had seen better days. Apparently the Jews were in the process of buying it, against stiff opposition from the Christians who had owned it for generations. The money that should have been spent on hotel upkeep was all being used to fight legal battles to try and retain ownership. Apparently that was the status of many properties in Jerusalem. The Israelis are taking over all the properties inside the old city walls, regardless of any opposition.

We had arrived a few days before the rest of the volunteers so spent our free time wandering around the old city. Inside the walls the city is divided into quarters – Christian, Muslim, Jewish and Armenian. We walked round the city on top of the walls, getting our bearings, fascinated by the different character of each quarter. Then we explored parts of the city, dipping in and out of some tiny, ornate churches and visiting the Wailing Wall.

I love Arab markets, and so the souq in the Muslim quarter was a real treat for me. Occasionally the bustling crowds would get elbowed to the side of the narrow, twisting thoroughfares as groups of Jewish tourists were shepherded along the Via Dolorosa (places where Jesus allegedly stopped on the way to his crucifixion) at a desperately fast trot. These groups always had a loud, shouting leader, a number of armed human sheepdogs at the side, and a rear gunner heavily laden with automatic rifle and emergency medical equipment, sweating to keep pace at the back. They shoved locals and other tourists out of the way with unnecessary force. I found that rather intimidating, but the local people melted into doorways and seemed to accept it as quite normal.

After a couple of days the rest of our volunteers arrived. We were taken via another check-point to a village in the West Bank.

On the way out of the city I noticed The Wall. You couldn't miss it.

The Wall winds for miles through the West Bank, cutting off many Palestinians from the majority of their land. It had been bulldozed through olive groves, blocks of houses and streets with no regard for the needs of local communities. I was told of families being separated, children unable to get to schools, people unable to access medical facilities. I suppose the Berlin Wall had split communities apart in the same way, but it looked and remains brutal.

We were taken to our host village in an old minibus. Everything about the landscape started to fill me with unease. Modern coaches swept past, but they were reserved for Israeli citizens. Palestinians had to use their own buses which were considerably older and less frequent. I was told there is a deliberate policy of keeping the two communities separated.

We passed a few Palestinian villages but the road access to them had been cut off by banks of earth. To get to any of the villages required a long detour.

Occasionally we passed the access road to one of the illegal Israeli settlements. They always seemed to be on a hilltop and recognisable by their bright-red roofs and abundance of greenery. The entry roads were often lined with magnificent palm trees.

'I'm surprised to see these palm trees looking so lush,' I commented to our Zatoun leader, as I gazed at the rest of the dry, rocky landscape.

She laughed. 'Yes, the Israeli settlements use whatever water they want. They have gardens and swimming pools up there.'

'So, what about the Palestinian villages? Do they have a good supply too?'

She sighed. 'Look, you see those round rubber water tanks on the roofs of that village over there,' she said, pointing to a dusty-looking Palestinian village. 'They're all empty. The Israelis use them as target practice. They're full of bullet holes.'

'Er, so what do locals use for water? There must be wells around here,' I asked.

'Oh, yes,' she replied, 'but the Israelis pump so much water up to their settlements and illegal farms that the groundwater here is getting lower and lower. And if the locals want to dig their wells deeper they have to apply to the Israeli authorities for a licence, and guess what? The licence takes years to come or never arrives. The village we are going to paid a quite exorbitant sum for a licence over five years ago. They are told that it's still being processed.' She shrugged.

Eventually, we reached a turning off the main road and the minibus wound down a lane for several miles back the way we had come. If the previous turning hadn't been blocked off the journey would have been much quicker.

In the village we were shown into a large room, with toilets and a couple of showers at one end. We were a mixed group of all ages, mainly women, some couples, about fifteen of us in all. We unrolled our sleeping bags, and some local women brought in large platters of rice, with tomatoes and olives.

We had arrived!

Helping to pick the olives could have been a really pleasant holiday. It was fun climbing up the tall three-legged ladders, picking branches full of olives into baskets, and gathering the fruits from the sheets spread out on the ground. The olives and leaves were full of wonderfully aromatic oil so that by the end of the week my hands felt soft and silky.

But picking olives wasn't really why we were there.

We were told that a licence had been granted to pick olives in one area the next day. We set off across the terraced hillside the next morning. The farmer I had been allocated to had quite a good grasp of English, which was useful for answering my barrage of questions. He showed me which of the terraced fields belonged to his family, how old each row of trees was, and which of his ancestors had planted them. He knew a lot about each tree. Some were well over a hundred years old.

The land was gently sloping and he explained how the terraces had been created centuries ago, and were still maintained by the village. He said that because the land had been in his family for generations from a time when there were no legal documents to prove ownership, the Israelis now wouldn't allow them to claim ownership. It was a big legal problem that was costing more than they could afford to sort out.

The farmer and members of his family started picking. Before long someone came across from the village with the news that trouble was brewing. Sure enough, a group of Israelis from the new settlement near the village could be seen coming along the track towards us. A TV van arrived and reporters from an American TV company started filming.

They interviewed an Israeli first. I listened from the sidelines. The settler was explaining in perfect English how the local Arabs were trespassing on Israeli land and stealing the wild olives which grew there.

I had to stop myself laughing out loud as I thought, *I've never seen wild trees growing in straight lines.*

But it was annoying to hear such lies being broadcast. The Israeli spoke in measured tones about how disruptive the Palestinians were, that they were troublemakers and thieves, often resorting to criminal damage of his and his neighbour's properties. He sounded very plausible. If I'd been watching this TV report, I could well have believed him.

Then a Palestinian man was asked to respond. His English was so poor, and he was so emotional that I couldn't understand what he said. I don't think anyone else could either. He was certainly providing a terrible case for farmers trying to pick their own crops.

I wondered if he'd been specially selected by the TV channel because of his complete inability to put forward a coherent counter to the Israeli settler's argument. It occurred to me that the ability to communicate in clear English must have a huge influence on someone's credibility.

Most Americans watching those two interviews would surely have sided with the Israeli.

Yet standing there on the ground, watching what was actually going on, I knew that the facts were completely at odds with the impression that this report would be giving.

The Palestinian family were continuing to pick, glancing anxiously over their shoulders at the huddle of men and TV cameras. The Israelis were starting to get angry and were shouting at them and waving sticks. Some of them had rifles.

I was getting nervous.

In the meantime, several cars had stopped on the main road and a few men were scrambling up the hillside. They were part of a Jewish group called 'Rabbis for Human Rights'. They reached the scene huffing and puffing with the effort of climbing across the terraces. They joined in the heated dispute, trying to calm what was an escalating row. These Rabbis are a group of moderate Israelis who try to mediate in situations such as this, and often get thoroughly abused by their hard-line fellow citizens for doing so. Brave men.

The TV cameras rolled, and, as previously instructed, we stood on the sidelines, watching, filming and taking notes.

Phone calls were made, the shouting eventually calmed down, the olive pickers were told to come down the ladders and go home, and everyone started to disperse.

As the tension reduced, I asked what had happened.

'Licence to pick today is withdrawn,' said our farmer in a flat monotone. And we walked back to the village.

Later, I asked him about the licences.

'We need licence for everything. Everything! And all licences cost money. Big money! We need take care of our olive trees. See, these sharp weeds.' He indicated the mass of thistles growing around the olive trees. 'We need cut them in spring before they seed. We ask, we pay for licence, but they give no licence. After the seeds spread, then they give licence, so now, full of weeds.'

He sighed heavily before continuing, 'Also, we need prune the trees, but they don't give us licence when we need prune. They give us licence now, in October. Not possible prune now. Wrong season!

'They tell TV, radio, the whole world, they let us Palestinians do what we like, just need to apply for licence. Ha! Licence! We apply, but they don't give us licence! Picking also big problem. Another licence! Olives are our only income. No olives... what do we do?' He uttered another huge sigh and shrugged.

Another day, and another attempt to pick olives from a different area of hillside where a licence had been granted. All went well for a few hours, then someone spotted an Israeli armed vehicle, a Humvee, loitering on the far hillside. Those of us in bright western clothes made ourselves as visible as possible. Our farmer was looking especially nervous. He had had to park his van over where the Humvee was because Palestinian vehicles were not allowed any closer to these olive groves. We watched while the Humvee pushed his van, none too gently, off the side of the road into a ditch.

Eventually the Humvee made its way closer and parked behind some scrubby vegetation. A rough voice shouted and the farmer's son, a young man in his mid-twenties who was a member of the Palestinian Police Force (an organisation responsible for public security and emergency services) came down his ladder and reluctantly walked over to the vehicle. We were unable to see what happened or hear what was said. After a few minutes he walked back towards us, looking visibly shaken. The Humvee moved off.

I asked him what happened.

He shrugged and looked away, but his eyes were brittle and red-rimmed. His father later told me, 'They threatened to break his hands,' but he wouldn't tell me why.

We continued to pick and towards the end of the afternoon two donkeys were brought from the village to carry the olives back home. A good day, apart from the incident with the Humvee.

Next day, the village had not been granted any licences to pick. The farmer took some of us for a clamber up the hillside at the back of the village.

The view was fantastic. A rolling landscape of terraced fields, olive trees and rocky outcrops. I could just make out two or three Palestinian villages, but the stone houses blended into the scenery so well that they were almost invisible. To our left, in the direction of Jerusalem, the bright-red roofs of two new settlements could be seen on the hilltops.

The farmer pointed to another hilltop, where I could just make out a couple of buildings and a tall mast.

'That, there,' he said, 'That is next settlement. They start like that. Not legal, but what can we do?'

He pointed further up the hillside behind us.

'Look. See the fence?'

I hadn't noticed before but another Israeli settlement was being built directly above his village.

'Come, I show you. This what they do.' We walked along the edge of his field where he had recently planted some young olive saplings. The saplings had all been uprooted or broken off.

Feeling impotent and depressed, I scrambled back down to the village and wandered around. Inside one barn was an olive press, with a large notice outside saying it was a gift from the United Nations. I stood and watched the olive sacks being hauled up some steps and tipped into a hopper. There was a loud grinding noise, and oil ran out of a channel into a barrel while the waste slid out through a different exit. The whole process released the wonderfully comforting aroma of olive. In fact, the whole village smelled of olive because the waste of olive stones and pith was spread around the base of village trees and over the fruit and vegetable patches.

The steep roadway through the village was only passable by four-wheeled-drive vehicles. The houses leaned against each other for support or were separated by tight alleyways. They were all intensely private, hidden behind high windowless walls, with tall gates of corrugated iron or heavy wood. The windows on the upper floors were tightly shuttered.

The only glimmer of colour came from the posters. Every wall was covered in posters and all the posters were essentially the same.

Each poster featured a photo of a young man, some smiling, but mostly looking fiercely patriotic, brandishing a gun of some sort. Some posters were torn and faded, looking as if they had been up for years. Others looked depressingly recent. They were all images of local martyrs, either shot dead, killed, injured or disappeared in some other way, or in an Israeli prison.

It was chilling to think of the waste and heartache that this conflict generates.

A few of us women were invited into one of the houses. Through the heavy iron gate was a little courtyard where a goat was tethered. We climbed up the steep steps to the front door, then up more steep steps which opened into the first-floor kitchen. It was a large room with a big table in the middle and a selection of old chairs, full of women and children of all ages. They stopped chatting and smiled encouragingly at us as we entered.

We were politely invited through into a formal living room where a large sofa and armchairs were still covered in the protective plastic they'd been bought with. I sat on the squeaky seat and looked around the room. The coffee table and dresser were heavily varnished. A small vase with red plastic roses sat on a highly embroidered table mat. The dresser was covered in family photos.

On the walls were posters similar to the ones in the village. The lady of the house proudly pointed to each one explaining, with the help of her family as she didn't speak any English, who each young man had been – sons, brothers, cousins. She described each one with pride, rather than regret at a life lost. I wondered if this hardened reaction was natural or whether it was learned through social pressure.

Now I understood why all the local women I'd seen were either pregnant or with young children in tow. The Israelis were encouraging immigration to swell their population, and the Palestinians were doing what they could to swell their numbers too.

A tray filled with small glasses of sweet mint tea was brought in and passed around. We sipped politely. One of our group asked whether soldiers came into their village. Once the lady of the house understood the question she pulled the lacy net curtain open and showed us the tears in the fabric.

'Bullets,' she said, and beckoned us into a bedroom. The glass in the window had been recently repaired but the wardrobe was peppered with bullet holes.

'Last month,' another woman said. 'They come all the time.'

'Why do they come here?' one of our group asked naively.

'They know every family. Know where boys live. Sometime good boys, they take to prison. No reason. Sometimes boys come back – sometimes not. My son, he eighteen. He good boy, no trouble. Now, he in prison – no reason.' The women in the room shuffled uncomfortably.

Two of the young boys in the house pulled at my hand and led me up more steep steps onto the roof. It had a high wall around the edge. They wanted me to play football.

'You English!' they shouted at me. 'Manchester football. Good!' and we kicked a ball around between the lines of washing until I grew tired.

In a pause while I got my breath back I asked the usual question, 'What do you want to do when you grow up?'

The older boy just shrugged.

The younger of the two surprised me. 'Doctor,' he said. 'Want to be doctor.'

I smiled at him, but his brother was already kicking the ball again.

'Football!' he shouted, 'Play football.'

He was still kicking the ball back and forwards as I left them to it and went back down the stairs.

My time in the village was making me angrier and angrier. When I'd come I'd had no idea what these people were having to put up with. It felt intolerable, but what could any of us do!

I felt like screaming, 'Where are the political leaders who genuinely want peace?'

By the end of a week I'd had enough. We all said our thanks and in dribs and drabs caught a Palestinian bus back to Jerusalem for a debrief.

Sitting on the old bone-shaker, I gazed round at the weary faces of the men and women sitting near me. I was unbelievably glad to be escaping this madness, but felt so sorry for the ones who couldn't just leave it all behind.

We were stopped by a random security patrol.

Soldiers with sub-machine guns circled the bus. A tall soldier and a young lass who looked about fifteen got on. The girl's uniform looked several sizes too big for her. She swung her automatic weapon from side to side as she strode confidently up the gangway. All the passengers looked away with deadpan expressions, looking down at their laps, out of the windows, anywhere but at her haughty gaze.

But I couldn't ignore her. Chin held high, I stared hard at her, daring her to meet my eyes. As she walked the length of the bus, I swivelled round and stared at the back of her head. She turned and strode arrogantly back down the bus, looking everywhere but at my eyes which were drilling into hers.

I honestly don't know what I'd have done if she'd singled me out. But more to the point she probably wouldn't have known what to do with me either. Anyway, the two soldiers got off, and the bus carried on.

Jo and I spent a week in Jordan, floating in the Dead Sea and scrambling around the ruins at Petra. I was still smarting with anger and frustration at what we'd seen the previous week, and how little we seemed to have achieved.

Writing this story sixteen years later, nothing seems to have changed in Israel and the West Bank. If anything, the situation has become worse. Living under 'occupation' is not legal and it's far from fun.

Both sides are guilty and both sides are victims.

It's what happens when people are taught from the cradle to hate each other.

Ticket to Ride

2012

The 'toy train' to Ooty Hill Station
and a steep forty-six-mile climb through the Nilgiri Hills.

For a while it seemed that opportunities for adventurous travel were sadly lacking. I obviously needed to do something drastic!

I opened my filing cabinet and reluctantly pulled out my old and dusty teaching qualifications. Was this the only way to go exploring again? I started asking around. One of my nieces, Lennea, knew the headmaster of an international school in Southern India and suggested I write to him. With a sigh of resignation, I did, sent off copies of my qualifications, and was soon teaching English at Kodaikanal International School.

The little South Indian town of Kodaikanal is situated over seven thousand feet high in the forested mountains of the Western Ghats in Tamil Nadu. These mountains rise steeply from the sweaty heat of the Indian Plains. The climate was refreshingly cool while I was there in the early part of the year.

The teachers and students came from all different corners of the world. As well as teaching, I was asked to take part in various extracurricular activities, many of which were great fun. I kept a sharp lookout on the activities notice board for interesting outings when one day something caught my eye.

The girls' football team had a tournament in Ooty the following weekend.

Ooty! Ooty was one of those romantic place names like Timbuktu or Samarkand, place names that used to fill me with illogical longing when I was young. Ooty – the little hill station in Southern India with the iconic narrow-gauge, bright-blue steam train that I'd always longed to go on. It is one of the oldest mountain railways in India, climbing up nearly two thousand metres on the steepest track in Asia.

I had to go!

I put my name forward as a chaperone and scuttled off to the school travel office to buy a ticket for the once-in-a-lifetime trip on the little train. If the school coach dropped me at the bottom of the mountain, I could catch the train, fulfill a dream, and meet the school party in Ooty at the top.

I wasn't prepared for the answer – there was a two-month waiting list for tickets! However, I was offered a tiny glimmer of hope. Sometimes, not every ticket holder turned up, and there could be some tickets available on the day. There is only one train a day so you had to get to the station very early in the morning, and there was usually a big crowd of hopeful tourists.

Undeterred, I boarded the coach with the girls' football team on Friday morning. That night, after a five-hour drive, the coach deposited me in the town of Mettupalayam at the bottom of the mountain. The girls' faces peered anxiously out of the rear windows of the coach as they waved me goodbye in the dark. When they'd heard I had no train ticket, and no hotel booking, I'm sure they never expected to see me again.

In India, there is always someone around who can speak English, so I asked for directions to the railway station and a cheapish hotel. Next morning, I found my way to the station hoping to buy a ticket. By five o'clock there was already a large crowd of eager young westerners with travel-stained rucksacks and hopeful expressions.

At five thirty the ticket office opened and the grumpy vendor repeated, 'No tickets. None left. Go talk to the station master!'

The station master's office was on another platform, so we swarmed across the tracks and besieged his office. Rumours spread that there might be one or two tickets available but we would have to wait.

'Go catch the bus if you need to get to Ooty!' he shouted, getting increasingly angry as the crowds pestered him. But of course, the whole point of going to Ooty was the train ride. I sat down to watch and wait.

The bright-blue carriages were shunted to our platform. There were only two small passenger carriages and a luggage wagon.

It was entertaining watching the crowd. Youngsters crowded onto the platform from all over the world: from Australia, America and Europe chatting in groups, meeting up with fellow travellers, joking or looking earnestly for the first signs of the engine arriving. Listening to snippets of conversation, it seemed that if there were any spare seats the station master would give out special chitties which had to be raced across the tracks to the ticket office, the ticket bought, then raced back again across the tracks to get onto the train before it left.

I noticed two German-speaking youths striding confidently up and down the platform. They were quite close to me when one of them plucked at the station master's sleeve and offered him some money. I was acutely embarrassed to see such a blatant attempt at bribery. The station master glared at him, brushed his arm away and walked on.

At six thirty precisely and looking to my eyes just like Thomas the Tank Engine, the miniature locomotive puffed out of the shunting yard and manoeuvred into position at the rear of the three carriages. Travellers with tickets found their seats and the station master started issuing ticket permits to those who had missed the train the previous day.

My heart started sinking. The seats filled up. There was no way I was going to get on.

The station master made his way past me back to his office. He seemed to have one or two pieces of paper left in his hand. Did he notice me sitting patiently on my own? I'm not sure.

The crowd surged after him into his office, where he stood sternly surveying the scrum. Big men and big rucksacks presented a solid wall between me and the station master. But there was a tiny gap between some of their legs. Bending low, I squeezed through the gap and looking up, managed to catch his eye.

'Just one person, sir.' I smiled up at him. Miraculously he handed down the last of his permits. Clasping the all-important piece of paper, I dashed across the tracks to the ticket office and thrust it across the counter. The ticket cost the equivalent of ten pence.

The platform was lined with disappointed, disgruntled faces, some of them openly glaring at me as I slid triumphantly into a small gap on the bench seat of the second-class compartment.

I'd done it. I was ON!

The four-hour ride didn't disappoint. The train stopped to draw breath and take on water at stations with names like Hillgrove, Lovedale and Fern Hill. The station posters and information boards were those of a bygone colonial age. Only the scenery and the playful monkeys reminded me that I was not in the Home Counties.

Near the top, the train passed acres of tea plantations and an ammunition factory before puffing with a long hiss of steam into the final station.

I'd done it. A dream fulfilled.

It was only then that I realised I had no idea which school the girls were playing at. I consulted a gathering of tuk-tuk taxi drivers, before being whisked away by one of them through the outskirts of the town. I did find the school, and managed to watch the end of a match which our school won, but I was so exhausted that I slept on the coach all the way back to Kodaikanal.

The girls thought I had been quite mad to get off the coach at the bottom of the mountain. But their ambition that weekend was different from mine. Fortunately we each attained our goals. Great weekend!

Carry on Camping

2012

A muddy walk around the lakeside, boating on the lake surface, using a zip wire and some dangerous wild bison near the campsite!

Things I hate: anything cold and wet, shrieking children, camping. As an English lady of a certain age (sixty-four by this stage) I enjoy a bit of comfort, peace and quiet. Or so I thought.

While I was teaching English at Kodaikanal International School, I'd been allocated a reasonably furnished apartment and given small groups of polite, respectful students to introduce to the mysteries of my mother tongue. Life was perfect.

I didn't even mind helping out occasionally at evenings and weekends – dinner duties, staring endlessly at a stopwatch on sports days, checking in dark corners during school dances. Each evening I could retire to the peace and comfort of my apartment and close the door.

So I didn't see it coming when Zai, my head of department asked me to help her accompany a group of eleven-year-olds on a trip to a local beauty spot. It actually sounded quite attractive.

'Love to!' I replied enthusiastically.

'It's a wonderful place,' she continued. 'There's a lake, miles of unspoilt forests, and lots of activities for children around the camp.'

'Camp?' I queried nervously, but she had already disappeared.

I asked around.

'Nothing to worry about,' was the general reply. 'The lake should be nice and warm at this time of year. It gets a bit brown, of course, because the water buffalo use it as well, and you'll need to check for leeches.'

I made a mental note NOT to pack my swimming costume.

'The children just love the freedom of wild camping. Some of them spend all weekend in the water. Just count them from time to time as we did lose one a couple of years ago. That was sad.' Apparently a boy had drowned. The parents hadn't pressed charges, much to everyone's relief.

'There's a fantastic zip-line down a slope through the trees. We got a broken hip last year. Silly boy! He let go and fell off.'

By now I was starting to feel a little apprehensive. Indian standards of health and safety were one thing, but how was I going to cope with the physical trauma of CAMPING!? However, I had a lot of faith in my head of department. She was a sensible woman of my own age who liked a degree of comfort herself and didn't stand any nonsense from the children. It's only for two nights, I thought, and if she doesn't mind going then it can't be too bad. This is India, after all. At least it won't be freezing cold and it probably won't rain.

The camping weekend was approaching. My head of department developed a cough, quickly followed by a bad cold.

I stared with a sinking feeling at the email from her which read: *Sorry, but unable to come this weekend. I'm sure everything will be fine...*

And of course, it was. No one drowned in the lake, and no one fell off the zip-wire. No one was shot in the eye with the bow and arrows, fell into the campfire, was gored by one of the wild pigs that crashed through the camp, was bitten by a monkey, slashed by the formidable horns of the huge and unpredictable *gaur* (wild bison) that roam these mountains, or got carried off by a tiger.

I was the only one to suffer a small mishap by falling into a particularly smelly patch of bog as I led a group of wildly excited children around the lake.

I lay awake on the second night. I'd asked for a couple of extra blankets to keep out the bone-chilling cold, and was listening to the rain hammering on the tent while waiting for the next flash of lightning. As I lay there, I remember thinking how unbelievably lucky I was to have spent an adventure-filled weekend with a group of active, cheerful children high up on a beautiful mountain in a secluded corner of India, that camping wasn't the nightmare that I had anticipated, and that no way would I have swapped this experience for a warm, comfortable weekend anywhere.

I had to admit, I was quite enjoying my retirement.

Healing Herbs and Sacred Snakes

2014

Kali and Irula men with cobras.

Extracting snake venom and Irula women working in the herbal plant nursery.

Zai Whitaker, my now-retired head of department from Kodaikanal, and I, had kept in touch. She has led a remarkable life championing wildlife and writing numerous books. She asked me if I could spend a few months working for a charity that she had helped to set up in 1986 when she had been moved by the terrible plight of members of the nomadic Irular tribe in Southern India.

Expelled from their forest home by international wildlife protection rules in the 1970s, these forest dwellers are often forced to live in pathetic roadside hovels and are being exploited by whoever needs cheap, easily manipulated labour. Zai and a few others had set up a women's group called ITWWS – the Irular Tribal Women's Welfare Society in a twelve-acre forest with the aim of educating and lifting a core group of these people out of their debilitating poverty. She was also concerned that their centuries-old knowledge of the medicinal use of plants as well as their unmatchable skills at catching snakes should not be lost.

Thousands of Irular are not so lucky and still live in atrocious social and economic conditions largely ignored by the rest of the world.

I've written the following story based around the Irular people I met in the ITWWS forest. I've changed some of their names and exact circumstances, but their plight is essentially exactly as I've written it.

* * *

Vijaya is my best friend. My very, very, very best friend. She is tall, for an Irular, with long dark hair. She brushes it every day with oil to keep it shiny. She is beautiful. She is quite old – about thirty, I think.

My name is Malliga and I'm twelve years old. I live in my father's compound with my stepmother and her two young daughters. My mother died when I was young after she was attacked by some young men. My stepmother doesn't like me very much.

Vijaya has always been kind to me. She is so clever. Her father was half-Hindu, though her mother is one of us. They made sure she went to school every day. She passed all her exams and even went away to the big college in Chennai. The women's group helped her with money and a lot of encouragement. She was very brave. She was away for three years. I really missed her. I hardly recognised her when she came back – she looked so grown up. But she was still my best friend.

She says it's important to look after myself. I'm quite small and my hair is brownish, short and dry which Vijaya says is because I don't get a proper diet. She also says I need to go to school and learn if I want to get a proper job.

Vijaya is still looking for a proper job. The women's group pay her a small amount for looking after the Irular Tribal Museum. She showed me what's in there. There are drums and pipes and musical instruments. My uncles and cousins make music with instruments just like the ones in the museum. Sometimes we have parties for weddings and things, and everyone sings and dances. We all love music. An outsider came once to listen and he stored the music on a cassette tape. When he pressed the buttons it played the music back again. It was magic!

There are lots of other things in the museum, like the forked sticks and baskets my uncles use for catching snakes. Vijaya says everyone knows that our tribe is the best in the world for catching them. Two of my uncles went to America to help the people there catch snakes. I've seen a picture of them holding some of the American snakes they caught. My uncles are brilliant at catching snakes. Here they take them to a special place where someone makes them spit their venom into a jar. And when the snake has done this three times, they make a little mark on its underneath so they don't catch that snake again, and then they take it back to the forest and let it go. We don't want to hurt the snakes because they might be gods. Everything alive might be a god. Even a tiny termite.

If you don't respect snakes they can bite you. Many, many people get bitten by snakes because they don't look out for them. And if they get bitten they die, or their leg turns black and drops off. That's what the snake venom is for. It gets turned into a special medicine which means the person doesn't die. Of course, our tribe doesn't use that sort of medicine. We have our own medicine. It's much better than the medicine from the hospital.

My aunts gather the herbs for all our medicines. They need a special licence to gather herbs from our forest. Many years ago, before I was born, we used to gather things from the forest. Everything we needed is in the forest. The elders used to exchange snakes for metal knives and axes, but apart from that we kept ourselves to ourselves. We knew what leaves and roots to eat, how to catch rats and other little animals to eat, how to plant and grow a few crops. We slept in huts made of branches and leaves, and never stayed in one place for very long. My great-grandmother has told me about the old ways. She said life was hard but much better than today. In those days the tribe was free and no one beat them or cheated them or looked down on them the way they do now.

But now we aren't allowed to live in the forest, and we need a special licence to gather anything. My aunts are very careful when they are gathering herbs. They only gather a few leaves from here, and a few from there so there are always plenty left in the forest. They bring them to the women's centre and dry them in the sun. Then, my uncles put them in a machine which grinds them into powder. People come to our herbal centre from miles away for the powders. They know that our recipes are much better than the pills they can buy in the hospital but they don't know which herbs to gather or how to combine them. Our recipes are gentle and natural, and they work by healing the whole body.

I know a few of the basic recipes, how to use turmeric to heal infections, and hibiscus for hair growth, but there is so much more to learn. My great-uncle has been learning the recipes since he was a boy. He says he is still learning. It takes a long, long time to be a great herbalist and he is very well respected. People always ask for him at the herbal centre. But if he doesn't teach the younger ones like me then who will know how to make up the recipes when he passes on?

I asked Vijaya if she wanted to become a great herbalist, but she said, 'No'. She said she's more interested in helping our Irular tribe stand 'shoulder to shoulder with the outside world'. She said it's not right that most Irular don't go to school, and that because we can't read and write, most of us aren't registered, so we don't get basic food rations, houses or medical help if there's an accident, the right to vote, or any of the rights that other Indians are entitled to. And because most Irulars don't understand how banking works, or the rules about working for a daily rate, we get cheated and treated really badly. She looked so angry when she was explaining this, I could see how much she wanted to make things better for our tribe. She did once represent us at a big meeting of very important people. But she came back rather quiet and sad.

Vijaya said sometimes we don't help ourselves. Many of our younger men earn small amounts of money on building sites and working in the fields for rich landlords. But then they spend the money on alcohol.

Vijaya is married to one of my older brothers. I know he spends money on getting drunk, and then he beats her.

I'd like to be clever like Vijaya. I'd like to do well in lessons but my stepmother says I needn't worry about reading and writing because she has already found a husband for me. But I've seen him. He's old and ugly, and I don't like him. He only has one arm. The other one got cut off when he was working in a saw mill. So now he's got no money.

Vijaya helps me with reading and numbers, but I have to work for the women's group too. I help Mangamaa with preparing food and I take cups of tea to any visitors who come to our herbal centre.

Vijaya was very excited last week. She said a lady from England was coming to stay with the women's group for a few months and that maybe she could help us learn English. Vijaya already speaks some English but she wants to learn more. She showed me some pictures of England. A tall red bus, and a big stone building where the queen, who is a sort of goddess, lives.

Vijaya said everyone in England is free to do what they like and they are all rich. She wants to go to England one day.

The lady from England has arrived! She is going to live in the concrete room on top of the museum. According to Jacob in the women's group office (he's non-Irular and deals with all the paperwork), she's sixty-seven years old. This morning I took her a cup of tea. She is very pale but isn't as wrinkled as my grandmother. She smiled and said her name was Sue. Then she asked me my name – at least, I think that was what she asked me.

Mangamaa has been told to cook her three meals a day and I'm to take her a cup of tea every morning and afternoon.

I see Miss Sue every day now. She sits with a 'computer' just like Jacob in the office, and makes words. She showed me some labels she is making to stick on bottles in the herbal centre. Sometimes she goes to the other side of the forest to our plant nursery. Tenmozhi looks after the plants. When people come to buy herbs or young trees she helps them choose. She knows a lot about plants, like where to plant them, how big they grow and what you can use the leaves for. There is a big notice board in the plant nursery with the names of all the plants written in English and Tamil. I can read some of the Tamil letters. I like going to the plant nursery and Tenmozhi teaches me how to water the pots and keep the plants in the shade with nets over the top. Miss Sue has written all the plant names in her book. There are a lot!

Sometimes we get a visit from a school – children with proper teachers. They are very noisy and bossy. Sometimes there are about a hundred of them all crowding into our big meeting area and Miss Sue stands at the front and talks to them. Vijaya said she talks to them about looking after the world. I suppose I'm part of the world but no one seems to look after me. I want to learn in a proper school, and get a job and look like Vijaya. I don't want to marry a smelly old man as soon as my periods start.

Today I helped Mangamaa cook a meal for some important people. We cooked rice and noodles and special herbs which Jacob had bought. And we made soup and pickles as well as dosa pancakes. I wasn't allowed to eat anything until the visitors had gone. Mangamaa is such a good cook – it all tasted wonderful. Much better than the rice or lentils my stepmother leaves for me. Mangamaa cooks it all on the outside fire, though sometimes she uses the gas ring in the little concrete hut where she stores dried chickpeas, rice and lentils in special tins. We have to keep the window and door locked, even when we turn our backs to stir something on the fire because of the monkeys. They are very quick and steal anything they can. They drink from our water tap by turning it on, but they never turn it off again so we are always running out of water.

Having water from a tap is brilliant. Where I live there is a water tap near our compound which everyone uses. Grandma says before I was born they had to go to a pond or a spring in the dry season when water was difficult to find.

Miss Sue is teaching English to anyone who wants to come to the lessons. I went to her lesson yesterday, but today I had to do a lot of washing so I couldn't go. Miss Sue wrote big letters and words on the chalkboard and asked us all to say the sound. Then she got everyone to recite a greeting, and answer what their name was. That was so good. Now I can now say 'Hello' and 'My name is Malliga' in English. But then Vijaya wanted Miss Sue to teach her some different things and I didn't understand what they were saying. So I just sat there. It felt good to be in a lesson with a pencil and a piece of paper but I didn't understand anything else. Anyway, Miss Sue still gave me a sweet at the end. I wish I could go to lessons every day.

On the last day before Miss Sue went back to England, she gave us all some special certificates for being 'the best students she had ever taught'. Then Vijaya knelt down and kissed Miss Sue's feet. Miss Sue looked a bit embarrassed. Then she left, and I never saw her again.

* * *

Towards the end of my three months with the Irular people, I was walking through the forest to the little palm-thatched hut where I took my meals. Birds were shrieking high up in the tree canopy and a huge butterfly settled on a bright-red hibiscus flower flanking the path. For anyone who doesn't know how the Irular people living here are disempowered and mistreated, this place might seem like paradise.

As I rounded the corner of the meeting area, I noticed three young Irular men with forked sticks, peering down into the undergrowth. They motioned to me to be quiet, pointing down into the tangle of bushes. 'Cobra,' one of them whispered in a loud hiss. 'Careful, madam. We see cobra. Need be very careful.' I tiptoed forward.

They indicated with circular hand motions where they had seen the snake. I stared down into the mass of vegetation and low bushes. It would be almost impossible to see a well-camouflaged snake in there.

The men inched forward through the tangled foliage. One was wearing flip-flops and the other two men were in bare feet. I glanced down at my open sandals and gingerly climbed up the two steps into the meeting hall.

Peering down on the search area, I suddenly saw the cobra's head. It reared up out of the vegetation, looking first towards the advancing men, and then straight at me, its tongue flicking in and out to scent the air.

I pointed. The men nodded as they had spotted it too.

The cobra's head disappeared back down. The men advanced slowly, circling the area where the head had been.

Cutting off all avenues of escape they crept forward. They looked, and they looked. But as if by magic, the cobra had vanished.

Eventually they gave up. Before walking away laughing one of them spread out his hands and said to me, 'Not a snake. It was a goddess.'

I must have looked surprised.

'They do that – disappear. That's how we know. Yes, it was a goddess.' Then he gave me one of those wonderfully enigmatic Indian head wobbles and hurried off to join his friends.

Afterthoughts

Saying goodbye is always a wrench – especially if you know you're unlikely to see each other again. But I never say '*never*'. Who knows where I might be heading next.

There is so much of our planet I haven't seen yet, so many landscapes to marvel at, so many people I've yet to meet.

Life is a journey and I'm still travelling, wondering what I'll find round the next bend. Maybe I'll meet you there.

'*Safari Njema*' as they say in Kiswahili – Safe Journey!

Jeannette's Stories

Jeannette's Introduction

Laughter, Tears and Fears

My mosaic of travel memories ranges from deepest black to glorious gold. I seize each picture as it jumps into my head, thinking, '*I must write about this...*'

I relive sailing away into the blue of the Aegean Sea with a German expert windsurfer. I suffer again the agonies of vertigo as I stumble along a rope tree walk suspended above a magnificent Malaysian forest. I shy away from the horrific memories of Bali where the devastation of the terrorist bomb still haunts me.

Stepping away from my Middle England bubble into the outer world I'd so longed to experience was both exciting and challenging. Forever vivid, I recall the laughter, tears and fears of each journey etched indelibly in my mind. These stories have become the fabric of my written tales, capturing the essence of an important part of my life.

Sighs, Smiles and a Restless Heart

Mid-1950

The Royal Observatory, Greenwich. Early 20th century.

We watched the scarlet globules of blood drip slowly onto the bright emerald grass as we smiled at each other. Solemnly we pressed finger to finger. 'You are now my blood sister,' I said. 'You are *my* blood sister,' she repeated. 'We are forever conjoined,' we chorused together.

Sitting under the lee of the ancient Royal Observatory in Greenwich Park so long ago, those two overly romantic English schoolgirls enacted a ritual practised by the faraway Sioux Indians wishing to form a deep bond with each other. Wanting a sisterhood the accident of birth had denied them, they performed a ceremony as old as time. One was an only child, the other was a lonely child, both instinctively feeling that life would change, all too soon.

Our convent school was a step away from the park, across the road in Crooms Hill, Greenwich. During the summer term, which was filled with boring tennis lessons, careful planning allowed us to regularly escape the eagle eye of our tennis coach in order to slip through the forbidden side gate of the convent grounds and enter our own world of girlish privacy.

As we lay together on the grass that sunny day, we discussed what we would do with our future lives. We often had these conversations, believing we had complete control over destiny and what we planned would inevitably come to pass. Our desires varied as the years progressed, from living in a land where you could buy gobstoppers whenever you wished, to more mature chats about boyfriends, the mysteries of sex, and clothes. At the age of sixteen, we confidently felt we would live forever and be fully able to map out the pattern of our future destinies. *She* was going to get married and have five children, live in London overlooking the silvery ribbon of the Thames and never move away. *I* was burdened with a restless soul. *No*, I'd thought, *that's not for me*.

Scrambling to my feet, I walked a few yards nearer to the ancient Royal Observatory building. There in the grass was a bright and shiny bronze line with a zero beside it. The meridian line zero runs through Greenwich Park at that point, on its lengthy journey to the North and South Poles. *Fantabulous concept!* I thought. I straddled it, foot on either side, and looked down at the mundane vision of my white schoolgirl socks and brown sandals. With one foot in the eastern and the other in the western hemisphere, I made a vow, I was going to 'Put a girdle round the Earth in forty minutes.' We both laughed. I knew I didn't have Puck's magic powers that Shakespeare had given him; trotting more sedately round the globe was more likely for me. *I'll probably get married first anyway*, I thought, which I instinctively felt would be a bit of a handicap to any travels. I wanted a boy and a girl child to love too. Pushing a pram on my trotting expeditions never entered my head. I only knew I had to wait until the time was right.

Our futures were bathed in this golden light of expectation.

I never imagined then, the reality of early widowhood or the fight it took to keep my much-loved adopted children with me after my husband's car accident. Money had never been important to me, but the spectre of that time of extreme poverty we endured, haunts me still. I never imagined my inherent empathy with most living creatures, beginning with the little colony of snails I adopted in my lonely early childhood, would end with my wonderful animal family that sustained my soul through thick and thin. And never in a million years did I anticipate the loss of my blood sister whose support I treasured through every trauma, and who left this life much, much too early, leaving me utterly bereft. I did suspect my travels might be a little delayed but there was no doubt in my mind that one day I was going to see that world out there, waiting, just waiting for me to taste it.

It took me about twenty years to fulfil that childish vow. During that time I managed just a glimpse into foreign living. Hating my job in London, I wrote to my old convent school to ask if they could suggest an alternative. They found me a place as a teaching assistant in a French convent in the heart of Normandy where I spent a rollercoaster year learning to live alongside French, American, and Spanish girls of my own age while trying to fit into the life of the Ursuline teaching nuns. A veritable vertical learning curve. The good, the bad, and the downright scary experiences I encountered on my travels started with that life in the middle of a non-English-speaking French rural community. I was inadequately equipped with my GCE foreign language certificate which I arrogantly thought would open every door, I was wrong of course – every French word I'd ever learned left me when confronted with fast Norman speech – I was dumb for at least a month! Undeterred, my itchy feet eventually took me to many adventures in many other fascinating countries.

So here we go...

First Foray

Early 1960

A church in Normandy.

It was pitch black and the tall wrought-iron gates were locked. No lights to be seen anywhere. I knew I was in Rue St Pierre, just outside Caen, waiting at the entrance to Couvent des Ursulines in rural Normandy. But now I felt lost and uncertain about what to do next. *Help*, I thought, *what now?* My long journey from London to my placement as an English tutor in a French school in the middle of rural France, had given me time to wonder if I had made the right decision. I'd left my boring secretarial job in the centre of London, which I hated, in the hope that this new project would give me ideas as to what I could do with the rest of my life. A bit unrealistically dramatic, I know – but I *was* only eighteen.

The old bicycle torch had run out of battery ages ago. The taxi driver who left me at the end of the street had gabbled directions in very rapid French before he drove off. Too tired to understand a word of what he said, I just walked blindly down the street in front of me until I reached what I thought was the entrance to the convent garden. Putting down my suitcase, my exploring hands eventually came across what appeared to be an iron bell-pull, at the side of what felt to be tall, freezing, iron gates. I pulled it. The bell was astoundingly loud in the silence of the night. Without warning, a door opened, slightly to my left, casting candlelight onto the paving at my feet. I stepped back in surprise, nearly falling over my suitcase. In front of me stood a little nun, face encased by a white wimple covered by a black veil clutching a hot water bottle to her bosom. She peered at me through Harry Potter-like spectacles. Another figure dressed precisely the same and smothering a yawn appeared beside her. 'Enfin ici,' they chorused, and continued talking in extremely fast French. I had no idea what they were saying. I was so bemused, I didn't even try to understand. One picked up my suitcase, the other took my arm and indicated I should continue walking with her down the street. We left nun number two to close the door, who then broke into a fast trot in order to catch up with us. It was a pretty chilly night, frost just hovering in the air waiting to pounce, so I was glad of a brisk walk to get my circulation going. I tried to ask where the convent was – had I got the address wrong? They replied in chorus – but again I didn't understand a word.

The darkness didn't seem to bother them, but I was glad I was sandwiched between my two sure-footed guides. My London home street was bespeckled with light, no dark corners anywhere – safe, familiar, reassuring. After what seemed like an endless dark tunnel, we arrived at an extremely large building, and met a man guarding the entrance. He greeted my companions, opened a door, and we entered a dimly lit corridor. The bespectacled nun led the way. We tiptoed down the corridor and came to another door on the right, she opened it, and said, 'Entrée, mademoiselle.'

There was a faint light from a lamp on a bedside table. The two nuns pulled back the bed covers, produced a hot water bottle each, placed them under the coverlet, chorusing 'Bonne nuit, dormez bien,' and left. Just like that. I was alone in a decidedly chilly bedroom, weary and homesick. Having passed a 'toilette' on our way in, I made for that and returned 'toute suite', shivering. Taking off my outer clothes, I tumbled into the blessedly warm bed, closed my eyes and went out like a light.

I woke up the next morning to the sound of marching feet. Getting out of bed, I padded barefoot across the cold floor, murmuring to myself, 'Brrr, it must have been pretty cold last night.' As I scraped the frosty window clear with my fingernails, I could just make out about twenty men in line, marching across the courtyard below. They were accompanied by four men in uniform, two at the front of the line and two at the back.

I couldn't quite believe my eyes, they looked weird and out of place. The men in uniform were obviously in charge, but what they were doing on convent premises, I couldn't imagine.

Hunger overtaking my curiosity, I put on my shoes, made for the door and opened it. Peering out, I saw a child trotting down the corridor towards me, dressed in school uniform, she must have been about twelve years old. She smiled and waved at me, and said something to me in rapid French. 'Er, bonjour,' I began. She regarded me somewhat pityingly, and replied in halting English, 'I have come to take you to Reverend Mother. Come with me. Bring your luggage. Put your coat on.' She grinned suddenly. 'We take a short walk.' Without waiting to see if I was following she skipped back down the corridor towards the exit. I hurriedly pulled up the bedclothes, put on my coat, grabbed my bag and left. I found her waiting at the door I'd come in last night. ' We go,' she said.

It was sunny, slightly misty and cold, there was frost on the ground. I was feeling hungry and thirsty by then, wanting my breakfast, hoping my interview with Reverend Mother was short... Curious about where I had spent the night, I turned and looked back. I could just make out a sign above the front door. It read 'Établissement Pénitentiaire'. It took me a second to work out what that meant. Surely 'Pénitentiare' meant prison? Unbelievingly, I looked at the little girl, and I pointed back at the building we just left. 'Is that really a prison?' I asked in slow French. 'Yes, yes, I live there. My daddy is governor. You sleep in visitors' room. You arrive very late. The convent closes at eight thirty. The gates are locked and the nuns go to bed.'

I looked at her unbelievingly. Had I slept my first night of my French adventure in the company of criminals, in a French prison? My legs suddenly felt wobbly, imagining what those ruffians I'd seen could have done to a lonely female. Almost involuntarily, my words spilled out, in English, 'Exactly what crimes have those people committed to be sent here?' She looked at me uncomprehendingly for a moment. After a few seconds to work out what I meant she replied, 'Oh, murderers, bad men who hurt people. Don't worry. My daddy keeps them in rooms with doors that don't open. He says, "Don't think about them, Colette", so I don't.' She spoke very slowly, struggling for words, making sure I understood.

A sharp frisson of fear slimed down my spine. I shivered, as I suddenly remembered my bedroom door had been unlocked all night. I immediately wished I'd known that I had been surrounded by 'bad' men. I would certainly have made sure my door was securely double-bolted with a chair lodged under its handle for extra security. Noticing my reaction she smiled at me reassuringly, took my hand and we carried on walking down the road towards those big wrought-iron gates. No wonder they were padlocked shut every evening. They were still locked this morning, but Colette knocked on the small door beside the gates. It was opened by a pleasant-looking dark-haired lady slightly older than myself. 'Bonjour, Colette,' she said. Obviously thanking her for bringing me to the convent, she indicated that I should come in. I turned to say goodbye just in time to see Colette take the hand of one of the guards from the prison who had unobtrusively followed us in order to escort Colette home. I learnt later that every time she left the prison premises Colette was allocated a security escort, for fear of kidnapping. Apparently one or two attempts had already been made.

Poor little girl, I thought to myself, *what a life for her and what a worry for her parents.*

My meagre French enabled me to understand that my soon-to-be friend, Michelle, was to be my mentor, until term started the following week. We were in what I later found out to be 'The Gatehouse', which only had the small door we'd just come through on that side of the building. No windows, nothing but a tall wall of stone was all that could been seen from the outside. A bit daunting – I began to feel as if I'd come to yet another prison! The ground floor of the Gatehouse was one large room containing an imposing spiral staircase, leading to the next floor. Michelle took my suitcase and started to climb the steep spiral stairs. I followed very carefully as I don't really like heights. You could see from the top of the staircase right down to the carpeted floor below, quite a long drop. Averting my eyes, I focused on Michelle's muscular backside as she athletically climbed upwards. Arriving on the last step she turned to smile at me, speaking very slowly in French, 'Welcome, Jeannette. I'm sure we'll have some fun together. I hope we will be friends.'

At the top of the staircase was a comfortably furnished sitting room. A few deep, squishy-looking armchairs, a big low table in the middle of the room covered with magazines and a bookcase extending the length of a wall. The whole effect was welcoming and cosy. French windows looked out onto a pretty grass square – edged with autumn shrubs. It was all very neat and tidy.

One more staircase to climb. This led us to the third floor, which was divided into three rooms with a bathroom between rooms one and three. I was allocated room three which contained a large bed, an armoire, a desk and a chair. The view from my French windows showed me a very large house painted a soft yellow, windows outlined in white and a sizeable main door, all rather imposing. I had a tiny balcony which thrilled me. I opened the windows and peered out, feeling very like Juliet, looking in vain for her Romeo. I sighed, shut the windows and turned to find Michelle looking at me with an amused smile on her face. I guessed she could read what I'd been thinking. I blushed, but by this time, my hunger was quite acute, so I just said to her, 'J'ai faim.' 'Come with me,' she replied in French, 'we go to the kitchen. We meet Reverend Mother after lunch.'

We negotiated that scary, steep, spiral staircase again. This time, I focused on Michelle's dark curly hair which helped me forget the long drop to the floor below. We left the Gatehouse through French doors at the back which opened on to the neat shrub-edged grass quadrangle and made for the back of the imposing château-like building. More steep steps led down to the door into a simply cavernous kitchen. The smells were heavenly – coffee, baking bread, and a delicious smell of dinner-to-come.

'Oh my gosh. I've been waiting for this, it seems forever,' I muttered to myself. It was deserted, except for a little nun busying herself at the large kitchen range at one end of the room. A well-scrubbed farmhouse-type table occupied most of the space in the centre, big enough for about twenty chairs to fit round it. We sat down at the end nearest the range, where two places had been set with a large bowl, a knife and a plate each. The little old nun turned to me, revealing a smiling wrinkled face, intense blue eyes, and a small pointed chin. In a slightly quavering voice, she introduced herself as Sister Cecile. She was very old, bent over, with rheumatic-twisted hands.

'I give you coffee,' she said in heavily accented Norman French. She produced an enormous jug, rather shakily filling our bowls to the brim. She then placed a basket of warm bread on the table between us, patting me on the shoulder as she slowly made her way to the other end of the kitchen table, wielding an enormous knife. I had no idea what to do with this large bowl full of liquid. Michelle, however, picked it up with both hands and drank thirstily from it. I giggled as I noticed she'd acquired a very fetching moustache of café au lait! There were no handles on the bowl so I followed suit, putting my hands either side of it. I gingerly lifted it to my lips – the coffee was absolutely delicious.

She grinned at me, helped herself to a large hunk of bread and tucked in. Sister Cecile had quietly returned to our end of the table carrying a large platter of some kind of meat, resting it on the table in front of us as she wagged her finger at me. 'Greedy girl,' she scolded, 'not butter *and* jam, never, never.' And she shook her head at the overindulged, slightly overweight spoilt English girl. I guiltily regarded my loaded plate. I tried to explain that in England, we would have bread, butter and jam or toast, butter and marmalade for breakfast. Unfortunately, my French was not up to it. She just smiled sweetly at me, shook her finger at me again, then shook her head, and turned back to that enormous range, depositing her freshly cut meat into the saucepan, ready for our forthcoming dinner. I did carry on eating, but felt very embarrassed. I made a resolution that in future I'd look carefully at everyone around me, so that I followed the customs of this strange new environment.

I later learnt a bit more about this sweet little Sister Cecile. She'd been found clinging to those formidable wrought-iron gates about seventy years before, unable to say more than a very few words. The nuns had taken her in, cared for her, and as it became apparent she was what they called 'simple', helped her feel a useful member of their close-knit community. She decided at the age of sixteen to join the Ursuline Order and became Sister Cecile. No one knew her real name, so the nuns had called her Marie; she'd called herself Cecile when she was ordained. She was the happiest, kindest, least polluted soul I had ever met. She'd put her whole life into the hands of 'Le Bon Dieu' she told me, she felt loved and valued and had experienced a very happy, contented life. The nuns had been kind, and one of them had taken her under her wing and shown the affection-deprived child how to be loving and giving. They'd taught her basic reading, writing and arithmetic, they'd taken her to their mother and baby refuge and helped her to care for the babies there. As she was very fond of animals, she was shown how to look after the goats, chickens and geese on their self-sufficiency farm. She told me she wouldn't have changed anything in her life. Happily accepting everything fate threw at her as 'the will of her God', she'd lived a life as one of service to others. She did confess to one sin, however. I asked her, 'What could that possibly be?' She hung her head and whispered, 'I pray for an early death, I am in such pain,' and she showed me her swollen distorted hands. 'I should accept it but I can't. It's so much hurt.' Turning to me she asked, 'Do you think Le Bon Dieu could forgive me, and allow me to be with the angels?' I swallowed the lump in my throat and said, 'I am sure He will. Of course He will.'

I discovered the only pain relief the Ursuline Order allowed themselves was aspirin.

Not much use to stop the pain of that rheumatism-wracked body of my little Sister.

She died just a few months after I left the convent a year later.

A Different World

1960

Church of Saint-Pierre in Caen, Normandy.

The reality of life in a convent was quite a shock. I don't know what I expected, but somehow I felt it would be a very easy lifestyle with everything provided for, and all you had to do was pray every so often. It turned out to be quite different. The nun's day started at three thirty am. Electricity had been turned off at eight pm the night before. Candles were used in emergencies. Their daily life was governed by bells, morning, noon and night, calling them to worship in their beautiful little chapel. Their Order was divided into teachers and 'workers'. The teachers were addressed as Mother; the nuns who looked after the pastoral side of the convent were addressed as Sister. Everyone was treated with equal respect, regardless of the tasks they had to do, from the menial to the most important, which made everybody feel equally valued. It seemed to be a tranquil, ordered life with Reverend Mother having the responsibility for the smooth running of teaching pupils, pastoral care including the cooking, the maintenance of the building – and us, the foreigners. She must've been a bit of a whizz-kid as everything seemed to flow effortlessly. All the time I was there, I never heard a voice raised in anger, nor any complaint about the running of this complex multitasking establishment.

We three foreign students, plus Michelle, our resident French teacher, enjoyed the independent privacy of the Gatehouse. Our only restriction was we were expected to be back in the Gatehouse not later than eight o'clock at night, when the door would be locked, and Michelle would pocket the key. Thankfully we were not expected to follow the rigid routine of the nuns across the way in that large château-like building.

Personally, I was particularly glad not to have to get up at three thirty am as I am definitely not a morning person. Happily I wasn't alone in this. Conchita and I were nearly always the last to get out of bed. Conchita Ramirez, Spanish; Betty Mitchell, American – and me, English, represented an interesting mix of cultures. It was difficult to predict how we would get on together, but with

Michelle's – French – help, we soon felt part of a cohesive group, tendrils of friendship sprouting from the very first day. The Gatehouse was delightfully cosy but bedroom space was limited. As there were four, one of us had to share a room with Michelle. Conchita's bedroom was the largest with a heavy brocade curtain across part of it, the beds either side enjoying almost complete privacy in a sizeable space. We voted *her* to be the one. She told us she was happy to share, she had a maid sleeping in her dressing room at home anyway, so she'd never slept alone. Betty and I looked at each other, we were both taken aback at this particular revelation. Neither of us could imagine the kind of restrictive life this pampered, protected, only child led.

During the enforced silence of my first week due to my insecure French, I felt very lonely in spite of Michelle's efforts to encourage me to speak. I just felt such an idiot, understanding nearly nothing, struggling with the unfamiliar Norman accent. I was extremely glad to meet up with Conchita who arrived, in tears, a few days after me. Her parents had organised her trip and placement without her consent and she hadn't wanted to come. Her English and French were basic, better than mine, but still very halting. I think we gave each other courage to try and speak, even if it was slowly. Michelle and the nuns were very tolerant and happy to supply errant words when needed. It took about a month before I became fluent. It was then I realised I was actually thinking in French, such an achievement! This facility eventually enabled me to speak much faster, almost as fast as the natives. When Betty arrived just over a week after Conchita and I, we were really glad to meet her. She was a breath of fresh air from a country that was known to both of us, mainly through Hollywood films. We expected a glamour puss, so it came as a bit of a shock when she turned up with what we'd now call a backpack, calf-length skirt, patterned with rather loud checks, white socks, and what she called sneakers.

The French, Spanish and English girls' dress was rather drab, our dark-coloured skirts and tops looking so boring compared with Betty's more colourful wardrobe. She greeted us all with a wide smile, and hugs all round. Obviously very pleased and relieved to be with us.

She won our hearts with her friendly personality and her generosity with the goodies she produced from her backpack including the shocking, forbidden chewing gum.

Somehow, she made us feel as if we were in an Enid Blyton tale of the Famous Five, even if we were only four! I think it was the fact that she excluded the adults around us from our real lives, which we lived in the Gatehouse. It was somehow a very comfortable feeling.

I discovered I really did not like thirteen- to sixteen-year-old French schoolgirls. My task every afternoon was to supervise the boarders' homework session. They did not want to be there and behaved accordingly. They eyed me knowingly up and down. As I was not the first young teaching assistant to be given this particular job, they were able to take advantage of me incredibly easily. I knew they were mocking me behind my back but I didn't know what they were actually saying, which was extremely aggravating. They were noisy and undisciplined, they weren't doing their homework, but spent their time passing notes to each other under the desk. And they were becoming increasingly difficult to control. I found it extremely hard to keep order and retain some authority when I had no idea what anyone was saying either to my face or behind my back. Added to that, I was only a couple of years older than the sixteen-year-olds I was supposed to be supervising. My French was basic, good enough to give instructions, but not good enough to understand the local Norman French accent, nor the fast slang they were speaking to each other. Very frustrating for me, anxious to make a good impression on the nuns who employed me. After consultation with sympathetic Michelle I was allocated a 'minder'. Apparently that was not so unusual in French schools. Teachers teach their subject and were not necessarily expected to have to do anything else.

My 'minder' was an undergraduate from Caen University. He was allocated to my classroom for the first half term after which it was assumed my French would be good enough to understand anything these horrible teenagers were likely to say and also to be able to keep law and order.

I have to say I fell in love with Lucas at first sight.

He was a handsome, dark-haired, blue-eyed, serious scholar, studying French literature. He loved poetry and he used to recite it to himself, I think learning it, during my supervision time. I didn't understand what he was murmuring under his breath, but the rhythm, and the tone of his deep voice was enough to win my heart.

Here was my Romeo, and I actually had a balcony, outside the French windows of my room just waiting for him.

The fact that the fifteen or so teenagers also fell in love with him made my task of engaging his attention that much more difficult. They passed notes to him which he just stuffed in his pocket, they left little presents on his desk. They gave him adoring looks as he came and sat at the back of the class, oblivious of everything they tried to do to catch his attention. They really irritated me. One young sixteen-year-old hussy had the cheek to drop her books at his feet as she was going out of the door. As he bent to pick them up, she smirked at me provocatively over the top of his head.

Unfortunately, she was very pretty, and only a couple of years younger than myself. Our hero was probably about twenty, definitely too old for her, I thought! He was a good influence on the behaviour of the girls though, as they all vied for perfection in the hope of winning his praise... He never really noticed them or me. He arrived in the morning, sat at his desk, occasionally said something in French when they got too rowdy, got up to go at the end of the session, nodded goodbye – and went. We were all devastated at his lack of awareness. Love unrequited was painful for all of us.

Betty and Conchita, on the other hand, had been assigned the roles of classroom assistants. Their teachers had been pleasant, encouraging nuns. Discipline was not an issue, so they enjoyed their time in their respective classes.

The timetable was arranged by Mother Bernadette who assured us that the policy for the foreign teaching assistants was to assign them different classes throughout the school to enable them to get a good understanding of every level of education there, and to enable all the children to learn about our respective cultures. I took comfort that no assignment was forever. So I had to be content with the idea my classes would be rotated, along with those of the other foreign students. I was especially looking forward to the task of helping in the French literature class as in the back of my mind I hoped I might be able to attend Caen University French literature courses. The nuns had mentioned it as a possibility when I arrived, as I had expressed an interest in French literature.

I enjoyed our cosy evenings together in the Gatehouse learning a bit about what it was like to be Spanish or American. Michelle often joined us so we got glimpses of French culture too. Betty was related to Margaret Mitchell, the author of *Gone with the Wind*, set in the Deep South during the Civil War.

Interestingly, the family ostracised Aunt Margaret because they thought her book was unseemly and lurid. In spite of the fact she was a renowned philanthropist and used her considerable fortune in charitable enterprises, they remained unimpressed. Aunt Margaret was making thousands out of her book and the film that was made, set in Georgia, during the American Civil War, featuring Clark Gable and Vivien Leigh. Both the book and the film received many accolades, and became world famous. *Gone with the Wind* is now regarded as an iconic movie. The book itself had been written before I was born and was already a classic by the time I came across it. I loved it and adored the film.

I was rather horrified to be told by Betty that in 1940 it was banned by the Vatican as unsuitable reading, and she seemed slightly scandalised that I'd read it. She told me her family had not allowed her to. Neither Conchita nor Michelle had even heard of it. I didn't quite understand or appreciate the power that unreasonable prejudice had to stop my friends from enjoying an epic piece of fiction. I felt it was so unfair. I became quite close friends with Conchita, in a way I felt very sorry for her. At home, she led a very regulated life, her parents organised absolutely everything for her from when she got up to when she went to bed. She had a small group of female friends which she met regularly, but they'd been chosen by her parents, and she didn't feel any real connection with any of them. She was actually very lonely.

She was apparently from a rich family, part of the Madrid upper crust. She confided to me that her parents were worried about fortune hunters so had found a nice young man, an architect, who would be very suitable for her to marry. Under some pressure, she had agreed to become engaged. Her ring was beautiful, a sculptured square sapphire, surrounded by diamonds. She didn't like it, so she kept it under her pillow in her bedroom as a protest against being made to marry a man she had no feelings for.

As she told me her story, her tears began to flow.

'He's very nice, but I don't know him,' she sobbed. She brought out a photograph of a good-looking, dark-haired, dark-eyed young man with a smiling mouth. 'He looks just like a film star to me,' I said. 'I promised to write to him every week,' she told me, 'but I don't know what to say.'

'Why don't you just tell him the story of our life here? He would probably like to get to know you better too,' I suggested. I just couldn't imagine what her life was really like to live; mine, at home, was so incredibly different. Hers sounded like a wildly romantic plot for one of those chick-lit novels.

One of the glorious aspects I discovered about French culture was wonderful fresh bread, baked two or three times a day. Napoleon had apparently passed a law that bread should be baked in a wand-like shape, about eighty centimetres long, so that his soldiers could carry their bread ration in their uniform pockets on the way to battle. By law only four ingredients were allowed: salt, flour, water and yeast and it had to be sold fresh from the premises that baked it.

That's how the famous French 'baguette' was born.

The boulangerie opposite opened its doors at about five thirty. However, the aroma of newly baked bread woke me pleasurably later, at around seven o'clock. Although our door was supposed to stay locked until nine o'clock, Michelle used to steal across the road and come back with delectable, mouth-watering baguettes and dark chocolate. Put a piece of dark chocolate in a warm, French baguette and you're in paradise, combine that with a secret coffee machine hidden in Michelle's side of the bedroom, add some milk and we were all on a high! We adored Michelle, she was quite happy to bend any rule if it enhanced our Norman experience...

After that start to the day it was no hardship to quickly wash and rush downstairs to be in time for another breakfast at nine am ready for our classes at nine thirty. (One of the first comments on my return home by the way, was how much weight I'd put on. Kind people said it suited me – I wasn't quite so sure...!)

'Did you know that the convent's beautiful château-like building and much of its contents were inherited by one of the nuns just before World War II?' asked Michelle as I stood gazing up at the beautiful façade of the nuns' main residence. She went on to tell me the Ursuline nuns had moved in, in about 1937/38, just before the start of the war. They became renowned and admired for their dedicated education of girls, their charitable activities, and, during the war, the help and protection of any vulnerable people who came to them, during the brutal occupation of the Nazi Germans at that time. All around the château was evidence of its past grandeur. Original paintings on the walls by various famous artists, beautifully polished wooden floorboards, and parquet flooring could be found here and there. The dining room had a great mahogany table, seating at least forty people. It had superb solid silver candle-holders set all down the middle, interspersed with silver bowls. This room was only to be opened on feast days, Michelle told us.

The nuns used an extremely large, comfortable sitting room which also housed a magnificent grand piano, for their relaxation hour. Once a week we students were invited to sit with them during their evening leisure time. It was usually incredibly boring as they were read to, in French, from various 'good books'. But every so often, Mother Angelique would be given permission to open the lid of the polished, ebony grand piano. She must've been a concert-level pianist as her playing was mesmerising. For the first time in my life, I was regularly exposed to the music of the classic composers, Ravel, Chopin, Scriabin to name a few. She must've learnt everything by heart, her mind echoing with all the music she had ever heard, as she never seemed to falter for an instant. I will never forget the tension-building introduction to Ravel's awe-inspiring *Bolero.* Apparently, she was allowed an hour and a half every day for practice as a special dispensation from her teaching duties. No one ever saw a single piece of sheet music anywhere near that piano.

It remains a mystery as to what her hidden story was, and why she had chosen to subjugate her talent and dedicate her life to a teaching order in a small convent in Northern France.

Surprisingly, the nuns had managed to hide the treasures of the château from the German invaders during World War II, and by the time I got there, there were lots of indications that this had been an extremely gracious place to live.

My first 'impression' was literally just that. It started with my bedlinen. This was a soft cream colour, pure linen, embroidered along the edge in deep red with what I assumed were the initials of the previous owners of the château. The pillowcases were enormous square, sumptuous additions to my ancient four-poster bed. They too were liberally sprinkled with large red embroidered initials surrounded by fleur-de-lys. Waking up rather groggily on my first morning, I hazily noticed red back-to-front large letters embossed, slightly tinted pink, on my left cheek. Conchita confirmed this phenomenon, and we both went into my bedroom to inspect the bed. Sure enough, round the edge of the sheet, and on the pillowcase were very large prominent embroidered initials. Mine was the only bed graced with those special antique sheets. (Apparently a normal size sheet doesn't fit large, ancient four-poster beds.) My cool, clean linen sheets and pillowcases were definitely a luxury to sleep with, but I was not so sure about the impromptu, semi-indelible 'tattoos' impressed on my cheek from the pillow, and on my shoulder from the top of the sheet. It took a couple of days of vigorous washing before the red dye faded from my fair skin. The next night, I turned the pillows back to front and the sheets bottom to top – problem solved – no more vaguely pink 'tattoos' to be found anywhere on my body, except possibly my toes!

The Gatehouse was about the same age as the château and apparently the big four-poster bed was built in situ in that bedroom, which is why it remained there for me. The task of dismantling it would've been formidable, I guessed. I didn't enjoy sleeping in it much, I kept hitting my ankles on one of the posts in my restless sleep. Later, I did appreciate the privilege of sleeping in a four-poster that had probably hosted more aristocratic bodies than mine between the sheets. I really regretted not making a note of the initials embroidered carefully on the linen. It would have been wonderful to know who the previous users had been. Unfortunately most historical research was extremely difficult as so many documents had been destroyed during World War II, whole libraries bombed, archives lost and valuable evidence bonfired to ashes. I never found out who had used those sheets before me. So frustrating.

My time in France went by all too quickly. Our timetables had been adjusted to allow us one weekday free from commitment. Conchita and Betty decided to explore the shops in town, but I asked Mother Angela if I could visit their farm as I was really interested in the animals. I could hear the occasional distant 'moo' as we crossed the beautiful garden on our way to breakfast. She explained that the farm was run in such a way that it supported the convent almost completely in food stuff and also supplied their charitable enterprise. 'I will leave you to find out what that is,' she said smilingly. 'I think you might have a bit of a surprise. Sister Claire and Sister Marie will accompany you as they go every day to help.'

The farm was about twenty minutes' walk away from the main convent, heading out towards the countryside at the edge of Caen. The nuns walked at a brisk pace, very used to walking everywhere, but it took me some effort to keep up. *Time for less bread and more exercise*, I thought to myself. We eventually arrived at a farm gate, the entrance to a neat and tidy yard leading to a sizeable house, behind some farm buildings.

We were met at the door by a nun dressed in a white habit with a spotless apron and a watch pinned high on the right-hand side of her bib. She let us into a small hallway, smelling vaguely of disinfectant and through into a large room that was absolutely full of babies. Some in cots, some being breastfed by their mothers, and some being cradled by nuns sitting on comfortable, low chairs. A few cried a little, but most of them were obviously very content and drowsy.

'I am Mother Mary Bernadette. I take care of the mothers and babies here. Our mothers are local girls who become pregnant, but who are not married. We offer them a refuge during their pregnancy, help them look after their babies when they're born and give them a means of earning a living for when they leave us. They stay with us for three months after the babies' birth. Most of our mothers leave here with skills and opportunities to support themselves and their children. Some of them go back to their homes, with their babies, and are welcomed back as useful members of the family. Very few stay with us and earn a small wage by working on our farm.' She paused and added, 'Feel free to wander and meet any of our girls and babies. I'm sure they would love to talk to you.' Mother Mary Bernadette then turned and left the room with the two sisters who had accompanied me, leaving me standing, slightly embarrassed, at the door.

When one of the the mothers beckoned me over, and handed her baby to me saying, 'Please could you put her over your shoulder and pat her back, I will return in a minute,' and disappeared, I was petrified. This little mite was only the second baby I'd ever held in my life. Scared I'd drop her, she was so tiny, I hastily sat down in the chair, baby draped over my shoulder. She gave an enormous burp, wriggled a little, then turned her little face towards me, snuggling into my neck. I looked around the room. A couple of babies were doing the same as mine. Most of the others were sleeping, cradled in people's arms. It was suddenly a wonderful experience to be there. The warm little bundle aroused feelings in me I never knew I had. Mother came back and reclaimed her little one, smiling at me. 'Her name is Rosalie,' she said. 'She's only a week old.' She looked proudly down into her baby's face, looked up at me and said, 'Isn't she beautiful?'

'Oh yes,' I breathed, 'She certainly is.'

As it was a sunny day, the French windows into the garden were open, letting in fresh clean air. One of the mothers stood up and asked me if I'd like to look round. I gladly accepted, stepping out with her into the bright sunlight. I realised the vista before me was actually an extremely extensive mix of vegetables of every kind, not a flower to be seen. Nuns and girls were dotted all around working busily among the varied rows of plants. I could see wheelbarrows piled with root vegetables, and in the distance, there appeared to be extensive orchards. Large white birds, which I was told were geese, grazed peacefully among the trees, helping to keep the grass at a reasonable level.

Further afield, you could see cattle; even further away, flocks of sheep. As my guide turned our steps towards the farm buildings she explained I would see a milking parlour, a large, airy building where pigs were kept in straw pens, with piglets already born or expectant sows waiting for even more piglets. They didn't keep a boar, she said, he just came to visit at the appropriate time. Housed further away were the goat pens and milking area for goats, and an extremely large barn filled with straw on one side and hay on the other.

'This has got to last us for the winter,' she told me.

'I am full-time here,' she explained. 'I'm in charge of the livestock. I have help every day from some sisters from the convent, and I help train new mothers in the art of milking and animal care.' She went on to say she'd been there for five years. Her little boy attended kindergarten, soon to be going to primary school. She lived in accommodation provided for people who worked on the farm, a one-up and one-down cottage, where she and her child lived. He would stay with her until he went to boarding school at the age of eleven. She expected to spend the rest of her life in the convent and planned to become a sister when she felt the time was right. 'I only have one day a week available,' I said, 'but could I come and work here, do you think?'

She looked me up and down, appraisingly, and smiled.

'Well, I think it would do you good!' she replied. I suddenly felt self-conscious about those extra pounds that wonderful French bread had so kindly donated. 'Yes, it certainly would.' I said, 'Thank you.' She said, 'I will discuss this with Mother Mary Bernadette, and I will send a message to you by one of the sisters confirming that you can come. I'm sure you will be very welcome. By the way, my name is Christelle.' With that, she picked up a spade and fork, put them over her shoulder and marched towards the pig pens obviously ready to 'muck out'. I wandered back to the baby room and found the French windows half open, curtains drawn and most of the babies asleep in the cots. Cool, calm and quiet.

A few mothers sat between the cots, softly talking to each other, nearly all of them with knitting in their hands, supervising the tiny sleeping tots. They smiled at me as I tiptoed to the exit. In the small vestibule a sister was sitting saying her rosary. She nodded goodbye. As I walked back to the convent I pondered about what I had just seen. I vaguely remembered hearing one didn't talk about unmarried mothers. I'd never met one. I wasn't sure what actually happened to them either. I found later most were pressured into having their babies adopted, extraordinarily sad.

I felt that the nuns here had a great idea.

Everyone in the mother and baby home had a place to have the baby, to keep it safe, and to learn how to earn a living.

It also ran a nursery school that mothers could bring their children back to when they were working. They stayed there until they were able to attend primary school. The whole arrangement seemed to me a pretty wonderful project. It wasn't charity, either, it was a system that was productive and self- supporting to a great extent, enabling mother and child to live a life with hope for the future. I was amazed to realise many of those mothers were about my age, one or two even younger. I couldn't imagine such a situation for myself and shuddered at the thought of having a baby torn from me against my will, which I later learnt happened in so many cases. The non-judgemental and supportive atmosphere together with the expertise available to everyone, was an invaluable help to those girls. They were so lucky.

Conchita was returning home at the end of the week. She said she'd write to me. I did hope so. I wanted to keep in touch with all of them. It had been suggested I could spend another academic year in the sister convent in Spain. I was sorely tempted, but I was homesick, actually, and just wanted to go back to England at the end of this term.

I'd been lucky enough to attend Caen University as an 'associate student'. The coursework for that term was an in-depth study of *Le Bourgeois Gentilhomme*, by Molière. I'd really enjoyed the eighteenth-century French, even though it presented many difficulties – a bit like a French person reading the English of Shakespeare for the first time.

As I got to know my difficult teenage students better, they explained some of their slang to me, and as I grew more fluent in the language, I found I enjoyed hearing their conversations – entering very briefly into their world. It became a fun session as they shared with me their homework difficulties and some hopes and fears about their futures, most expecting to find a husband to settle down with and have a family rather than even considering a career.

They were interesting and even fun, once I began to understand them. I felt very settled with our Gatehouse friendship group. It was such a privilege to have a glimpse into other cultures, it soon became obvious that under the skin we were real kindred spirits sharing the same concerns, the same problems, and quite often similar dreams. I never lost that fellow feeling wherever I travelled, everywhere I went, there was a camaraderie of shared life experiences that never seemed to fade.

This first taste of travel was in a very secure bubble with support on all sides with sympathy and affection on a day-to-day basis which was an invaluable experience.

I was so torn about what to do next – homesickness warred with a desire to stay where I was – I would've loved to have worked in the Home for Unmarried Mothers, probably focusing on the animal husbandry aspect of their self-supporting farm. I seriously considered transferring to Madrid in the hope of continuing the friendship of Conchita and the exploration of yet another way of life. But the call of home and family was too great, and in the end, with tears and hugs I said goodbye to Michelle, Betty and Conchita.

I had my interview with Reverend Mother who kindly offered to keep me on for the next academic year in Caen. She also offered to give me a reference if I wanted to go to the sister convent in Madrid. She gave me a kind embrace and a kiss on both cheeks, as I said goodbye.

I cried again.

I still miss my brief involvement in a lifestyle that was so alien from the one that was about to evolve for me.

I didn't know it, but I had reached a very important crossroads and I unwittingly chose the tougher route in the hope of fulfilling the dreams I'd spelt out as an early teenager lying on the grass, in Greenwich Park, with my blood-bonded 'sister'. That girl wasn't me anymore. My first solo foray into Europe had enabled me to evolve and mature into the person almost ready for the next instalment of what life had to offer.

A Very Real Cowboy

Late 1970

Postcard from New Mexico depicting a delicious lunchtime snack.
First, take your rattler...

Choking on chilli is no joke.

'Si, si, Señorita, very, very good, very very leetle chilli...' and the waiter trailed off, embarrassed at me choking over the Mexican rice dish in front of me. Other customers hid their amusement at these pale English not being able to cope with the fiery New Mexican cuisine. Red and green *chiles* (chillies) historically becoming the definition of local food meant I faced a couple of weeks of near starvation, during my stay in Albuquerque, New Mexico. After staggering to the ladies, rinsing my mouth out with cool water and swallowing an antihistamine pill, I returned to my table. The waiter was rather anxiously engaging in a conversation with *mi esposo*. In a mix of English and Spanish he tried to explain my *chile* allergy... I resigned myself to a healthy basic diet of *el pan* (bread), possibly cheese and fruit for the duration.

As an accompanying person on my husband's visit to the Sandia National Laboratories, I was mainly free to explore the delights of the intriguing historic south-west. Eager to explore the country the Navajo and Apache Indians had roamed and perhaps meet a 'real' cowboy, I decided to aim for the foothills of the Sandia mountains that lay about ten miles east of where we were staying. I intended to snatch a quick paddle in the Rio Grande on the way. It's one of the longest rivers in the US, springing to life in the San Juan Mountains of Colorado, eventually emerging in the exotic waters of the Gulf of Mexico, nearly two thousand miles downriver. In all the best cowboy films I'd ever seen, it was a wide rushing river depicted with herds of cattle being driven across it, wading and swimming, struggling to reach the opposite bank. No more: it seemed a mere trickle compared to its former glory, no longer a '*grande*', more a '*pequeño*' Rio. It had shrunk.

On its long journey south-west it fed fields and cities, farmsteads and towns not to mention being dammed every now and again. Its seemingly everlasting resource was showing the strain. The Rio Grande National park did not disappoint however. There were many things of interest in such a wildlife-rich environment. I went there hoping for a glimpse of a coyote or even a mountain lion. No such luck, but I *was* entranced by a pair of rare great blue herons wading in the shallow waters, heads bent, beaks just above the water's surface, obviously stalking fish as they then stood stock still waiting for a sizeable one to spear with their long razor-sharp beaks.

Boating, swimming and other water sports were on offer but I was satisfied by my tentative paddle, imagining my toes capturing those travel-weary droplets on their way to the Gulf of Mexico. I bent down and surreptitiously half-filled a small bottle, guiltily denuding the Rio Grande of about a quarter of a litre of precious water. 'More travel for you, *pequeñitas*,' I murmured as I tucked my bottle in the bottom of my bag ready for it to make the long journey back to England, to join my quirky collection of travel memorabilia.

Gazing at the rose-hued granite of the legend-laden mountains tantalisingly near, I walked briskly to my waiting car, kindly provided by our hosts. 'Now to Cedar Crest stables, please,' I instructed my driver, who had been sitting patiently reading his newspaper. 'Sure, ma'am,' he said, and we headed out into the foothills. I was hoping that my horse would be a willing, easy ride. Western riding is so different from the English technique I'd learned, I was beginning to regretfully realise I could make a complete fool of myself – even fall off!

On arrival I was led into a big barn where there seemed to be enough hats, boots, saddles, bits and bridles to equip an army. Picking out a pair of boots and a cowgirl-type hat, I was left to my own devices. Whilst waiting apprehensively at the door of the barn, a tall rangy-looking guy dressed in jeans, check shirt, and the ubiquitous cowboy '*sombrero*' appeared, leading a pretty grey mare and a big chestnut horse. He looked me up and down, appraisingly, and handed me the reins of the grey horse. 'I understand you can ride, ma'am. This is Canela, she's a part-bred Arab, quite lively, but very reliable. My big boy is Rojo.' Putting his foot in the stirrup of the chestnut, he mounted in one easy movement, leaving me standing uneasily eyeing the unfamiliar saddle with its very high pommel – that bit in the front. He looked down his nose at me and indicated I should follow him to a mounting block. Standing on the block enabled me to slip my leg over the saddle and settle into what felt like an armchair, held in place back and front. 'I've never used a deep saddle like this before, in fact, this is all new to me. I ride the English way,' I explained. He looked exasperated, and muttering something under his breath, he said, 'Waal, do what I do, lady, I ain't no teacher.'

With that he urged his horse into a trot, circling Canela and me. Using the rein on the neck of his horse, a slight pressure of his heels on its flank, he did several circles in each direction, and suddenly broke into a canter in ever decreasing circles, ending abruptly in front of us, raising a little dust-cloud around our horses' hooves. He looked as if he was born in the saddle, completely at ease and relaxed. 'Follow me, lady,' he said. Without waiting to see if I was ready he set off on the trail leading into the foothills of the sacred Sandia Mountains at a steady trot. After attempting the English rising trot, I gave up and just sat in the saddle and let my horse do the work. She was a joy – long-strided and comfortable. The slightest movement of the rein on her neck, and she changed course, the slightest touch of my heel on her flank, and she obediently moved to one side. My confidence grew with every yard. 'I'm Chuck, by the way – keep up, lady – what's your name anyway?' 'Jeannette,' I yelled, and urged Canela into a canter as Chuck's chestnut gathered speed up the rocky, winding track. Pines and juniper lined a deep gorge on our left, a vertical granite wall on our right gave little room for manoeuvre. I blessed the surefootedness of my little Arab. A missed step could have resulted in a very nasty accident.

Nearing the crest of the hill, Chuck slowed his horse to a walk. 'Had enough?' he drawled, obviously hoping I'd say yes. 'Absolutely not,' I replied, looking him in the eye. 'Okay,' he said slowly, 'newcomers usually yell out going at that speed up the gorge. Why didn't you, weren't you scared?' I patted Canela. 'No, I wasn't, I put my trust in her, she knew what she was doing all right – I didn't need to interfere.' 'Right,' and his sudden grin made him look like a mischievous schoolboy, 'would you like to see a *real* south-west trail?' he asked. I nodded enthusiastically. 'Follow me then,' and he turned on to a narrow path, slightly hidden in the undergrowth.

The dry clear air was invigorating, the April sun drew out the sweet fragrance of the juniper bushes mixed with the resinous scent of the pine surrounding us. I breathed in deeply, enjoying the unfamiliar aromas. Our fit and muscular horses willingly coped with the steep rise of the path in front of us. I leaned forward in the saddle, easing my weight on Canela's back so she could use her powerful hindquarters more easily. All I could smell leaning over her neck was the sweat of my horse, all I could hear was birdsong and an occasional piercing cry of a red-tailed hawk high above our heads in the clear blue sky, as we climbed higher and higher. I gloried in the fantasy that we were totally alone in an alien unexplored world. The terrain gradually changed as we rode up the steep slope. The path became narrower and was strewn with random rocks. We slowed to a walk, to allow our horses to pick their way carefully, keeping our eyes peeled for basking snakes – I was dreading meeting a rattler.

'Don't worry,' said Chuck, 'they are more frightened of you than you are of them. As long as you don't tread on them they will quickly move out of your way.' 'Well, that is one theory I don't want to put to the test,' I muttered to myself.

I'd never seen prickly pear cactus in bloom before, the vibrant splashes of orange, red and yellow against the arid backdrop of rocks and sparse vegetation gave dramatic emphasis to the unleavened monotony of the pink-hued rock. Focusing on the track in front of us, I hadn't realised we'd reached a plateau overlooking another steep gorge. A glorious view of the verdant Rio Grande valley spread out below us. A trickle of water seeped out of the rocks above my head and cascaded down to form a little pool beside a mesquite. 'We take a rest here,' announced Chuck, 'the horses can drink and we can sit under the tree.' He swung himself easily out of the saddle, taking a saddlebag with him, and relaxed in the shade, stretching out with his hat over his eyes. Stuck in my deep armchair of a saddle, I struggled to get my leg over the high back, and then over the front totally unsuccessfully. I was not happy about trying to slip sideways in case I fell right off onto solid rock. Feeling totally idiotic, I called out, 'I can't get off.'

I had allowed Canela to walk herself to the poolside and she had dropped her head immediately, slurping mouthfuls of water and blowing bubbles to clear her nose of dust. *I* was impotently stuck. Chuck lazily stood up and came over to Canela, put his hands around my waist and just pulled me to the ground and roughly set me on my feet, leaving me bandy-legged and stiff from my unaccustomed time in the saddle. I leaned against Canela for support. It was then I noticed a shotgun slotted into a holder on the side of the chestnut's saddle. 'Hey,' I yelled across to him, 'why have you got this?' Without looking up he opened his saddlebag and got out some apples, cheese and bread, and a couple of carafes of water. 'Catch!' he called, and threw a couple of apples at me which miraculously I managed not to drop. I was about to take a bite when he called out, 'No! Not for you – for them, Canela and Rojo.' They were both obviously expecting a treat, turning their heads towards me, eagerly accepting my offering.

I staggered over to the shade and rather carefully sat down. Indicating I should eat and drink, Chuck leaned back against the tree, staring at the view before us. 'We are sitting on holy ground here, you know,' he began, 'the Tewa Pueblo Indians tell of a flood that covered all the land you can see down there. A few survivors climbed the highest mountain they could find – Sandia Mountain. They prayed to the sun to dry the waters and bring life back to the land. Which it eventually did. Ever since then this area has been regarded as sacred.'

As I listened to his story, a slight breeze lifted my hair and rustled the pods of the mesquite tree. It was so peaceful, I relaxed and looked around me, revelling in the cool shade. 'Is there any proof that could be true, or is it simply a fairy tale?' I asked, thinking of Noah and his Ark. Turning to look at me, he said, 'Scientists found minute particles of sea creatures, all over this mountain so certainly at one time it must've been covered by sea. Difficult to imagine looking at the landscape now isn't it?' he replied.

Carefully collecting all the debris of our lunch, he placed it into his saddlebag. He offered his hand to pull me to my feet, and strode over to Rojo, attaching the satchel and checking the shotgun holster was secure. 'What *is* that thing for?' I asked again, as I walked rather stiffly over to the dozing horses. His face serious, he replied, 'One of the lessons you learn as a wrangler is you never go unarmed into unknown territory. With your agreement, we took a path that we don't normally use, mainly because this area has so many dangerous possibilities. You will have noticed a large number of rabbits, for example. This means some of the bigger predators will be hunting in this area.' Without warning, he put his hands around my waist and lifted me bodily back into the saddle, easing my foot into the stirrup. Mounting Rojo, he rejoined the rock-strewn path leading ever upwards, Canela following obediently. 'You'll notice some spectacular waterfalls on our way up.' he said. 'This means more vegetation which means hideouts for coyotes or mountain lions. I hope you're sensitive to your horse's reactions. Canela is famous for smelling mountain lions at a hundred yards. She will stop, snort, paw the ground, all signs of her sensing danger to you and her. If she does that, freeze.'

As he spoke he pulled the gun out of the holster, checked it was loaded, reins in one hand, he slung it over his shoulder. The terrain was gradually changing from arid desert-like conditions to a mix of pine forest and Alpine meadows. 'Watch out for signs of lion spoor, a sure sign a lion has been this way.' Chuck was turning his head from right to left as we progressed up the path. Suddenly Canela snorted and I could feel every muscle in her body tense. She stopped abruptly. We all froze. There, slightly to the right of us, resting under the shade of a rocky outcrop, lay an amber-eyed animal looking at us curiously. It had traces of blood on its jaws and the remains of a furry object between its front paws. I sat in the saddle, immovable, mesmerised. Its coat was a sandy colour, sleek and glossy – great camouflage for fading into a rocky background. It looked at us intently, trying to gauge if we were a threat. For a moment it appeared ready to rise to its feet and pounce.

'Do what I do,' said Chuck quietly, and he urged Rojo into a slow, careful walk. I followed with Canela. The path led away from the lion's resting place, putting more space between us. It pricked its ears as we moved, those wonderful eyes gazing at us, but it didn't get to its feet, it just lay there following our every move – looking. Chuck slowly eased the gun off his shoulder, as we processed past the outcrop of rocks, no one saying a word, gun at the ready. We all breathed more easily as we rounded a bend, following the path which led us slightly downhill away from the danger zone. 'All clear,' announced Chuck, 'I didn't think she'd follow.' And we continued our slow walk, allowing the horses and ourselves to relax, eventually changing from walk to trot to canter as the path levelled out, on its way down to the foothills from where we'd started.

Slowing Rojo down to an easy walking pace, Chuck fell back, so we were riding side by side. 'When was the last time you were in the saddle?' he asked. 'About a couple of weeks ago,' I replied. 'Why?' 'That explains your weird walk. You must be sore. I spend my life in the saddle, not just an hour every so often. I guess you don't often meet a cougar when you're out,' he went on conversationally. 'As a matter of fact, neither do I. We are not encouraged to expose our clients to danger – I could lose my job. So don't blab. Where do you hail from anyway?' 'I'm English,' I replied. Chuck smiled and leaned across to shake hands. 'I've never met English, I thought you were one of those northerners – New Yorker maybe, don't care for those – too much money, not much sense.' And he frowned.

'Glad to meet you, ma'am. It was pretty cool meeting the mountain cat, with her kits too.' 'Kits? Kits?' I repeated excitedly, 'I didn't see them. Where were they hiding? Let's go back. I want to see them.' He laughed. 'Oh no. We don't push our luck. It's because she was guarding her young that she didn't move. Also, she'd made a kill and would be teaching the little ones to eat meat. While she didn't feel threatened she wouldn't necessarily attack but I don't want to try again.' 'Thank goodness you didn't shoot her,' I said. 'I'd never have forgiven you.' 'I don't shoot for fun, I only shoot to eat,' he replied. 'We need to look after our wildlife, not steal from it.'

'Back there you said you were a "wrangler". What's that? What do you actually do?' I asked curiously. 'I guess you could call me a cowboy,' he replied. 'I hire myself out as a cowhand, that doesn't pay much so I go to rodeos, enter competitions to ride broncos, or calf roping. I win a lot of money that way.' I looked at him admiringly. 'That sounds a great life, but why are you working for Cedar Crest Stables then? It must be such a boring job compared to your other work.' 'Yep. It is mostly but a guy's gotta eat,' he said ruefully. 'What do you do with all your money then?' I wondered aloud. 'Medical fees,' he answered briefly. 'I've just got out of hospital with a broken leg and a couple of broken ribs – I reckon I've broken just about every bone in my body over the years – I'll be no good for rodeoing after this year. I've almost enough put away to settle down, buy a few cattle, breed a few horses...'

His eyes grew dreamy. He pulled his hat down over his nose and broke into a trot, embarrassed at revealing his emotions. Canela followed suit. Calling back over his shoulder, 'What you doing after? Want a game of pool at the clubhouse?' he asked. Taken completely by surprise, I replied, 'Er, no thanks.' 'Why not, we could have a good time?' And he turned his head to give me a sideways smile. 'Well, I'm married for a start – and I can't play pool.' 'Married? Well, that doesn't matter to most girls,' he said. 'It matters to my husband,' I replied. 'Really? Well, don't worry, that'll soon wear off.' With that he stood up in the saddle and turned to look at me, slightly unbelievingly, leaving Rojo to carry on unerringly making for his stable. 'How long have you been married anyway?' 'Twenty-four years,' I said. His jaw dropped. 'In all my life I have never met anyone married that long.' He looked at me in awe. 'My folks parted when I was five, I went with my dad, I heard my mom married for the fourth time late last year. I didn't like my dad's third so I split. I guess that was about fifteen years ago. I ain't seen either of 'em since.' I digested that in silence.

'Erm, you married?' I eventually asked. 'She left me when I spent the last of my money on Rojo.' He turned to pat him. 'He's sired a couple a good 'uns. I'll use him when the time comes.' I stared at his back trying to visualise the bleak loneliness of his life. 'I'm really sorry I can't come and play pool...' I began. He fell back so we were side by side again. 'Stick with your man,' he said curtly. 'Better that way.' I opened my mouth to say he'd misunderstood me, but closed it again. The gate to the yard was open and both horses aimed for the water trough. Chuck dismounted and lifted me out of the saddle, gently this time. He gave Canela a pat on her rump as she walked past with Rojo, led by the stable girl. 'Mine too,' he said proudly. 'She's beautiful,' I said, looking up at him. 'Thank you so much for a wonderful ride. It was very special.'

He grinned again. 'You got a weird accent as well as a weird walk,' he said. '*Adios, Inglesa, eres especial.*' He took my hand, held it, touched his hat and strode away. At the edge of the barn he turned to see me still watching him and yelled '*Vuelve cuando estés libre.*' And waved.

* * *

Sitting in the luxurious limo on my way back to the hotel my thoughts were still with the poor little five-year-old Chuck left motherless, who turned into a tough wrangler breaking bones for a living, dreaming of a future breeding horses.

Thinking of his lean, lonely, rangy figure, coolly shouldering his gun in order to protect his horses and a perfect stranger from a 'clear and present danger', I wished my 'real' cowboy well. '*Buena suerte*,' I said to myself, '*Mantente seguro, mi amigo*. Good luck and stay safe, my friend.'

The Lone Star State

Late 1980

A real-life roadrunner... and not a coyote in sight!

Austin-Bergstrom International Airport, Austin, Texas.
Guns. Every official carried one, capturing my attention, while everyone else seemed totally unfazed. My initial alarm subsided as I relaxed a little, remembering it was usual for American police to carry arms. However, the reality remained unsettling. I didn't think I'd ever get used to it!

My husband, Graham, was a member of various international commissions that research the aftermath of events like high-rise building collapse, such as the recent bombing in Oklahoma. The meeting was in Austin, the capital of Texas – famously known as the Lone Star State due to its flag bearing a solitary star. This emblem, once the state flag until 1846, still proudly waves throughout the region. Texas became the twenty-eighth state to join the United States in 1845. Accompanying Graham on this trip was an exhilarating experience, even if I was just considered an 'accompanying person'. I was eager to explore more of this vast and intriguing territory.

The heat hit us as soon as we left the chilly air-conditioned airport. '30C', the illuminated sign told us.

We were staying with friends, Tom and Lucy Grimm, who had an enormous house on the outskirts of the city. In fact, everything about Texas seemed to be outsize! Tom himself was a large figure of a man who lived in the widest-brimmed Stetson hat that I had ever been close to. I presumed he took it off in bed; I didn't dare ask!

Walking down Main Street we were surrounded by tall men, all wearing Stetsons, cowboy boots, and chaps – those leather leg protectors used when horse riding. Some were even wearing holstered guns on their right hip. All this gear appeared to be normal everyday wear. Cowboy film sets must have been similar! 'Jeannette, I apologise for the heat; our climate must be quite a change from back home,' Tom remarked as he escorted us to his car. 'Don't worry, we'll have you more comfortable in just a minute.'

He gestured towards an enormous, sparkling white limousine parked a few yards down the street. Graham and

I exchanged a glance, both thinking, *Is this Hollywood-inspired extravagance just for us?* It was truly impressive! Personally, I embraced the luxury, relishing in the unfamiliar opulence. The warmth and generosity of American hospitality welcomed us everywhere we went.

On our first evening, we were taken to Chez Zee steakhouse for the famous Texan Longhorn Steak. In spite of jet lag, and the fact I don't like steak, after our sidewalk amble, nostrils assaulted with delicious smells from every direction, I was exceptionally hungry. 'Howdy, ma'am, I've got the biggest, juiciest, best-cooked steak in the whole of the US ready for you here,' announced the white-aproned chef in his lovely Texan drawl. And unbelievably, there it was on the table in front of us, certainly the largest hunk of melt-in-the-mouth fillet steak I'd ever seen. Most of the commission group were Europeans, some from Eastern Europe, and I think we were all in a haze of culinary bliss, jet lag, and amazement at the sheer largesse laid out before us.

Around us, the American conversations centred on the glories of Texas and what we should all see and do during our hectic, and all too short, visit. 'You must try and visit NASA; it's only one hundred and sixty-five miles away in Houston,' said the man on my right to the German delegate. Scraps of conversation reached my increasingly sleepy ears. 'Our oil fields are the biggest in the world.' 'We have the largest state building in the US, bigger than the White House,' said another and 'Don't forget The Alamo...' said a third.

I came to with a jerk to find myself in that luxurious family limo again, Lucy at my side with Graham and Tom in the front. I think I dozed off, how embarrassing, but fortunately, our kindly hosts made no comment. They just ensured we had everything we needed as I collapsed into oblivion on the huge emperor-sized bed.

I woke the next morning to find husband Graham and Tom had gone to the ubiquitous seven thirty talk session, leaving me still sleeping. After my much-needed shower and glass of milk – no tea to be seen – I was ready for the day. 'I'm meeting some friends for lunch down in San Antonio, it's only eighty miles,' said Lucy. 'I want to introduce my English friend to them, we're leaving now, okay?'

'Er, wonderful,' I replied, slightly bemused that a one hundred and sixty-mile round trip was the norm for lunch. Americans are well known for their large comfortable cars, and this was no exception, with the air-con on full blast it was slightly chilly, but as I relaxed into the passenger seat, I realised Lucy was a very fast, experienced driver. The road to San Antonio was long, straight, and empty except for the occasional passing car, most in the opposite direction. As the speedometer touched over ninety miles an hour, I nervously asked, 'Erm, isn't the limit here seventy? What happens if you get caught speeding?'

'Oh, Tom is a judge, don't worry,' said Lucy, laughing.

As I started to digest the implications of this, I found myself focusing on the cerulean-blue haze either side of the road. A startlingly vibrant sky seemed to have descended on us as we sped along. 'Bluebonnets,' volunteered Lucy, apparently oblivious to their beauty, 'named after the hats pioneer ladies wore to protect themselves from the sun. They're our national flower, related to the English lupin,' she continued. 'How they survive our searing sun and sometimes minus six degrees, I don't know, but they come back every year.'

Enjoying the dreamy sensation of floating along in a cobalt cloud, I forgot my concern about our actual speed and relaxed, eyes half-closed. My interest was aroused again as I realised we were being followed by a roadrunner – the bird made world-famous by the well-known Looney Tunes cartoon. Lucy slowed the car so I could see him more clearly. His extended tail was bobbing up and down as he just about kept up with us, jogging alongside the car on his long legs at about twenty-five miles per hour. His mottled brown and white feathers would be great camouflage in the desert he called home. Goodness knows where he thought he was going or why he chose the harsh and arid habitat of the Texas desert, I didn't know. Apparently roadrunners thrive there, getting both food and drink from prey. I was fascinated to see it in the flesh.

Our children would be pretty jealous when I told them I'd actually seen a real one close up. Long straight roads with little change in the landscape tend to be a bit boring but not this one – loping along on my left were two male figures. After all the Cowboy and Indian films I had seen, somehow these were unmistakable. Tall and lean, running with sinuous synchronised grace, these two guys were definitely Indian. Black-haired, dark-eyed, they glanced without curiosity at our gleaming white car. 'Stop, stop, Lucy, they must be going to San Antonio, they might need a lift,' I said urgently as we sped past. She looked at me in horror.

'Absolutely not, Tom would never forgive me. We don't give lifts to such people. Anyway, they've probably come from Austin. We're nearly there, besides, they're used to jogging everywhere, not many have a car.' She muttered all this to herself in one breath. I subsided reluctantly, suddenly feeling really angry at the prejudice and lack of care that comment showed. It was definitely not what I would've done.

Arriving in San Antonio, we aimed for the River Walk at the heart of the city, rivalled only by the Alamo mission a mere few minutes' stroll away off the main square. I was so excited at the thought that one of those many foreign fighters who died there might be one of our own family – I'd heard that Scottish troops were involved. My ancestors had fought and failed in their fight for freedom on bleak Culloden Moor, so far away. I somehow felt a fellow feeling.

Lucy handed her car keys to a parking attendant who drove the car away to that haven in the sky where all good cars wait to be collected by their owners for the return journey.

'Lucy, this is magical,' I breathed as we sauntered along the bank towards Ocho, *the* place to eat. We were surrounded by a wonderland of flowers, sunny sparkling water, and restaurants, offering food from many nations, as we briefly accompanied the San Antonio River wending its long way down to the Gulf of Mexico. As soon as we entered Ocho, we were besieged by a bevy of perfumed, beautifully turned-out females, hugging us both mercilessly. I tried to catch my breath, feeling totally overwhelmed, but Lucy nonchalantly greeted everyone, took my arm, and led me to the chair at the head of the table. I was obviously the guest of honour; I blushingly sat down. In spite of the wonderful food and sumptuous surroundings, I just wanted to escape. Feeling slightly claustrophobic, I felt I couldn't breathe, the *smell* of wealth was smothering me.

Lucy raised a hand to stop the conversation, indicating me, and said, 'This is Jeannette. She is from England visiting with us, she loves Texas already, don't you, Jeannette?'

There was a brief pause, and Lucy's friends round the table carried on speaking, but in lower voices. 'Yes,' I said inanely, 'it is simply beautiful...' There was instant silence, and all faces turned towards me. 'Oh my, what a wonderful accent,' everyone said at once. 'Say something else, we just love to hear you speak.' Immediately tongue-tied, I managed to stammer something about 'tomahtoes' and 'tomaytoes'... so stupid. Saved by the waiter bringing our food, the conversation turned to fashion, make-up, and husbands. As soon as I could, I whispered into Lucy's ear, 'I've got to disappear, remember I told you about my mission to look for a possible ancestor in the Alamo fight? Do you think I could go now? I won't be missed, surely.'

She smiled at me. 'You go on, I'll meet up with you in the main square in a couple of hours' time.' Thankfully, I slipped away, nodding goodbye to my nearest neighbours, and followed my map to the ancient tree in the centre of the square. I was told prospective guides to the Alamo congregated in its shade but all I could see was a solitary figure who turned out to be an oldish chap with a long black plait, dozing on one of the benches.

He woke up slowly as I approached and smiled tentatively at me. From his cotton-fringed overshirt, baggy cotton trousers, and soft short boots, he looked exactly like pictures of local Indians I'd seen in a book about Texas back at Lucy's house. I smiled in return and asked if I could sit down on the bench. He nodded. The heat of the early afternoon was really hard to bear. I fanned myself with my folded map. Looking up into the branches of the weird-looking tree with its long-hanging pods and vicious-looking spines, I asked the man, 'Do you happen to know what type of tree we're sitting under?'

'We think of it as the tree of life,' he replied, 'it's called a mesquite tree. Our people rely on it for so much.'

'Really? How do you mean?' I studied his brown wrinkled face with its small intelligent eyes. 'Tell me,' I said.

'I belong to the Tigua Indian tribe, and this tree gives us fuel for our fires, bedding for our horses and cattle. We also extract medicine for our children and use the ground-up seeds to make flour for our bread. It is a good tree, God's gift to us,' and he smiled, showing uneven white teeth.

'Well, I'm Scottish,' I told him. 'I've come to see if any of my clan died here at the mission in that famous 1836 Battle of the Alamo. I understand lots of Europeans came here to help in the fight for Texas's freedom from that horrible Mexican regime. I am looking for a guide,' I added. 'My time is short, so I want someone who knows the inside of this church and can show me the list of names of the dead.'

He stood and offered me his hand for me to stand up too.

'We'll go together; I can show everything. I know San Antonio church well.' As we walked up the path towards the open wooden doors, he pointed to the grove of cottonwood trees surrounding the building. 'Los Alamos,' he said. 'We call this area The Alamo – Spanish for the cottonwood tree.'

I already knew some of the legendary names of the men who died there, James Bowie of lethal knife fame, King of the Wild Frontier, Davy Crockett, and Commander William Travis. Iconic figures, martyrs even, leading just two hundred men against General Santa Anna's Mexican army of seven times that many. Suicidal really, but freedom fighters never give up. Sadly, all defenders of this mission were slaughtered. I drew a deep breath; I couldn't wait to find out if one of my kin had died there.

The church itself was tiny, built around 1720 for the Franciscan monks intent on converting the locals to Catholicism. Today, it was teeming with people. 'Is it always like this?' I asked my guide. 'Yes,' he replied sadly, 'not possible to pray quietly there.' I glanced at the crucifix around his neck. Probably a Catholic then. I was getting worried about Lucy and our meeting in the square. I didn't want to be late, so we rather rudely pushed our way into the crowds, and my kindly friend fought to get me to the wall plaque listing about two hundred names of the people who died there. Alas, there was no mention of my immediate ancestors, but I did find a John McGregor, Scot, among the dead from England, Ireland, and Wales. There was no grave; they'd all been burnt on a pyre on Santa Anna's orders. I stared at it blankly, vowing to myself, *I'll try to find out more from that book when I get back to Lucy's house*. I held that thought with tears in my eyes. 'My' John McGregor – my aunt's husband – had been my favourite uncle. He'd played the pipes that I loved as a child, even though everyone else put their fingers in their ears! He was jolly, kind, and affectionate to me. He had died a couple of years ago; I still missed him. My heart was racing, and then, I caught a glimpse of a display case with Jim Bowie's knife in it and, further on, Davy Crockett's raccoon-tailed hat.

Suddenly, I shuddered, feeling like I couldn't get out of there fast enough. Goosebumps rose on my arms, and chills crept down my spine. Feeling decidedly giddy, I grabbed my guide's arm and gasped, 'Out now, please.' He took one look at me and shouted, 'Lady here's feeling sick.' The crowd magically parted, and we made our way to the exit. 'I'll come with you to our seat,' he told me. 'You can wait for your friend.' 'I can see her,' I exclaimed. 'She's over by the tree.' Taking a deep breath and relishing the warm air now, I hurried over to her. 'The car is ready for us; let's go. We'll be late,' she said, waving at the waiting chauffeur.

'Thank you so much for your help. I felt really faint in there,' I told my guide as I handed over the envelope of money I'd prepared. He smiled at me. 'God go with you, lady,' he said. 'And thank you.'

After giving some dollars to the guy waiting with the car, Lucy, without more ado, jumped into the driver's seat, and we made our way out of San Antonio along the long, straight road back to Austin. I hadn't quite succeeded with my search for an ancestor in the Alamo Roll of Honour, although aunt Marion had told me Uncle John's grandfather had joined a 'crusade' across the Atlantic in the USA. The dates were right, McGregors were famous pipers of the day and uncle John McGregor's brother had crossed the pond to meet up with family just before Uncle John had died. Multiple coincidences do tend to point to likely facts. It would be wonderful if my random visit to the state of Texas led me to solve a family mystery that had puzzled us all for years.

I wasn't really hungry, but we'd promised to be back in time for the dinner at Texas University, where the Explosives Conference, the main object of Graham's visit, had been held that day.

Back in the delightful suite of rooms at Lucy and Tom's house, Graham and I hurried to put on our finest attire in time for the farewell dinner. 'It's been a most interesting and rewarding meeting – sorry I can't talk about it, you know, Official Secrets and all that,' Graham growled while wrestling with his black tie. 'Help me with this thing, will you?' he asked, blocking the whole front of the mirror. We were both a bit grumpy as we vied for a glimpse of ourselves, getting ready to meet our official hosts, the chancellor and hierarchy of Texas University, one of the largest in the US, renowned for its well-funded engineering research programs. This time, a Hollywood-style stretch limo arrived at our door to pick the four of us up and take us to the chancellor's white-pillared residence. We were entertained in his chandelier-besparkled reception room, along with about two hundred other guests, for the pre-dinner drinks party. 'Well, we're in pretty select company,' Tom whispered in my ear, pointing out various Deans of Faculty, influential businessmen, and a few fellow judges. He introduced us to numerous people whose names and faces became a blur as we were plied with cocktails.

Lucy looked resplendent in a beautifully styled cocktail dress adorned with real diamonds in her ears and at her throat. I have to say I felt incredibly dowdy in my best Marks and Spencer's 'formal wear' dress, but I did wear my tiny diamond engagement ring with pride. I was relieved that no one remarked on my accent, although several ladies enquired about our weather situation and the incidence of rainfall and fog, obviously feeling their sunshine was superior to ours. 'Oh, yes,' I agreed, 'so much more of it and hotter too,' and I smiled sweetly at their blank response. The familiar feeling of wanting to escape the situation was becoming more insistent as the chancellor's wife signalled it was time for honoured guests to withdraw to the dining room and the rest of the guests to disappear into their waiting limos.

Glancing discreetly around the table, I found the familiar faces of the European contingent sprinkled among the unfamiliar delegates of the conference. However, Graham was nowhere to be seen. It turned out he was seated beside the 'first lady' at the other end of the table, obscured by a mix of flowers and candles. Sandwiched between two unfamiliar men, I prepared to eat, drink, and be bored.

'Hiya, I'm Jacob, who are you?' asked the man on my right. 'You don't look like an explosives expert.'

'No, I am not,' I replied. 'I'm here with my husband, but I have to say I really prefer bows and arrows.' He looked at me hard and suddenly grinned. 'Actually, I don't agree with those either,' he said, his eyes twinkling. I felt a surprising connection. 'I'm here because I'm really good at bombs,' he continued. 'I'm one of those people who knows which wires to cut. My best buddy is this guy.' He fumbled in his pocket and drew out a wallet bulging with dollars and photos. Flicking through the many mini pictures, he stopped and held one up for me to see. 'Jack,' he said proudly. 'He's a star.' And there was a delightful Jack Russell staring straight out at me! 'We're partners; he finds them, I take them apart. His nose is the best ever,' he said and turned his attention to the plate in front of him.

In between mouthfuls, he explained that he chose Jack because he could take him everywhere easily, and his Austin wife loved dogs. 'I love him too; he's saved my bacon more times than I care to remember. Bombs, mines, any kind of explosives are my enemy,' he explained. 'Jack and I are on a mission – get rid of 'em all.'

'Did you say Austin wife?' I suddenly realised he'd hinted at more than one. He stopped eating and looked at me. 'Yes, my other wife lives in Utah,' he said. 'I'm of the Mormon faith. Are you interested? I'm not limited to two, you know.' He grinned as I opened my mouth to hotly deny any such thing. 'Just kidding – I love shocking people.' He carried on eating, and I looked at his undeniably handsome profile, suddenly understanding how he'd attracted two wives in modern, emancipated America. How on earth would it work though? I felt the stirrings of feminism coming to the fore, but before I could say a word, the chap on the other side of me leaned across and addressed Jacob, 'Hey, buddy, are you upsetting our English guest? Give it a rest!'

Turning to me, he said, 'Ignore him, ma'am; he's not worth listening to. I'm Ben, and I know your husband;

we've met on several commissions. He's quite a guy; glad to meet you.' He extended one of the largest hands I think I'd ever seen and engulfed mine as he held it briefly, glaring at Jacob. 'We're no fans of Mormons here in Texas, especially those who have several wives. You're not even a real Mormon for f**k's sake – pardon me, ma'am – they stopped that sort of thing when they became a part of the US of A, turn of the century, I think. Unchristian heathens.'

I shrank down a little in my seat, and I muttered to myself, the stress of the moment bringing my primary school Cockney accent to the fore. 'Oh, gawd,' I said to myself, 'Jacob wouldn't stand a chance against this giant of a man.' There was a pause in the conversation around us, and several people looked at my companions expectantly. I realised these two were old adversaries. Jacob turned red and visibly refrained from expressing what was on the tip of his tongue. He glowered at Ben, and pointedly turned his back on both of us. 'Coward,' muttered Ben disappointedly, as the man opposite me grinned and gave me a wink. Conversation resumed, and the moment passed. Ben took a swig of beer and said, 'I'm one of the explosive research fellows here at UA; do you want to know how to make a bomb?' I choked on my steak.

'Wow, that's a conversation stopper.' I laughed. 'It sounds as if you're asking me if I can make a Victoria sponge.'

'Nothing funny about bombs, ma'am; I'm serious. We're surrounded by people who can make bombs; they only have to go on the internet.'

'Internet?' I repeated doubtfully. 'I am not familiar with anything like that.'

'Of course you are; hasn't your husband got a computer? He must have if he's doing research.' He answered his own question. I remembered the typewriter 'thing' Graham had on his desk at work. 'Oh, maybe; this "internet" is fairly new, isn't it?'

'Well, the "worldwide web" has been going for a couple of years. I think it's going to take over our lives. I'm not sure I like the idea, but you can find out about anything if you use it,' he looked thoughtful, 'including how to make a serviceable bomb.'

'I don't think I need a recipe for a bomb, thanks, erm, I'm against bombs.'

'Well, so am I; I'm here to help repair bomb damage, but to do that, you have to learn everything you can about how they operate, how and where they're made,' he looked sharply at me, 'and who is going to use them.'

I was indignant. 'This is ridiculous, surely you don't think...'

'No,' he replied, 'we've checked on you and your husband; you're clean.' And he turned away to answer someone across the table. I opened my mouth and closed it again. Flabbergasted wasn't quite the word in my mind!

He started scribbling busily on a napkin as I carried on eating automatically, not really tasting much. I took a sip of what was in my glass and turned to him as he turned to me. 'I've written you the recipe,' he said. 'You obviously didn't think it would be universally available, but you'll see it is, and this is the evidence. Where's your purse?' Taking a second to realise he meant my evening bag, I dumbly handed it to him. He opened it, folded the napkin, pushed it in, and closed it shut. 'There you go, ma'am; don't forget it. I've gotta go now; my wife is having a baby tomorrow, and I promised I wouldn't be late home.' He stood up, frowned at Jacob, who still had his back to us. 'Honoured to have met you and your husband. We'll meet again, I'm sure.' And with unexpected grace, he gave a funny little bow and left.

To say the rest of the evening was an anticlimax would be an understatement of vast proportions. The way home was enlivened by Lucy's scurrilous comments about various dignitaries present. She closely questioned Graham about the first lady's dress, jewellery, and conversation, but his observational skills on ladies' attire and retention of gossip added up to a total of 'nul points'. When Graham denied any knowledge of the number of mink coats the first lady owned, her smug retort about keeping hers in the freezer brought the conversation to a surprising yet humorous halt.

Feeling the effects of the alcohol and a reaction to the stress of the evening, I retreated to the novelty of a jacuzzi bath in our en suite. Lucy, decidedly the worse for wear, was escorted to her room by Tom, who got out a bottle of bourbon on the way, saying, 'See you in a second for a nightcap' to a less than enthusiastic Graham.

Next morning was a very quiet time. We all drank coffee in wan silence. Vowing eternal friendship, we thanked our hosts, and I hugged Lucy, clutching the last-minute present she gave me. After joining the rest of our European compatriots on our coach to the airport, I opened the present. I held in my hand a nineteenth century edition of an illustrated copy of Grimms' *Fairy Tales*. Inside was an inscription: '*To Jeannette, a real lady, with affection from Thomas Grimm, the great, great, great-grandson of Jacob Grimm, co-author.*' 'Wow, what a fantastic present.'

I'd spent years looking for antiquarian children's books. I'd got a small collection, but this was very special.

I shook my head in disbelief, trying to get my mind to take in the reality of the parallel universe I was just leaving.

A mix of history, bombs and antiquarian books.

I could hardly believe we lived under the same sun, gazed at the same stars and enjoyed the wonders of the same civilisation as the people we'd just met.

I'd certainly lived and learnt a lot on this trip.

I couldn't wait for the next.

Memories are Made of This

1990

The sea eagles of Langkawi (seen here superimposed over a map of the Langkawi district) have a wingspan of two metres.

Blinded by dark, deafened by silence. I held my breath.

The smooth progress through the gently heaving water and the gradual twilight gloom revealing unfamiliar shapes, intrigued and soothed simultaneously. It was very hot and steamy in the gloomy tunnel of trees. I could just make out weirdly twisted roots and trunks emerging from the brackish water; the branches intertwining above my head hiding all sight of the brilliant blue sky left behind in that bright world outside. I could smell rotting vegetation and hear stirrings of unknown creatures as the boat drifted along. My blouse was wet with the sweat running down my back. Breathing was hard work. Peering over the side, I could make out the sinuous shape of a water snake among the roots of the nearest tree, I could hear chattering coming from behind the screen of trees on each bank which seemed to follow our progress downstream, and I became aware of the Malay skipper speaking. 'We stop here. We plant here.'

The boat gently rested, prow on bank. His young-boy crew jumped out into the swampy mud, pulling the stern with them so all six passengers could reach the uninviting bankside. 'Here. Take,' said the skipper and he handed me a sapling about a foot long. 'Plant... You first.' And he beamed. 'Like this.' Holding the sapling just above root level he plunged his hand wrist deep into the brown squelch, pushed slightly, half-rinsed his hand in the murky water and wiped it on his trousers, leaving a dark-brown stain. 'You now,' he said. 'Erm...?' He firmly took my wrist and guided my hand down into the soft warm goo and pressed slightly. I let the sapling go and hurriedly pulled back my hand, globs of mud dripping into the water as I tried to shake it clean. I was handed a grubby piece of cloth to finish the job. Miraculously the sapling remained anchored and upright. 'You here forever, now,' he told me, 'mangrove live forever.' Everyone clapped.

I looked more closely at the trees around me, noting the different stages of growth and realised the impact tourists were having on this swampy plantation. *We're planting forests*, I thought. *My tree could be here for over a hundred years... not quite forever, but awesome, totally awesome.* After each one had been planted, we cast off, the boat floating dreamily down-channel to our next destination, a small beach-like clearing that could be seen on the far bank. Everyone was quiet, observing, absorbing.

The chattering on the bank grew louder and more insistent, small brown creatures could be seen excitedly congregating along the muddy beach among the trees and in the shallow water. Little brown macaque monkeys. Mothers and babies, mostly. 'A nursery? Oh, I do hope we can get closer,' I murmured to myself. The boat slightly picked up speed and the skipper brought out a bucket of fruit and bread.

Mmm, I don't think I'm that hungry, I thought, looking at it distastefully, feeling threatened by a possible impending campylobacter invasion! The skipper laughed at the look on my face. 'This not for you,' he said. Focusing on the beach just ahead, my heart melted at the sight of the numerous young, clinging tightly to their mothers, who were wading out into the water. Hoping to get even closer I leant forward over the prow and to my utter amazement a baby brown head bobbed up in front of me followed by a wet brown hand and a larger head. 'Give banana,' urged the skipper, 'here.' As quick as lightning the little hand stretched further, grabbed the fruit, put it in its mouth and dived under the water to emerge several yards away from the crowd to a quieter bit of the bank where mother and baby shared the spoils in peace. Monkeys don't swim. Usually.

'These are amazing,' I said, looking at another mother just about to dive, its baby obviously taking a deep breath ready for the immersion. 'They're everywhere.' I grabbed a random handful of fruit and bread, throwing them piece by piece to the expectant monkeys surrounding the boat.

They moved quickly, zigzagging and diving, mother and baby each grabbing what they could. The tinies riding piggyback, holding tight with their legs, arms full of precious banana. As the bucket emptied, the monkeys gradually dispersed back to the bank, disappearing one by one into the sheltering mangroves. The boat drifted on as if nothing had happened to disturb the unruffled velvet surface of the water. *I would like to linger*, I thought. *We've got hungry followers*. And I turned to look regretfully at the vanishing small brown heads, swimming after us. Gradually the jungle noises began to fade, as the boat drifted, silently drawn into the faster flowing current of the wide Kilim river. I closed my eyes, savouring the images of my first mangrove swamp and the intrepid monkeys, fixing them in my memory. I wouldn't easily forget those delightful baby macaques.

The boat drifted on, picking up speed as it entered the faster flowing river. We were heading to another feeding ground, nearer the sea. But as feeding the inner man came first we stopped at a floating restaurant, apparently resting on a substantial raft. This was surrounded by mesh 'tanks', through which the water flowed, filled with exotic fish. A much healthier environment than some fish farms which suffer from so many infection issues. We all disembarked, and after walking round, admiring the fantastic fish in the mesh containers, we made for the table already laid with the most superb mangoes, other local fruit and homemade bread. Cold coconut water to drink enhanced the absolutely delicious lunch. After the meal our Malay boatman bid us farewell, coming round the table to each of us, holding out the bucket that still had remnants of the fruit and bread stuck in the bottom. We took the hint and donated a tip for his 'expert navigation skills', hoping he would include the young lad who'd helped him.

Replete, after our sumptuous meal, we boarded a slightly larger vessel with a much more powerful engine. A bucket of dead fish was handed to each of us as we scrambled on board. I put mine as far away from me as I could, actually on the seat in front of me, the smell was really not enticing!

The skipper of this boat was Australian. He started the engine, took the tiller and our boat sped away downriver, to a far more turbulent and open stretch of water. As we left the protection of the mango trees, we became aware of powerful wings, beating the air above us. Looking up, we could see the white head and white underbelly of an enormous eagle, who was immediately joined by most of his numerous clan, hovering at what seemed to be just a few feet above our heads. The sky was filled with beating wings creating an unforgettable noise, and breezes that ruffled our hair, filling our senses with their indomitable presence. Extremely, scarily intimidating. The boat party had enlarged itself to include six other guests; three of those ladies screamed their heads off and ducked. The men looked very anxious, one went pale, almost green actually – he fumbled for his handkerchief, or maybe he was hoping for a paper bag.

I looked on. I was mesmerised by the beating of wings above our heads. The birds took no notice of us at all, they continued flying, their seven-foot wingspan forming a canopy of glossy brown feathers above us, creating a false twilight. As I gazed upward, intent on a closer scrutiny, I became aware of their formidable talons and curved, vicious, razor-sharp beaks, much too close to my face for comfort. Their normal food source is live fish and one of them executed a superb dive, wings close to him, neck outstretched as he almost immersed his upper body in water, emerging in about one second flat with a wriggling fish in his beak which was swallowed whole as he flew away, soaring into the upper stratosphere. What a fantastic, awesome exhibition of prowess.

I stood up to watch as another bird also spotted an underwater fish and made the same expert dive, coming up with a sizeable catch, which he swallowed whole. I suddenly realised what my bucket of fish was for, and I threw one into the water. 'No, no,' yelled our Aussie skipper above the turbulence. 'Like this!' And he picked up a fish, stood up, and held out his arm, holding the fish in his hand. To my horror, one of the eagles turned its head, fixed its beady eye on that fish – and swooped! Again, with absolute precision, it folded its wings and dived directly for our skipper's hand. 'Oh my God,' I breathed, 'it's going to take his hand off.' Instead of diving deep into the water, it picked the fish delicately out of his hand, and swooped high in the air, eating it in mid-flight. It soared above us, circled round and joined its friends, hovering over our boat. As we moved downriver, I became aware of other boats also with fish and brave people standing holding out their contribution to the population of sea eagles on that river.

I pulled my bucket of fish towards me, picked out the biggest one and moved to stand beside our Aussie friend. 'I want to feed them too,' I said.

'Well, good on you.' He looked at me, obviously thinking, *She'll never do it. She will drop it and duck!* I held out my arm as I'd seen him do, my fish glinting in the sunlight that filtered through the winged shadows. One of the eagles high up in the sky spotted the glint of the fish and prepared to dive straight at me. It pulled its wings in and came down at a speed of about seventy miles an hour, then oh-so gently took my fish and swooped skywards again, those magnificent wings opening as he devoured the fish on his way up, only to circle high above us as he prepared to dive for more. The sudden injection of adrenaline made my heart race. What a thrill. 'Yes, yes,' I yelled in my excitement. 'Oh, yes.'

The Aussie man exchanged my bucket for one of his which contained sizeable, gleaming,unrecognisable fish. 'Carry on,' he said. 'You don't need me.' My friend of the seven-foot wingspan circled round, eyed the fish in my hand and swooped again. I swear he was aiming for me. His eye was friendly in that split second we made contact. He returned again, and again, as our boat made its way down that ever widening river flowing into the waiting Andaman Sea. My bucket was empty. I held both hands out up to the sky, indicating there was none left. With a final swoop and circling round our boat, that awesome bird seemed to say farewell, and thanks. That was probably just my fantasy but I didn't care – I was high on adrenaline. The privilege I had of being so close to such a dangerous, enormous bird of prey left me in awe at the raw magnificence of nature. What a wonderful, extraordinary world. It was an extremely emotional moment, I had stopped breathing for a second.

My Aussie attempted to put his arm around me, but as I stepped out of arm's length he grinned, and said, 'I knew you had guts. Usually there is only one per boatload, also usually it's a man. This time it's you!'

I turned to look at my fellow passengers and sure enough, all of them seemed huddled together, low down in their respective seats looking at me in some amazement.

Their buckets were still full of fish. Straggling behind us were about half a dozen other ships, lingering, with people standing up, holding out their fish lure. However, obviously this was a set session and most of the eagles had flown off. Presumably they'd had enough to eat for the time being, just the odd bird high in the sky, circling round, occasionally diving for the fish in hand. Our skipper opened the throttle and we sped downriver, hugging the bank, aiming for our home port and the coach taking us back to our cabin on the beach.

'I finish here when I'm moored up, fancy a beer?' he whispered in my ear, obviously aware I was not alone.

Tall, tanned, blond, and handsome though he was, I resisted the temptation, grinned at him and introduced him to my partner, who glowered. 'No,' I replied, 'but I can't thank you enough for the experience of a lifetime. I'll never forget it.'

He shrugged, turned away, annoyed, muttering, 'You win some, you lose some.'

I'd forgotten him already as I disembarked, my head full of that wondrous bird, its vicious talons, its razor-sharp beak and the powerful seven-foot wingspan of glossy brown feathers. This fantastic image was etched forever in my memory, as vivid now as that day on

Langkawi, the island not far from Penang, off the coast of Malaysia.

The vision that was planted in my brain still remains.

One Surprise After Another

Late 1999

Shock City: Pristina, Kosovo. Razor wire protecting vulnerable buildings. UN headquarters on the left.

I hadn't been in Tetovo, Macedonia, very long when I discovered the seemingly sleepy town was not quite what it appeared. My job there was working for an Austrian NGO, Wochenklausur, who were trying to help the Albanian refugees fleeing the Kosovo conflict. I was to be an educational coordinator/teacher/liaison officer.

Stefania, my counterpart in Vienna, was to arrange a series of educational supplies via various couriers on a regular basis. She also organised a member of the Austrian diaspora to deliver a Volkswagen people carrier to me in Tetovo. They drove the long arduous journey down from Vienna and left it in the parking place behind my flat, giving the keys to the man behind the counter in the small shop nearby.

They'd assigned me wheels, as some kind of transport was required if I was to travel regularly from Macedonia to Kosovo. It was clear that I needed to, in order to liaise with professors based in the University of Pristina.

I would be delivering educational supplies mainly consisting of books, paper and writing materials but including eventually very valuable and eagerly awaited computers. The only route to Pristina from there was through the unmapped tracks of the Šar Mountains. These convoluted trails had been hammered out by successive generations of patient donkey feet; it wasn't until relatively recently they had been used by motorised vehicles.

I was pretty apprehensive about that particular joy, as I had not yet driven on what to me was the 'wrong' side of the road. I was particularly apprehensive about exiting my only parking area which was on the bit of scrubland behind my apartment. The only access to it was negotiated through a very narrow, if short passage. I was dreading trying to drive out onto the main street. Another problem I knew I had to face was the fact that women never drove. I could imagine my local reputation would be sullied with yet another black mark for encroaching onto a male domain. My 'partner' local NGO was run by a group of hardcore Muslim Albanians, who were already having difficulty in coping with this stubbornly weird English unfeminine female.

Temporarily putting all this to one side, I focused on what was needed to set up our educational programs. It was pretty disconcerting though, when for example, trying to organise my various language classes, one of the prospective teachers suddenly yelled 'Poshte' (Down) in Albanian, and the whole group dropped to the floor, leaving me standing like an idiot, staring. I must've been extremely noticeable as I was wearing a light-blue 'Marks and Sparks' dress at the time. The few casual gunmen bespattering us randomly with bullets from their car window as they drove leisurely by, thankfully missed me, but broke quite a few windows. They occasionally shot in the air, apparently just for fun. I guessed if they'd really meant to kill me, I would have been laid out in a morgue pretty sharply!

As peace returned, the men rose sheepishly to their feet, one of them apologising and saying, 'Oh, we forgot, you don't speak the language yet.' I managed to utter, 'Anyone hurt?' and collapsd on to the nearest chair in shock. Fortunately no one was even scratched. We'd barely got our breath back when we all froze as the door to the street suddenly opened and a tall, heavily armed soldier walked in. He said something in Albanian to my group, ignoring me completely. I rose to my full five foot three and demanded in my best, if slightly shaky, headteacher voice, 'Who are you? What are you doing in my classroom with all those guns?'

He looked at me in some amazement that the only female present had the temerity to question him. There was an uneasy shuffling of feet behind me, but his only response was a very hard stare. Gathering a smidgeon more courage, I said, 'Well?'

He suddenly looked slightly amused, and replied in perfect English, 'You must be the English woman I've heard a lot about.' 'What's that got to do with anything?' I retorted, beginning to feel annoyed. 'I *don't* allow guns in my classroom.' He looked around the chaotic room and stared a me appraisingly, apparently memorising my appearance.

He announced as if issuing a series of commands, 'I am Ramush, I've come to tell you there will be no more gun incidents. While you are here to help Albanian refugees you are under my protection. This is my territory. No one is left unprotected while I'm in charge.'

With a somewhat ironic salute to us all, he turned on his heel and strode out, annoyingly leaving the street door wide open. He boarded the army truck waiting outside which drove off at some speed, down the street towards the Kosovo border. His abrupt exit left me, and the prospective teachers, shellshocked and momentarily dumb! My Albanian teacher of German eventually said to me, in some awe, 'That man is an extremely important member of our liberation army, he has a very scary reputation for "removing" people he takes exception to. He is our famous commander, Ramush Harudinaj. You wouldn't have lasted a minute if you hadn't stood up to him!' he added.

There were murmurs of agreement from the other men, but I said, 'Look, we are not here to wage war, we are here to help anyone who needs some extra skills to find a job in a world we hope will emerge at the end of this conflict. I hope our classes open up opportunities for our pupils in the rest of Europe after this is all over. That is what we're here for so let's get to work and organise some education – we can use this room to start with.' I picked up my schedules from the floor, shook the debris caused by the temporary fracas off them and began putting the chairs and tables in reasonable order, with some of the men doing the rounds examining the windows with bullet holes, discussing, I was told, how to repair them. We needed to get things in order before the next week when classes were due to start.

We couldn't let a few misplaced bullets stop our work, so we didn't, we carried on.

Slightly unbelievably, the sun still warmed the street outside, the shop opposite reopened its shutters, and the smell of food from the café across the way floated through our open door, reminding us we were all hungry. The momentary blip was forgotten. No one mentioned the attack, no one mentioned Ramush's unexpected visit or his involvement in the protection initiative giving us tacit approval for our work. No questions, no answers, ever.

Little did we guess that in the future he would be tried for war crimes in The Hague, allegedly committed during his command of the KLA (Kosovo Liberation Army), acquitted, and eventually would become prime minister of his country of Kosovo. A very dangerous man I was told. After our experience, I believed it, he exuded power and ruthlessness.

I began to realise local attention was focused on my every move. I was certainly the first and only woman who attacked the sanctity of a male domain – the local coffee house. I decided to go one evening to drink their excellent coffee and read my book. My entry caused every conversation to cease, and every head to turn to look resentfully at me. The only person who welcomed me, was the waiter who pulled out a chair, and brought me coffee and the usual glass of water. Men frequented coffeehouses regularly at all times of the day. They could be seen reading newspapers and talking earnestly across their coffee cups; women were simply not allowed. The waiter was a pleasant young man who obviously was intrigued, rather than appalled by my entry into the erstwhile male domain.

However, his clients were obviously not of the same opinion, and did not like this pushy, western unveiled woman in their café.

My flat was pretty bleak and lonely; no TV, no radio, no phone of any kind and no internet. It didn't even have a postal address. My only communication source was the little shopkeeper next door who had apparently been paid to receive post and messages for this strange English woman, living alone in an apartment owned by what the

Albanians perceived as an 'opposition' family. I didn't know it, but I was in an invidious position. Firstly, it was unheard of for a woman to live on her own. My kindly landlady, who took me under her wing, suggested I hang some men's underwear on my little washing line, giving passers-by the false information I had a male protector in situ.

Secondly, everyone seemed to know my mission was to set up help of various kinds for the Albanian refugees who had flooded that area fleeing the Serbian-attempted genocide. What they didn't understand was why I had 'chosen' an anti-Albanian landlord. I was unknowingly living in a frontier town, with the stresses and strains consistent with a country next to a country at war. German soldiers walked the streets, casually carrying guns on their shoulders, and their purchases from the local market in plastic bags hanging from either hand. They came from a NATO camp located just outside Tetovo. I stood out like a sore thumb as being a westerner and was hailed by them as a fellow European. Most of them spoke pretty good English and we had pleasant conversations as we did our shopping in the fantastic market. The locals were not happy about this strange woman conversing with the military in public; her behaviour was so alien to their own customs and ideas of what was proper. The Muslim women were convinced that I was out to steal their men. I was verbally attacked in the street one day by a very angry, veiled lady who was apparently under the illusion I was out to get *her* man.

Not understanding a word of what she was shouting at me, I stood dumbly and totally astounded. When she finished I simply turned my back and retreated across the road towards the haven of my apartment. It was my landlady's daughter, who spoke a little English and who had witnessed the whole incident, who explained in a rather embarrassed way, that apparently the woman thought I was a harlot. Unfortunately, my hair is reddish blonde, the traditional colour harlots dyed their hair when they wanted to advertise their wares – or so they'd thought. I looked questioningly at her as she spoke, and she smiled wryly and shook her head. 'No, we don't think anything like that,' she assured me.

I was vastly relieved. I'd visualised for a moment instant eviction for 'dubious practices'. Her father would almost certainly have implemented that course of action. He'd lost an argument with me about whether I needed a bed or not, in my apartment. In his book, women sleep on the sofa – or a floor. I'd got the bed. Actually in the bedroom, after a tedious, lengthy argument. Much against his will, it was included in his rather exorbitant rent. He had not liked losing an argument to a woman.

My next task was to visit, by local bus, the neighbouring town of Gostivar, an Albanian refugee stronghold.

My appointment was with someone I nicknamed Mack (the Knife).

Oh, the shark, babe, has such teeth, dear,

And it shows them pearly white... (Apologies, Kurt Weil.)

He was a very handsome Albanian wheeler-dealer – in the jargon of my childhood, 'a real fly boy', who had set up another NGO, theoretically aiding the refugees fleeing Kosovo. I felt absolutely sure that hidden somewhere on his person he carried the legendary jack-knife. It was only instinct, but my first impression was, *Don't trust this guy.* He looked very surprised when I turned up, apparently, no one had told him I was female. After his initial effort to reject me, his face showed he accepted the unavoidable and was working out the pros and cons. He obviously came to the conclusion that he could deal with a couple of women – me and my Austrian contact. I would be his liaison with the affluent west of Europe through my employer, Stefania – another female. I don't think he'd had any experience of bossy headteachers or educated, emancipated women. Between us he was faced with both, unfortunately for him we were not the pushovers he hoped we'd be. He started to give me instructions with reference to the requirements he felt refugees would have in the way of educational supplies.

It soon became evident that there would be some controversy about my ideas of 'educational materials' and his. He had assumed that any arguments would be won by the superior, intelligent and more powerful male. Mmm, not if Stefania and I could help it.

My first assignment was to carry some wooden boxes which were marked 'medical supplies' and some bags of correspondence into Pristina, the capital of Kosovo.

I explained I hadn't driven the Volkswagen yet, and he smiled, showing his pearly white teeth, saying, 'Don't worry, Mrs, I can provide a driver.' Looking him in the eye I explained that the insurance only allowed me to drive the vehicle. 'I have a driving licence that is valid here,' I told him. He looked unbelievingly at me and said, 'Women don't drive, they are not allowed licences.' 'Where I come from, I took a driving test, passed, and was awarded a licence. I drive a Land Rover at home,' I replied. 'I've driven since I was twenty-four – that's quite a while ago now.'

Smiling sweetly at him I then said, 'So, if you can send all the goods you need to be taken to Pristina, I will be going within the next week. I have some supplies from Vienna to be delivered to a Professor Metaj in the university. I have been instructed to ask you to let him know I will be arriving within the next few days.' He barked something at a guy in the other office and then assured me a message would be sent, and goods would be delivered directly to the Volkswagen in the Tetovo car park. His annoyance was palpable. At this point, his very pretty sister came into the office and after an anxious glance at the brother, smilingly indicated she would give me a tour of Gostivar, ending with being put on the bus which would take me back to my apartment. We'd been dismissed 'to go away and play, allow us superior males to do some work'. Irritated as I felt, his sister was delightful, and I certainly didn't want to be discourteous to her. I love unexpected experiences, and was determined to savour this one, but those of that afternoon were rather unusual – thereby hangs another tale...

It wasn't until the next day I went out to inspect my new acquisition, the Volkswagen. To my surprise, it was already loaded with chairs, a table and boxes, barely room left for my educational books and supplies that I'd been told were needed. Nonplussed, I went to the little shop man to ask about the keys. His English was very limited but we established no one else had used them so far. I took him out to show him the loaded vehicle. I mimed my amazement at its contents. He sort of grinned, shrugged his shoulders and indicated Albanians don't need keys, and walked back to his shop. A good lesson learnt, I thought – never leave anything you want to keep private, or that has value, in a vehicle in Macedonia locked, or otherwise! My first effort at driving out into the sparse traffic of Tetovo High Street was sweat-making. I was absolutely terrified. Not quite sure why as I had been driving for years, but it was so disconcerting to have traffic on the wrong side of me. Fortunately, it was a European-manufactured car so at least the controls were on the correct side, but they also took a bit of getting used to.

Another unexpected complication was that I'm cross-lateral. Naturally, extremely left-handed, I had always had problems distinguishing my left from my right, leading to quite a few misunderstandings when trying to instruct another person which way to turn left – or right.

I was extremely nervous of turning into the traffic from the car-park exit as I was never quite sure whether I was going into the traffic, bad idea, or with the traffic, great idea!

Scary in the extreme. Fortunately my tutor, a good friend visiting Tetovo from Vienna, was cool, calm and collected. He didn't turn a hair at my sometimes toe-curling mistake of direction! After being hooted at several times and enduring three separate hourly lessons during the next couple of days, my confidence grew and as the deadline for leaving for Pristina got near I felt I was just about ready to take a journey, hopefully where I wouldn't meet many vehicles on the way.

I packed a small bag for myself and stuffed it under the seat, the rest of the Volkswagen was filled to the brim with supplies to be left at the university in Pristina. Nowhere could I locate a map of the Šar Mountain paths I needed to follow, which worried me a lot. When asked, my landlady's daughter had replied in surprise, 'We don't need maps here, we know where everything is.' From her reaction to my request, I guessed visitors were rare, so I resigned myself to the fact I'd have to find my own way. A friendly taxi driver had shown me the track leading to the forest at the end of the paved road in downtown Tetovo. So I simply drove to the end of the tarmac and carried on along the rough track, leading into the forest and up into the mountains.

It was an absolutely beautiful day. The sun was shining through the trees, dappling the path with sunbeams and shadows. Birds were singing and creatures were rustling in the undergrowth, busy going about their daily lives. I began to sing, glorying in my sense of release. Changing gear, I realised the trail was rising, twisting and turning, so I focused totally on my driving. I really did not want to end up face to face with an immovable tree. It was a bit eerie up there. There were no sounds of any human activity. No sounds of any vehicles, not even the plod of a donkey's hooves. I carried on upwards, feeling reassured that at least there appeared to be only the one track leading to my destination, thereby ensuring I was unlikely to get lost.

When I was forced to come to an abrupt halt, facing an extremely deep ravine with a badly damaged bridge spanning the sizeable gap, I was horrified. Once there had been a wide, safe, solid bridge. Not now.

It had evidently been attacked by a bomb. I got out of the vehicle and peered into the abyss. I could see the bottom of the ravine was strewn with great rocks, gouged out of the hillside above my head that had rolled unimpeded down to meet their fate. It was a sizeable drop, and I stepped back hastily, feeling giddy and sick, suffering my usual symptoms of vertigo. I looked at the bridge, there were no railings left. From where I was standing it just seemed to be an endless stretch of narrow stone with an enormous bite taken out of the side of it on the left, at my end.

I got back into the driving seat and sat there, trembling slightly. This was my first real evidence, apart from the soldiers I'd seen, that a war had been fought. Television in England had shown pictures of war-torn cities and ravaged countryside. Newspapers had shown photographs of lines of desperate refugees, trying to cross the border, back from where I had just come. But it had all seemed like an unreal film to me, living as I did in safe, Middle England.

As I sat there I suddenly realised the well-worn track I'd been travelling along had been honed smooth by desperate people on foot, going in the opposite direction.

The bomb-damaged bridge brought it all home to me.

War is real, senseless destruction, and isn't just a moving picture on a screen in my cosy living room. I got out of the cab again, and leaned against the bonnet of my vehicle, looking at the deep ravine, with its very, very narrow bridge. Unwanted tears trailed down my cheeks, I couldn't go on. I simply couldn't risk crossing that damaged narrow strip of road. The stress of being shot at, and shouted at, during the last week or two and the fear I was feeling now, threatened to overwhelm me. I wanted to lie down on that road and sob.

I didn't even know whether the wheels of my vehicle were narrow enough to negotiate the bit of the bridge that had the enormous bite out of it. I closed my eyes, trying to visualise myself inching across, waiting for my vehicle to make traction on the air beneath its wheels, inevitably pitching bonnet first, down onto those unforgiving razor rocks. I let out a strangled squeak – as usual my imagination had run riot. *No, don't put yourself through this*, I told myself, *your only sensible recourse is to turn round and report back that the road was not negotiable.* Right, about turn.

I looked down, surprised to find the toolbox open and a tape measure in my hand. I got down on my hands and knees, trying to measure the width of my wheels. I then crawled forward as far as I dared along that damaged bridge and tremblingly measured the width of the beginning of the 'bite'. I found myself thrusting the toolbox back where it came from, sitting in the driving seat, starting the engine.

According to my calculations there was about six inches to spare at the narrowest part of the bridge. Praying the weight of my vehicle and me would not prove too much for the stability of my 'tightrope' of a road, I inched agonisingly slowly forward. I dared not look anywhere except straight ahead. I knew if I looked out of the side windows and saw nothing but air I would freeze and be stuck in that nightmare forever. Vertigo is a terrifying experience because you lose your sense of balance and you are impelled to lean forward and let yourself go, feeling you could fly, but knowing damn well you could not. Suicidal, sweat-making, stay well away from heights, I had always told myself.

I was too scared to move the steering wheel even slightly left or right in case the six inches I had calculated was wrong. My knuckles whitened as I gripped that wheel for dear life.

I've no idea how long it took me to cross my Rubicon. My bright sunlight had dimmed to gloaming when I realised I was driving once more on a rough, pothole-pitted track. I put my foot on the brake, turned the engine off and sat there.

I was panting, as if I had just run a marathon. I needed air. I opened the car door, negotiated the potholes and sat thankfully down on the grass verge, my back against the trunk of the nearest tree, surrounded by its protective lower branches. No idea for how long I hid there like a frightened animal but I did find out that what I thought was the 'gloaming' was simply tears in my eyes, dimming my sight.

I was so grateful to that tree for lending me its generous foliage as I faced the fact I'd just had my very first panic attack. I felt such a coward. I felt ashamed of myself. I had no tears left to shed. I got to my feet, I had to get to Pristina before dark. Looking around me, I was so thankful no one could see my ravaged face, up there alone in the heart of that deep forest.

Believe it or not, the sun was still shining, as I crossed the road, preparing to get back into my vehicle and to finish the journey to Pristina. The trail was extremely bumpy along here. The number of potholes seemed bigger and more numerous. I found myself zigzagging from side to side in an effort to avoid damaging the suspension by bumping in and out of what looked like fairly deep holes. Progress was frustratingly slow and I was very aware that I didn't have many hours of daylight left. I had no idea how many more miles I had to travel either. I was still travelling uphill, so I guessed I would eventually drive over the top and then downhill, into the city. Suddenly, with absolutely no warning, I was surrounded by soldiers. I hadn't seen them coming. I was travelling extremely slowly of course, so when one of them put his hand up to stop – I did.

I quickly shut my windows and locked the doors.

I could hear a cacophony of voices shouting at me but couldn't make out any words. The man who appeared to be in charge indicated I should wind the window down. I shook my head, and shouted, 'No fear.' I could make out a few words, surely they were swearing? Yes, they were, in glorious English too. I opened the window a fraction as I studied the uniforms. I nearly fainted with relief: they were British soldiers. 'What on earth are you doing here?' I yelled. 'I need to ask you the same question,' he yelled back. Feeling slightly ridiculous, I opened the window completely and said, pointing back the way I'd come, 'You can't go that way. There's a bombed-out bridge.'

'Get out of the vehicle, please, miss,' was the reply to my comment. It was said in a 'don't disobey me' kind of voice.

I did so, and was immediately surrounded by about half a dozen British voices all asking what I was doing,where I was going and where was I from. I turned to the captain and explained that I come from Tetovo carrying educational supplies, I was a teacher organising classes for Albanian refugees and I was carrying on to Pristina.

He looked at me and said, 'There's a severely unstable bombed-out bridge back there. We've come to survey this area looking for mines and bomb damage. You couldn't possibly have negotiated that bridge in that vehicle. Now tell me the truth. I haven't got time to deal with liars.'

I repeated that I had indeed come across that bridge and had been slowly making my way over the top of the mountains down into Pristina. The response to that was a flow of choice army words, most of which I had never heard of before. He ended by saying, 'You incredibly stupid woman. You could have died and never been heard of again. What the hell did you think you were doing? Kindly tell me how you think you did it.' I wilted slightly at the force of his anger, and the stares of the men who had gone silent. I explained I had crawled on to the bridge with my tape measure to find out how wide it was, and then measured my wheel span; as the bridge was about six inches wider than my wheels, I'd slowly driven across it. He took his hat off and scratched his head, ruffling his hair. He looked at me for a long moment.

'You're a mad, stupid, dangerous woman,' he said at last. 'Totally.' Turning to his group of men, he said, 'We'll have a ten-minute breather now. At ease.' He turned back to me, and said, 'Would you like some tea?'

I'd never heard more beautiful words in all my life.

I was handed a hefty mug of extremely sweet, hot tea, and digestive biscuits. Sitting on the ground, with that group of men and their leader were the best moments ever. They turned out to be a friendly, chatty, great group of lads.

Their captain quietly told me they were the cream of the mine-detecting squad. He explained that every pothole I had encountered, so far, was likely to have had a death-dealing mine hidden underneath in the soft earth. He went on to say, their job was to examine every single one on this refugee road between Pristina and Tetovo. Women and children were trickling back to their homes, hoping to find them intact. There had been one or two deaths reported, so the army had instructed a clearance operation, believing that dissident Serbs were planting death traps. I shuddered, thinking of the risks those brave lads were facing every time they dug out those small innocuous-looking bits of metal. This beautiful forest on a lovely sunny day was war-spoiled and fraught with unknown, multiple dangers. Scarred, damaged but still surviving, providing escape routes and shelter to all those who needed it. Somewhere, someone had protected me, miraculously I was still alive and kicking. 'It's safe for you to carry on this road to Pristina, we've cleaned it,' the captain said, and shook hands, with a warm smile.

'Glad to meet you, stay safe, you crazy woman.' I said goodbye to them all. 'I can't thank you enough for your wonderful tea and for your stupendous work. Stay safe too, all of you.' We waved goodbyes as most of them melted into the trees, searching for evidence of any dangerous objects left in the undergrowth. A couple remained with the captain, ready to carry on down the path, looking for, and disarming, mines.

My intrepid Volkswagen started first go, and we chugged along up a steeper and steeper incline over the top and down into the chaotic city of Pristina. Nothing in my life had prepared me for the rest of my journey. For a start, there was quite a lot of traffic which was not complying with any rules of any road I had ever travelled on. People were driving haphazardly anywhere, everywhere – on pavements, the road, the grass verges, even across people's gardens.

The worst was that nobody seemed to be travelling in the same direction. I met several cars and a couple of trucks, bonnet to bonnet, acquiring a bent bumper. There were quite a variety of vehicles on that road down into the city, from UN-marked people carriers to a few cars with photographers hanging out of windows, eager to take pictures of the aftermath of war. Fortunately, everyone was driving slowly. There were quite a few bumps and curses, but that was all. What horrified me most were the dead bodies littered haphazardly on that route into town. Cows, goats, a pig and many dogs. A few cats scattered here and there added horrific variety. It was a scene from hell.

My sickening dread all the way down that interminable hill was that I would see human corpses. I saw none, thank whatever god was up there, supervising.

I found the café where I was to meet Kadri Metaj.

I numbly parked my vehicle, locked it and stumbled into the smell of strong coffee and a man sitting at a table. He took one look at me, said in French, 'Bonjour. Je suis Kadri Metaj.' He helped me to a chair, calling loudly, 'Du café, maintenant.' I closed my eyes, and the world disappeared.

* * *

Apparently I had a conversation with Kadri in halting French, while driving to the law faculty at the university where students and a couple of professors unloaded the contents of my vehicle. I fortunately prevented them from taking the toolbox, the spare wheel and my bag.

I'd been allocated a room for the night, in the Grand Hotel – a hotbed of film crews, reporters and photographers. Going straight to my room I raided the minibar... Kadri had escorted me there, promising to meet the following morning, for further consultation in my desperately slow French. Work went on, life went on. NATO troops started to restore the normality of peace, the UN and OSCE (Organisation for Security and Co-operation in Europe) started to repair and restore law and order and 'civil society' – we were all on a mission: UNMIK – United Nations Mission In Kosovo. Acronyms ruled the world in those chaotic, early post-war times.

Blind Encounter

Early 2000

Pristina, capital city of Kosovo.

The setting of the rector's office was unexpectedly serene. It was housed in a single-storey building in the middle of a rose garden at the bottom of Pristina high street, Kosovo.

I'd got an enormous surprise on my first day working in the rectorat, as I was shown into the palatial rector's office.

My computer had been put on an extremely large, mahogany desk, facing an equally imposing mahogany table surrounded by matching chairs, and a settee flanked by two armchairs. A superb Persian carpet lay on the polished oak floor. The previous Serbian rector obviously had had an eye for grandeur combined with comfort.

The war ending in 1999 changed all that.

A group of United Nations employees, of which I was one, were now responsible for the reformation, reorganisation and improvement of the educational standards of the now *Albanian* University of Pristina. My immediate boss, the interim international minister of education, had a suite of offices on the fifth floor of a high-rise erstwhile insurance building, known as Eximcos. He was on the opposite side of the street, and not as might have been expected, in the rectorat itself. There may have been a lift in Eximcos once upon a time, but it had become a casualty of war. I'll never forget the image of those interminable stone steps rising in front of me, challenging me to get to the fifth floor in time for my eight thirty morning meeting. Most of my colleagues who were younger and fitter passed me, struggling for breath, as they arrived cool, calm and collected ready for the meeting.

I usually arrived panting, pink-faced, dishevelled – and last.

My role, then, was to organise, recruit staff and begin working with the newly returned Albanian professors and students. My first task was to find a secretary for myself who would occupy the small outer room. Together, we would amass a group of reliable people to help us re-establish a university worthy of its name. It was not surprising really, that not everybody welcomed a female occupying the office of the highest official there. A replacement of the previous Serbian rector by a native Albanian had been made already.

He'd obviously expected to occupy the desk of honour.

Not unexpectedly, he resented my presence in what he considered his domain. His first encounter with me was to offer a tour of the rectorat. I naïvely, gladly accepted.

Swiftly walking towards the exit he paused by the ladies' toilets. 'Miss Xhanet,' he began, using the Albanian pronunciation, 'I understand you will be in charge here for a while, do you think you could get some flowers and organise some pretty paint to make the toilets more attractive?' With some difficulty, as I was taller than him, he avuncularly tried to put his arm across my shoulders as he spoke. 'I am sure you could manage that for me,' he said, and he smiled patronisingly. I moved away and turned to look at him. In my best headteacher voice I replied, 'I am so sorry, but I have no responsibility for the maintenance of this building or any other come to that. My role here is to assist in the re-establishment of a worthy educational university. I am directly answerable to Professor Daxner and under the umbrella of the United Nations. I am not available for domestic discussions. Apologies, but I have a business meeting to attend.'

I turned on my heel, and returned to the palatial office and the wonderful mahogany desk. I was upset and annoyed. I looked in the mirror hanging at the end of the room. I was dressed smartly in a jacket and trousers, hair tidy, a little make-up on. I held my glasses and a notebook in my hand and I felt I looked efficient and suitably dressed.

My lack of tact initially had bothered me a little but really my response was necessary to firmly establish the temporary hierarchy if we were to succeed in building a place of learning worthy of its name. I calmed down as I pondered on a culture that regarded women as much less important than men, and mainly a vehicle to produce children. The concept of women having a career was apparently yet to be recognised. I had to realise the fact I was female and foreign-looking was going to be a continuing problem. In Muslim society there and then, it was rare for many females to occupy positions of power; a few admirable, strong Albanian ladies were revered and respected, but they did not include unknown foreign females with reddish-blonde hair. It became obvious to me that no one knew quite how to cope with what amounted to a foreign takeover of the total administration of the infrastructure in Kosovo, including Pristina University.

The United Nations Mission in Kosovo (UNMIK) worked closely with NATO and the OSCE and the EU who were there to rebuild a war-torn country. The man in the street initially regarded us all as saviours, they adored Tony Blair, they revered Braveheart for his cry of 'Liria' (Freedom) and his valiant attempt to free his people from an oppressor.

The former officials, however, were not so sure. They suspiciously reserved judgement, rightly concerned that their present authority might be challenged.

The previous oppressive Serbian regime had been pushed back to Belgrade with less than one thousand Serbs left in Pristina by the time I arrived. 'Rilindja'– rebirth, renewal – had begun in an area that had been under Yugoslav/Serbian domination for over fifty years. Foreign troops walked the streets, strange foreign languages were heard everywhere. Tension was high and had to be carefully managed by us, the temporary intruders. Once it was established that I was there for the duration and 'accessible', I had a continuous stream of people from the university coming to me for information and sometimes help. The problems were diverse, and only to be expected in a recent war-torn country that was just beginning to settle down, and hoping to find its place in the world. One of the first students to visit me was a delightful girl. She'd come to ask me what I thought about a request from her professor to have sex with him.

He said she'd get a really good mark, if she agreed.

If she didn't comply, she would fail her exams, be expelled from the university and therefore not achieve her degree or follow her chosen career. She came to me because I was female and she felt I would understand. Her mother had warned her she'd never get married if she agreed to his demands, and she suggested the girl should leave the university at once and marry her fiancé. She was an ambitious medical student, however, and was hoping against hope that the new regime would be able to help her.

She looked at me with tears in her eyes. 'I am so very scared that my brothers will take revenge against the professor for this if they ever found out... they will kill him.' My stomach jumped at the thought of more murder. Too many deaths had occurred already. I took her hand, and said, 'My professor is an honest man. I must go to him and tell him what you told me. I promise no word of what happened to you will be spoken by us. Leave your problem with me. We will deal with it, but please, please, no violence.'

I assured her she would be safe, and certainly not harassed in that way again. She looked upset and doubtful that I would be able to organise this, she'd only come to me because she felt desperate. She was finding it hard to believe that equality and democracy were a reality, and hopefully soon to become the norm in her world too.

At a private meeting with my Professor Daxner, we managed to find reasons why her professor was not suitable to be employed at this university. It was made clear to him in no uncertain terms his behaviour was totally unacceptable in the new university life. It was also my unenviable job to give him his notice. He left.

She got her degree in the end with honours.

One of my other tasks was to ensure that the professors in the university became familiar with English.

Vioja, my interpreter, and I turned up at one of the old lecture halls for our first English session. We were faced with about seventy professors instead of the half dozen or so we were expecting. Undaunted, we carried on and introduced ourselves. As usual, I felt totally embarrassed, at being looked up and down with surprise – and some hostility. There wasn't a single person in that room, who didn't have dark eyes and dark hair, and, apart from Vioja, there were no other females present. I stood out like a sore thumb – I really hated that feeling!

Through my interpreter, I introduced myself and then asked the professors to tell me what languages they could speak, hoping for some English. Amazingly, nearly all of them knew about five or six. Albanian, of course, Serbo-Croat, Russian, German, French, Italian, some Turkish, and lastly, a little English. I wondered how many of our professors in England would have such a wide range to choose from – I thought nearly none. It was weird speaking through an interpreter though. Previously, I'd managed to communicate using my rather rusty French. I had to slow my speech speed down to allow Vioja to translate for a start, but we had a really good first session, and amazingly our 'students' stood up and clapped at the end of their hour.

The sessions were established for two days a week. I discovered I was really good at talking, not so good at the refinements of grammar! Vioja, on the other hand, knew her English grammar back to front. So the professors progressed well and their knowledge of spoken English grew apace. Vioja and I worked out a really efficient combination of team teaching, me talking about England and our way of life as a subject of interest, at their request, and her defining the intricacies of English grammar. Unfortunately, my duties as part of the administration team increased dramatically so I couldn't carry on with the class. I felt really regretful. I enjoyed the contact with most of the professors, who were looking forward to a more democratic governance and enjoyed talking to me about our English education system, hoping to gain ideas, I think.

One of the things I did discover was that the university was the main source of soldiers for the KLA – Kosovo Liberation Army. Whenever there was some fighting, students and professors would disappear, the campus would be deserted, lecture halls empty. Gradually people would filter back, some with bandages, some with small wounds and some wouldn't come back at all. Female students sat in half-empty lecture halls with red eyes and sombre faces. It took me some time to work out what was actually going on but eventually it became evident that the hidden centre of the Kosovo dream of freedom was right in front of me there, in the university.

I found my work fascinating. The various political shenanigans that were going on provided endless food for thought, and formed a basis of our reforms.

We gradually stamped out intimidation and bribery, we broadened and improved the curriculum throughout the faculties. In some cases, we improved the quality of the professors, gradually dropping those that were either dishonest or unqualified or both. It was a job that required total dedication and focus from eight thirty in the morning until about the same time in the evening. A long and tiring day. I had managed to swap my ancient Volkswagen people carrier that had carried me valiantly over the Šar Mountains to Pristina and bought myself a small car. My little rescue dog, Daxi, and I travelled usually at great speed (I was always late) to and from work every day. The parking area at the back of the rectorat was basically scrubland, muddy and bumpy. We had great fun off-roading, negotiating the bumps and puddles on the way down the track leading to the university building. It led past the shell of a Serbian Orthodox church, beautifully designed and outlined against the horizon, especially at sunset. I loved it. I gazed at it through my office window in moments of abstraction, whenever inspiration was required. It was surrounded by razor wire to protect it against possible damage from vengeful Albanian dissidents.

I'd found Daxi huddled in the rose garden in front of the rectorat being kicked by the doorkeeper who hated dogs.

I'd picked her up and carried her to my office, intending to find a home for her. I took her to the vet. She was healthy, but flea-ridden. She had her jabs, her flea deterrent and worm pills – and she ended up staying with us in our flat.

I'm not sure she appreciated the luxury of a home. She was feral to the core. I loved her though and told her she was safer with me than being gang-raped in the streets by packs of feral dogs. I took her with me everywhere I went. The locals regarded me as extremely peculiar, obviously concluding the English were weird. My Austrian boss, however, sympathised with my sentiments and allowed me to bring her to work as long as she kept out of sight.

One fateful evening, I was working very late on a special assignment. Daxi and I were feeling tired, hungry and fractious. I carried my heavy bag over one shoulder and held my keys and the lead in my other hand, we walked slowly to our car in pitch darkness. All the lights in the university were out, and all we could see was the outline of the Serbian church against the night sky. She was keen to get in the car and jumped in the back eagerly as I inserted my keys into the ignition, dumping my bag beside me, just about to start the engine. A knock on my window, made me sigh.

'Not another student problem...' I opened the window halfway down, and a voice said in perfect English, 'Good evening.' The handsome young man smiled at me with superbly even white teeth. I just had time to notice he had something in his hand when an awful, burning spray seared my eyes and I screamed. My dog barked menacingly from the back seat, I heard an expletive – very un-English – a thud and running footsteps. Daxi was barking frantically.

I was blind, totally, tears streaming down my cheeks, nose, lips, face burning. I'd had my hand on the ignition key. I turned it on and reversed in panic. The car hit the bank at the edge of the track with a loud thud, and temporarily halted, I managed to get into forward gear, turned the car and drove and drove and drove. I could see nothing. I could hear nothing, except Daxi's frantic barks reverberating round the car. My muscle memory must've followed the bumps and puddles of our daily drive in and out on that track, because miraculously I headed for the Serbian church with no further mishaps, aiming for the exit. I was blinded and deafened, and in shock-induced autopilot. Through the din I heard a blessedly English voice yell at me, 'Halt. Halt or I fire.' Hardly registering his actual words and having no idea where on earth I was, I pushed my foot on the brake, still in gear, and ground to a very abrupt stop, pitching dog and me forward, hitting my head on the windscreen.

At the same time, yelling back, 'I'm English, you bloody fool,' and burst into tears, mingling with the waves of pain from the teargas that had been discharged straight into my face. I could feel the car rocking slightly as it was surrounded by people. My little dog went absolutely hysterical, rushing from side to side and barking at each window in turn. I heard one of the guys say, 'I'll take care of the dog, it's just very scared.'

The first voice said, 'Open the window, miss, we'll take care of the dog.'

'No, no, who are you? Where am I? Who are these other people? I can feel my car being pushed.'

'You are blocking the entrance to a British Army facility,' said voice one.

'I don't believe you,' I stuttered, 'I haven't left my track. I can feel it.'

A more cultured voice spoke quietly through the half-opened side window and said, 'I'm Captain Haig, my men will push your car into our compound where you will be safe. We will look after your dog and give it a few treats and some water. It has had a shock, so have you. I will walk beside the car and when we're inside the compound I will ask you to open the door and allow us to lead you directly to our medical team.'

I dumbly nodded. 'Okay, okay.'

I sat in the driver's seat, immobile, panting. Tears were still coursing down my burning face. And my eyeballs were beginning to give me serious pain. I've no idea how I got from the car into the church and laid out on an examination table. I could smell antiseptic, I could feel several people around me. Someone took my hand and said soothingly, 'We will be washing your face and eyes with a cooling solution in a very few minutes. Your face will feel much better and hopefully you will be able to see a little, maybe shadows and light.' Captain Haig took my other hand and said, 'You are safe now' as I began to shake all over.

A cover was put over me and I could feel my face being thoroughly doused in a cool liquid. My eyelids were prised open and the merciful cool encompassed me and I think I passed out. Sometime later, I found myself sitting up, eyes bandaged, hair soaking wet and a mug of hot sweet tea in my hand. 'Your brave little dog is sleeping beside you – we've given her a sedative, she will sleep for an hour or two. She will be fine.' I put my other hand on her furry back, taking comfort from her steady breathing. 'We will leave you to rest,' said Captain Haig, 'and then we need to ask a few questions.' I heard the rattle of curtains and leant back after putting my mug safely on the floor.

I slipped silently into oblivion.

* * *

I felt a hand taking off my eye bandage. 'Sorry to disturb you, but I need to look at your eyes.' I blinked quickly and discovered I could see a little, but my vision was extremely blurry. Eye drops were put in each eye which soothed the burning feeling I was still having. 'I can't see any damage to your eyeballs,' said the voice. 'Can you see me?'

I turned to look at him. 'You are pretty fuzzy, but yes, I can make you out.'

'Good,' he said briskly, 'I will give you these drops, please put them in your eyes three times a day until they're finished. Your bag is here and I've put them in there for you.' And with that he left. I tried to look around me. I could just make out I was in what looked like a hospital cubicle, surrounded by white curtains, I think. Daxi was still snoring at my side on the bed. Three more people came into the little space bringing chairs with them. Two were in dark colours. The one nearest to me was in army colours.

He spoke first. 'We need to ask you a few questions. I hope you're feeling better after your two hours' sleep.'

And thus the interrogation began. It seemed to go on forever. Question after question about possible confrontations, why the attack occurred. Who they might be. Any descriptions. Basically I couldn't answer any of them. The man in khaki turned to the two people in blue, and said, 'Captain Haig will escort you to your car. This lady will be also be escorted out in about twenty minutes. Please will you take her home and don't leave her alone until she reaches her own front door. Thank you.' When they had gone, he turned to me and said, 'I am in command here. Until this moment no outsider has been allowed inside the church. You will see as you leave, evidence of occupation and usage of the interior of this building. You will be required to sign the Official Secrets Act. This is to ensure you don't discuss any aspect of the interior with anyone. We have security-checked you and your immediate superior Professor Daxner and made enquiries as to why you should've been attacked. Nothing has come to light so far. You are free to go home as soon as you feel able. You are a very lucky young lady. My men had instructions to shoot first and ask questions after. Our position here is extremely delicate.' He stood up. He bent to stroke my dog, and left.

Two minutes later, Captain Haig came in with a piece of paper and a pen and said, 'I'm afraid you've got to sign this. Can you see?' With screwed-up eyes I managed to sign what I hope was my signature at the bottom of the page. He looked at it and said it was fine. He called in a young man who carefully picked up Daxi, still sleeping. Another young man picked up my bag and handed me my ignition keys with the information that my car would be returned to the parking lot outside the rectorat and he was sorry, but it wasn't driveable anymore.

Captain Haig offered me his arm as I staggered to my feet. As I came out of the cubicle I became aware of quite a large number of personnel in various stages of relaxation, enjoying food and drink at a long table. We passed sleeping quarters, the usual facilities, which included showers. We emerged into what was obviously a field office with a desk, and what looked like bits of telephone and a filing cabinet or two. We came out into the fresh air at the back of the church, where a waiting police vehicle was parked. The guy carrying Daxi put her gently on the back seat, the guy carrying my bag put it beside her. They both nodded goodbye and disappeared back into the building. Captain Haig put his arm round my waist and helped me into the back seat also. 'Stay safe,' he said and murmured something to the police officer who replied under her breath. We drove back to my flat.

It turned out both police officers were female, they both commiserated with me about my attack and expressed indignation and disbelief that an Albanian would be involved, as according to them the whole population was grateful for our presence and efforts at restoration. By this time, Daxi was stirring, and was able to walk up the short path to the entrance of our flat. The ladies carried my bag and steadied me on our walk to my front door. One of them actually gave me a hug and said, 'The army recommend you are allocated a bodyguard for the next few weeks as they believe you may be targeted again.' They watched me as I inserted my front-door key, opened the door and walked in. My sight was clearing slightly and I was able to smile to them, goodnight. They waved as I shut the door and I breathed a sigh of relief to be in the place I temporarily called home.

My Girl Daxi

2000

Daxi's lookalike brother!
None of my little rescue dog's photos survived the move from Kosovo to Vienna, my next port of call. This is delightful Duke, a mix of whippet, greyhound and Bedlington, who could be her twin.
Thank you Tarcani Gundogs for the use of your photograph.

My colleagues were rather horrified when I called my little rescue dog Daxi, after our chief, the Interim Minister of Education, Professor Daxner. He, however, laughed when I told him my intention, and said he was honoured!

She was a small, undernourished youngster, black-haired, and of no known breed. She and others like her, wrung my heart. Many could be seen scavenging not far from where we were staying.

I never saw any member of the local population do anything other than abuse and throw any missile to hand at these poor animals. Pristina was plagued with packs of roaming dogs. People fleeing the city with goods and chattels had for the most part left their pets behind. These erstwhile pets had no idea how to look after themselves and spent their miserable lives foraging in rubbish bags, and on landfill sites dotted around the city at the time.

The army had finally received instructions to rid the city of the feral dog population. Groups of army personnel were deployed each evening to cull as many as possible.

As an animal lover, my heart bled for them. I spent a lot of time after I had finished work on my own, and I'd go into the bedroom, put my hands over my ears, with my head under the pillow until the shooting sessions were over. I can't remember how long it took to rid the city of most of the roaming dogs but the cull invaded my dreamscape for months; better a quick death than slow starvation, I'd told myself, and the army *were* crack shots. But it was an aspect of life in Kosovo that I found extremely difficult to cope with.

My work at the university occupied nearly the whole of my life, so it wasn't easy to cope with a feral puppy who patently was ambivalent about being constrained after being able to roam at will. She loved the food and the comfort and she began to put on weight and show affection to me, but not really anyone else. She behaved quite well during the day, sitting under my desk while I worked. Western Europe colleagues tolerated her presence, sometimes bringing her a treat. She gradually grew attached to my Polish colleague, Tomas. She hated the two Albanian bodyguards I'd been allocated after my assault behind the rectorat. She could probably sense their dislike of her.

The army and security were unable to find any trace of my assailant, or any motive for the attack. They found the canister of teargas that he had discarded in his panic. They told me that Daxi had probably saved me from a much worse outcome as most people were frightened of what they called the 'wild dogs'. To have one sitting on a seat in the back of a car was unheard of. As it happened she had a particularly deep scary bark which startled the young man so much he dropped the canister and ran. The instructions given to the bodyguards were that outside my place of work or my apartment, they were to guard me against any possible further attacks. The official UN policy was that if one of their people was under threat they would be sent home.

But I was determined not to be intimidated and decided that bodyguards would be sufficient safeguard, and that I would fund them out of my own pocket. Actually, I enjoyed their company. They were local guys, ex-police in a couple of cases, security-screened, armed and ready for any emergency. They came with me on my walks with Daxi, sat with me at lunch and accompanied me shopping in the Commissary, kindly carrying the shopping home.

There were six in all, on duty from the time I left my home at about a seven forty-five am until I returned home usually just before eight pm. They were cheerful and chatty, and at the end of the three weeks when it was deemed that I was likely to be safe, I regretted saying goodbye. No motive, no assailant, no justice was ever meted out to the person who'd had the effrontery to attack an international representative of the UN. As far as I know.

In those early days, there were many secrets that never saw the light of day.

My work carried on without interruption, and eventually the whole incident was forgotten.

Daxi became a problem though. It turned out, she was nearly impossible to house-train. My office had easy access to the garden. Regularly walked, it was pointed out to her in no uncertain terms that to relieve herself in any building was unacceptable. She never took that on board.

At the weekends, I often had access to a UN vehicle for recreation purposes, and we would go out into the countryside and walk. I began to realise that the only time that Daxi came to life was when she was on those walks.

Tail wagging, nose busy and ears upright, head going from left to right, obviously listening, smelling for evidence of other dogs. She did not want to get back in the car – her tail drooped, her head hung low, she looked a very miserable animal. I could see she was becoming more and more unhappy with her life. Things came to a head when we had an important meeting in my office, and there at the door was a fairly substantial puddle. Although it was hastily dealt with, orders from above indicated that Daxi could not continue to accompany me to work. I rang the kind army vet I had originally contacted about her vaccinations. I asked desperately if there was anyone he knew that could house a little feral female dog. I had already arranged for her to be spayed. I said I'd pay for that operation. He promised to make enquiries, but didn't hold out much hope.

A few days later, he rang back and said no one was in a position to take Daxi on. I told him about how miserable she had become and we discussed possibilities, but it became apparent that either I release her back into an extremely hostile environment or humanely put her down. I couldn't bear to think of her living the hazardous life of a street dog or being shot unexpectedly one night, so eventually I made the decision to have her put down. We agreed that the vet would come to our flat to make it less stressful for her.

One evening, he turned up with his bag, ready to put my little companion to sleep. She sensed that I was very disturbed and was quite agitated herself. As the vet came in she growled menacingly and jumped onto my lap. 'That's good,' he said, 'hold her firmly but gently, and I'll get everything ready.'

With that, the lights went out. Everywhere was in total darkness. One of the regular power-saving cuts decided that this was the moment to conserve energy.

After a couple of expletives I heard his voice say, 'Do you have any candles? Or even better, a torch?'

'No to torch, yes to candles. I don't want to let Daxi go – I know she'll hide under the settee,' I replied. I could feel her trembling and getting extremely agitated. 'If you make your way to the sink and put your hand down slightly to the left, you'll find a cupboard and the candles are in there together with a box of matches.' He muttered something under his breath, bumbled about, hitting the kitchen table and eventually found the sink. A few seconds later, soft candlelight revealed him standing at the table with his bag open. He'd found three candles, a couple of saucers and a plate and stuck all three on the table, shedding a reasonable amount of light.

'Surely you can't do this in candlelight?' my voice squeaked. 'Please, let's leave it to another time.'

'Better to do it now,' he said gently. 'Bring her to the table.'

My little dog began struggling frantically, as I stood up and carried her to the table. She *knew*. 'Hold her still,' he said. 'I will inject a relaxant into her muscle and then administer the anaesthetic.' I could feel Daxi saying, '*Like hell you will.*' And she turned and bit my hand and then like lightning, lunged forward and bit the vet's hand. He swore long and loudly, then, but still gently inserted the needle into her leg muscle. She relaxed into my arms and lay down on the table, he found her vein and injected the anaesthetic overdose and in a couple of seconds it was all over. I collapsed suddenly onto the kitchen chair. The golden candlelight lent a surreal quality to the whole tableau.

'Have you got any alcohol in the place?' the vet asked in gruff voice. 'Yep,' I said and I got out a bottle of whisky from the cupboard. I offered it to him and he took a long swig out of the bottle, then handed it to me. I wiped the top and did the same. We both sat there, somewhat stunned at the way things had turned out. He removed his gloves, rinsed his wound under the tap, fumbled in his bag and found a plaster. My hand had bled onto my skirt and a bit on the floor. 'Come here,' he ordered and held my hand under the tap for several minutes. 'I will take your dog with me. She will have to be incinerated for safety.' He got out a bag and put Daxi's body in it and sealed it with tape. He closed his bag of tricks and stood up, briefly patted my arm and made his way to the door, bag in one hand, Daxi under his other arm. 'I'll be in touch,' he said. And left.

I cleaned the floor, blew two candles out, carried one into the bedroom and crawled into bed. I could hear the guns in the distance. I put my head under the pillow. I didn't sleep well. I was ridden with guilt. I was responsible for the death of a creature that trusted me. That I cared for. I felt pretty miserable.

Work called me. At the eight thirty meeting, I received many sympathetic glances, but no one said a word. Life went on, and I became immersed in the jobs of the day. Later that afternoon I had a telephone call. 'Hallo there. I hope you've recovered from yesterday evening, but I have to ask you a question. Have you had your rabies injection?'

'Rabies? What on earth for? My dog has been with me for months, she didn't have rabies.'

'I have been instructed to have the rabies injection, and have called to instruct you to do the same,' the vet replied.

'Nonsense, I certainly don't need an injection. Thank you for your concern. How much do I owe you for last night?'

'Nothing, it's part of my job to rid the city of vermin. You must have that injection,' and with that he rang off. I muttered to myself I didn't need an injection, my dog didn't have rabies, my workload was too great for me to take time off, my car was off-road anyway... I carried on working. A few days later, my secretary showed a young soldier into my office. 'I've come with a message,' he said. 'I've been ordered to inform you our chief medical officer requires your presence tomorrow at two pm to have your first rabies injection. Should you decline to come he will arrange for a couple of military police to escort you there. Transport has been arranged.' With that, he saluted and left the room.

I was fuming to myself. What cheek. Who does the army think they are? I am not in the army, I an a citizen with rights. At the eight thirty meeting the next morning, I informed my boss that I'd been summoned to the army doctor for a rabies injection, expecting him to say, 'What nonsense.'

Instead he said, 'Good. Sensible. Go,' and carried on writing.

I'd heard all sorts of rumours about injections into the stomach that the rabies vaccine required. None of my colleagues had ever had the vaccine, no one seemed to know what it entailed. I was really scared. As I climbed into the waiting army vehicle, ready to go to the medical officer, my heart was jumping into my throat. My hands were clenched and I was slightly sweaty. I hadn't relished being escorted by the police, however, so I decided to bite the bullet.

The army medical facility was scrupulously clean and smelt of antiseptic. I was shown into what looked like a reception area, and told to sit and wait. 'I understand you were reluctant to come,' said the voice behind me. 'What was the problem? Surely this is a very sensible precaution?'

And an efficient-looking, white-coated man approached the desk and sat down with a tray of syringes and serum. 'Roll up your sleeve, this will only take a few minutes.' And he swabbed a spot on my arm and gave me an injection. 'Come back next week. You will need another injection and in a month you will need the third and final one. That's it.' He got up to go, looking at me, quizzically. 'Science has progressed over the last few years, no more invasive injections into other parts of your anatomy. I expect to see you next week.' I left with a feeling of enormous relief. The young man outside said to me, 'You'll be protected for life when you complete the course of injections. If you ever get bitten by a rabid dog or a bat your vaccine will protect you. You can relax now.'

I returned to work on a high. I patted my stomach, gently saying to that part of my anatomy, 'Science is wonderful, you've had a narrow escape! All our "bits" are safe now – at least until the next disaster!'

A Greek Soldier

2000

'Teetering on the edge'. Map showing the border between Greece and Macedonia.

A bright and breezy day in 2000 was the day I thought I was going to die.

As assistant to the international education minister, I was often sent on a variety of interesting journeys, sometimes by helicopter and sometimes in a United Nations vehicle. However, this particular journey was more than just interesting...

A young Greek soldier stood stock still, pointing his machine gun straight at me. He was scarlet-faced with anger and trembling slightly. The six of us stood in line at the edge of the road facing a people carrier with its large black United Nations logo and its green-faced driver sprawled across the bonnet, guarded by another Greek soldier. Behind us was a sheer drop into a quarry made by a company mining for chalk. I was on a special mission, having been granted a personal interview with a very hostile Austrian ambassador based in Skopje, Macedonia. Two of our Kosovar Albanian professors were hoping to attend a convention in Vienna later that month and needed visas. I was sent to persuade him to grant them. My travelling companions were five phlegmatic Finnish doctors due to contribute to a medical conference also in Macedonia. We stood in total silence – waiting – only too aware of the sheer drop behind us, a single false step away.

We had been in a line of cars, waiting to cross the border between Kosovo and Macedonia, sandwiched in a miles long lorry queue. We'd been stuck there for about three hours.

The border control painstakingly examined every vehicle minutely, checking for hidden arms or explosive devices, which delayed the drive-through even more.

Some of those lorries had been stranded for several days as they inched, agonisingly slowly, forward. Tempers were short. Our Albanian driver was getting very impatient with the Greek border guards who were walking up and down, imperiously waving their Kalashnikovs at any vehicle that dared deviate from the military-straight column moving inch by inch at a snail's pace. We were all waiting to be screened by the border customs officials. Our man had been muttering to himself for the last half hour, first in Albanian and then in Greek, his animosity towards the soldiers becoming increasingly evident. He kept revving the engine which eventually caught the attention of a young Greek soldier who gestured impatiently for him to stop. Secure in the knowledge that the UN would protect him, he shouted something to the young soldier, who went scarlet with fury and gestured violently with his gun for us to pull over to the side. Our driver tried to swerve the other way, I think in the vain hope he could make a getaway to the border which was about half a mile in front of us. That was a big mistake.

We were suddenly surrounded by a bevy of Greeks all shouting excitedly and waving their guns at us to go as directed. Wisely, the driver did. The moment we stopped, the driver's door was wrenched open and he was dragged kicking and yelling out of the vehicle and none too gently pushed across the bonnet as they frisked him. I don't know what the young soldier shouted at him but he went even greener and looked as if he was going to be sick, and suddenly froze.

We were ordered out of the vehicle at gunpoint and lined up in the classic execution format, backs to that sheer drop.

So there the teenager stood, pointing the machine gun at us, trembling, sweaty and patently very scared. One of his compatriots said something to him which started him crying but he unlocked the safety catch of his machine gun and pointed it directly at the only female – me.

His finger hovered over the trigger ready to press it at the slightest provocation. We all stood quite still.

I think I shut my eyes for a moment.

He was in a state of panic by this time as he appeared to realise he had passed a point of no return, he obviously didn't quite know what to do. He was caught in a situation of his own making, basically caused by him losing his temper. Backing down would mean an enormous loss of face, killing us would mean a major international furore.

He started swinging his gun from side to side, patently trying to decide which end of our line to start shooting at.

The beads of sweat were dripping down his face, he was obviously under enormous internal strain. At that point I realised my life really was in the balance and it actually might be the end.

My mind went blank.

After what seemed like forever we became aware of a Greek officer approaching the lad quietly, but swiftly, coming to a halt just to one side of him. 'Nico,' he said. 'Nico.' And he carried on speaking incomprehensible Greek words directed at the young boy, as he slowly lowered his gun. Never taking his eyes off it, the officer gently held out his hand, indicating it should be given to him. Slowly, oh-so bloody slowly, the gun changed hands. The officer replaced the safety catch and handed it to one of the nearby group of soldiers apparently transfixed by the whole incident.

Our soldier dropped to his knees, head bowed, as he collapsed into a heap onto the hard tarmac road. The officer went over to the huddled figure and quietly helped him to his feet, arm around his shoulders, turned and they walked haltingly to the waiting Land Rover which drove off down the road towards the border. No one made eye contact with any of us. No one uttered a single word.

Within seconds we were alone on that dusty road, still standing in line, dumbly waiting for our execution which never happened. Slowly our driver straightened up and walked shakily to the open door of our vehicle and got back into the driving seat. He sat there staring vacantly into the distance. The young doctor standing next to me, turned and looked at me. 'Naoki,' he said. 'Jeannette,' I replied.

He put his arms around me and hugged me hard. He took my hand and we moved to the open side door of our vehicle. He helped me in, we returned to our seats, and we were followed silently by the rest of the passengers. Naoki fumbled in his pocket and drew out his wallet. He opened it and passed it to me. In it was a small photo of a plain little girl and a sweet-faced woman. I touched it gently with my finger and handed it back, sudden tears streaming down my face.

Not a single word was exchanged on that endless journey to Skopje.

As the driver stopped in front of the Austrian Embassy, I stood up, still shaky, and still in shock. I picked up my briefcase, ready to get off, held out my hand to Naoki, and said, ‘Goodbye, thank you.’ He nodded and replied, ‘Stay safe, Jeannette, stay safe.’ I watched the UN people carrier drive away. I never saw any of them again.

A Right Royal Meeting

2000

King Leopold V designed his country's flag. It is believed to be the oldest in Europe. It was first displayed in 1250 and is still used on state occasions.

Climbing the steps to the embassy entrance, I felt I needed, first of all, the loo, then possibly a double whisky and a comfortable armchair to collapse into. Looking at the austere expression on the face of the young Austrian soldier demanding to see my passport, that dream faded abruptly.

I waved it under his nose, and he knocked on the door, which was noisily unlocked, opened and locked again behind me. Another very correct official indicated I should follow him. Leaving him striding towards the foot of a staircase, I hastily made for the corner of the large reception hall where a small notice said 'Toiletten'.

Having wiped the dry drips of blood from my chin, where I had inadvertently bitten my lip earlier, I made myself presentable and opened the door to find myself face to face with the angry official, who said icily, 'It is expressly forbidden for visitors to move round the building with no escort and without permission. Kindly *follow* me.' He led me back towards the stairs, his long legs climbing them rapidly. He almost thrust me into a room at the end of a corridor lined with portraits of previous incumbents. I chose a deep comfortable leather armchair, dropped my bag on the floor and settled into it. After a few moments, the door opened, and a charming blonde female came in carrying a tray of 'Kaffee und Kuchen', together with a glass of water. Setting it down on a nearby table, she asked if I had everything I needed and added, 'His Highness will see you in twelve minutes. I will come for you.' She smiled at me and left. In exactly eleven minutes, she returned and indicated I should go with her.

We walked a short way along the corridor, stopping outside a pair of tall doors. Checking her watch, we waited a second and she then knocked.

A deep voice said, 'Kommen.' She opened both doors so we could enter, gave a bow and left, closing them behind her, leaving me standing awkwardly on the threshold not quite sure what to do. The silence in the room was profound. Heavy curtains at the windows muffled any possible street noise and the building itself must have been soundproofed as not a peep could be heard from anywhere. The man at the enormous desk, flanked by the Austrian flag, looked up from his writing, and indicated I should come and sit on the chair, placed some distance away in front of him.

He raised his head and looked at me. Speaking in German, he said, 'I understand you have come to request visas for two Albanian professors. The answer is emphatically no.'

His face was impassive as he spoke, and his eyes cold.

'I apologise for not speaking your language,' I replied, 'but I have not understood a word of what you have just said. However, from your tone, I presume you are not in favour of our request.' He looked surprised and said in English, 'Your accent is excellent. Are you Albanian?'

'No. I am English. I represent the interim international governing body allotted the task of reforming the University of Pristina, under the auspices of the UN. We have two professors who have been invited to speak at a conference in Vienna. They need visas,' I replied, a bit pompously... He rang a handbell on his desk, and a hidden door opened behind him, and a young man entered. 'Yes, your Highness?' he said, bowing. The ambassador gave an instruction in German, the young man pulled up a chair and prepared to take notes. Turning to me, he commanded in English that I continue. 'As I said, two of our professors require authority to visit Vienna for a three-day convention from next Wednesday. Their request was approved by Professor Daxner, the International Minister of Education. I verified the authenticity of the convention and decided their presence would enhance the reputation of Pristina University. Hence the approval of their application. You have the paperwork in front of you in the file I gave in earlier. What objection do you have to this application?'

Both the young man and the bearded ambassador raised haughty eyebrows at my question. Obviously surprised at the temerity of this lowly female, the ambassador replied, ‘I presume you are unaware of the numbers of Albanian illegal immigrants disappearing into the Austrian diaspora, eventually becoming a burden on the state. We are actively trying to ensure no more illegals enter our country. Why should we make an exception to these two professors you mention? They too represent a possible threat.’

‘We believe that to be untrue,’ I replied. ‘They both shed blood during the Serbian regime in order to keep the underground university going. Their loyalty is proven. They both have young families that they would never see again if they disappeared into Austria. They have pledged to return and report on the convention outcomes. I am authorised to inform you that the university offers a guarantee they will return to Kosovo at the end of their visa limit, the reputation of their university is at stake here. Incidentally, I *am* aware of the “disappearing Albanians” problem. We believe the integrity of these two professors is unassailable.’

The forbidding expression on the ambassador’s face didn’t change but he looked at me for a very long moment. Turning to the young man, he handed him our file. ‘Erlaubnis erteilt,’ he said.

Standing up, he waited for me to do the same, gave a slight bow of dismissal, turned and walked out through the hidden door behind his desk. I stood there, feeling deflated and depressed. I had failed in my mission. My success had meant so much to the two anxious professors. It would have been their first visit to a western country for years. As I bent to pick up my briefcase, the young man said, ‘Congratulations. This is the first application to be granted for a very long time, please come with me.’ I followed him in dumb surprise to those tall doors, along the corridor back to the waiting lounge, guarded by a young soldier.

‘Wait here, I will send the paperwork along in ten minutes.’ Giving me the ubiquitous little bow, he went.

Ten minutes later, there was a knock on the door, a young female entered carrying a large envelope. She handed it to me saying in slow English, 'I am to escort you to the exit. Follow me.' In spite of getting extremely tired of the 'follow me' routine, I did just that. 'Auf Weidersehen,' she said as the guard unlocked the formidable front door.

'Gut bigh...' and she smiled at me.

I thankfully marched down that flight of steps, onto the road, walked a short way and turned the corner towards a waiting UN minibus. I gave a skip and a jump and a Highland fling of sheer joy and relief. *Mission accomplished*, I thought, *Mission accomplished. Everyone will be so pleased. Another small step forward for Pristina University.*

A Right Royal Reflection

2001

The United Nations logo.

The minibus carried half a dozen British Council staff on their way back from an R and R (rest and recreation) trip.

I chose a seat towards the back of the bus, wanting to be away from their happy chattering, in order to think about my recent interview at the Austrian embassy. The ambassador seemed so cold and remote, not what I thought an ambassador's attitude might be. He was so unlike the highly regarded David Slinn, our British representative in Pristina, who was a friendly, likeable chap. I remembered teasing him about his choice of tie at a reception we attended. I couldn't imagine the Austrian ambassador being teased about anything. I moved nearer the window as a bulky young man joined me in my back seat.

I closed my eyes in an effort to indicate I was not in a talking mood. My mind wandered back over the reasons for my interview and request for visas. The two professors that would be our first launch into the public eye were to my mind extremely special.

Professor Kadri Metaj was the first member of the university that I met on my very first visit to Pristina.

He and his colleague were very eager to represent their fellow academics at this important convention in Vienna.

As part of my duties in the rectorat at the university I had a lot of contact with many other professors, and I had become quite friendly with Kadri and his family.

It was his wife who showed me his bloodstained shirt he had been wearing during the peaceful protest against the unfair exclusion of Albanian students from their university in Pristina. He and his professor colleagues had been sitting in protest in the main street up near the Hotel Dea, actually just along from where we were currently staying. Serbian soldiers had been deployed to clear the street of protesters. To achieve this, they brutally beat up some, hauled some off to prison, summarily shot a few and left the rest dead or dying where they fell. Kadri's son, Artan, managed to get up there after dark with a vehicle, bundled him into a truck and took him home to his wife. His severe head wound was treated secretly by a doctor from the university medical faculty and he survived. He showed me the extensive scar just visible across his hairline, living proof of his brush with near death. It was he and his close colleague that had asked for the two visas. There was no way either of them would ever leave Pristina to join the numerous unknown Albanians absorbed into the Austrian population. I involuntarily clutched my briefcase containing those precious visas closer to my chest. My movement attracted the attention of my neighbour. 'You're not with the British Council are you?' he said, looking at me curiously. 'No,' I replied. 'I am with Pristina University.' I examined his dog tags which clearly stated he was with the legal department of the UN.

'I've just had an interesting interview with the Austrian ambassador,' I told him. 'Have you ever met him?'

He lowered his voice. 'I work with Bernard Kouchner,' he said. 'We've been to several meetings with him.'

A very austere – and influential – man.

'He demands all protocol required for his position to be followed exactly. Did you get to meet him?'

'Actually, I'm just pondering on my recent meeting with him. You're absolutely right about the protocol – everybody seems to be calling him "Your Highness". I must say, I thought that was a bit over the top.'

He looked at me curiously. 'Do you know anything about him?' he asked.

'Not much, I mean, only that he was very against handing out visas to anybody. I had an interview with him. He awarded me two,' I replied. 'I'm amazed you were actually granted an audience. He really is a "Highness". He is a descendant of the Archduke Franz Ferdinand who was bumped off in 1914. His murder triggered World War One, if you remember your history. You met Karl Hapsburg-Lothringen himself, he's related to probably the richest and most influential family in Europe.' He looked at me in awe.

'He obviously didn't eat you alive then,' and he suddenly grinned at me. 'No,' I murmured, 'he gave me what I came for.' The image of that hard, unyielding, bearded face came into my mind. His family had had a murder, lost an emperor's throne, and sustained a total change of lifestyle together with exiled parents all within relatively few years. A truly formidable series of traumas for anyone to cope with. I didn't envy his life experiences, his wealth or position. Sometimes there is safety in the lives of the common man. I did feel I understood the granting of those visas to people who had suffered greatly in the name of equality and justice, though, surely he must've empathised with them – and also trusted our assessment of their integrity. My rather resentful impression of the proud, aloof man who gave nothing of his inner thoughts away, giving no clue to his real character, softened at the thought of what he must have suffered. His appointment as Austrian Ambassador was witness to his loyalty to his country that he guarded so carefully against unwanted intruders. I felt privileged to have met him.

* * *

For your further information:

(Bernard Kouchner – French politician and physician known for his involvement in humanitarian efforts. Founder of Médecins sans Frontières. French Minister of Foreign Affairs and Special Representative of the Secretary-General and Head of the United Nations Interim Administration Mission in Kosovo (UNMIK) from 1999 to 2001.

A Judge in the Buff

Late 2001

The Fiji coat of arms.
The translation of the words on the scroll is 'Fear God and Honour the King'.

'Out,' commanded an extremely large, black, uniformed officer. He had waved me into a lay-by as I drove slowly in a traffic queue across the busy Macedonian border, back into Kosovo. He looked grim and unsmiling. '*Lock the doors, close every window and stay put if you are stopped. The Macedonian Police are unscrupulous with foreigners, especially females*,' I'd been told previously. So I hesitated.

'Out,' he commanded more forcefully this time, hand on gun, fortunately, still safe in its holster. I got out, very slowly. Not coming any nearer, he told me to stand straight, hold my arms away from my body and then waved what looked like a table-tennis bat up and down me as I stood there. He then held the bat under the vehicle and moving it slowly from side to side scanned everywhere underneath the chassis. He opened the doors and repeated the performance inside the vehicle leaving me standing there feeling slightly ridiculous with arms and legs still akimbo.

'What are you doing?' I asked. 'What are you looking for?'

He straightened up and looked me directly face to face, he indicated I should stand at ease and replied, 'We are on high alert for arms smugglers. We caught two so far. You clear. No arms here.' And he smiled slightly. 'Where you from?'

'England,' I replied cautiously, wondering if he had a chip on his shoulder about the English.

He grinned, showing extremely white teeth. 'I got good friend, Gor-don, he English.'

'Oh, great,' I said, preparing to get back in the car as quickly as possible, eager to get home. Just slightly curious, I asked, 'Where are you from, I don't recognise your uniform.' 'Fiji,' he replied. I paused, vaguely interested.

'I have friend from England back home,' he went on. 'He tell me stories of English life. I want visit after this is over. I want know more about England. We talk? Now?' He pointed to the small building behind him serving as a custom house café where some UN officers could be seen through the window. 'There, tea?' He looked appealingly at me. 'Only ten minutes, take tea break?'

I was thirsty, I'd had a long drive, there were safe, friendly faces in there. It was momentarily appealing. 'Oh, okay, thanks, but only ten minutes.' I left my car where it was, locked it and duly followed him. He was talking at me all the time as he opened the door and the warm atmosphere and cheerful noise of the canteen hit us. I found a seat, not too far from the UN guys, feeling if necessary I could call on them. 'Wait here, I want hear all about England. I come back quick.' And he disappeared into the crowd at the counter to return with two paper cups filled with hot, very sweet black tea. 'Here, for you.' And taking his hat off, dropping his rifle casually on the floor between us, he sat down. 'Time to talk.'

I sipped the black concoction cautiously, it was so strong I choked and nearly sprayed tea all over his pristine uniform.

'Sorry,' I spluttered, 'it's a bit strong for me, I usually have milk with it too.' I took a breath to allow my scalded tongue to cool... 'What do you want to know?'

'Where you live, near Big Ben?'

'No, not very, I live in a village, near Ashridge forest in a place called Hertfordshire.' And I went on to describe a world so alien to both of us, at that moment, that it seemed like a half-forgotten dream and I found my eyes unexpectedly filling with tears. Suddenly, sharply, I missed my dogs, my horses, my home... I turned my face away for a moment and felt an enormous black hand gently patting my arm. 'I tell you about Gor-don. He very funny,' he said. 'Back home, I police, I work with Gor-don. He very high judge. We friends,' he said proudly, 'he joke and tell stories. We travel round Fiji, he judge, I arrange tent.'

'Tent?' I asked, not quite able to visualise a tented courtroom. 'We move round Fiji, do judging, not too many buildings, so we take tent. People come, we take prisoners back in van to Suva. We go on many boats too. Gor-don very good sailor. It good life but I come here, make money and make peace.' He looked thoughtful for a moment. 'We have more Fijis in Pristina,' he added.

As I listened to him I gradually became aware that many foreign voices emerged from the hubbub around us, people from halfway across the world mingled with us Europeans, here to stop a war. We were all on the same mission, to restore and keep fragile peace. Awesome when you came to think of it, thousands of foreign military and hundreds of people like us, just trying to make things better. I felt a sudden camaraderie... I held out my hand. 'Jeannette, that's my name.' 'Ben,' he replied. 'I Big Ben.'

'Our "Big Ben" is a bell inside a clock, did you know?' I grinned.

'No, no, it clock. I see pictures, it clock,' he insisted. 'Very big like me.' And he laughed, his large frame shaking all over. 'I want visit Gor-don village, tell me where to go? You know Gor-don?' I shook my head, and said, 'Look, Ben, Britain has about sixty million people in it, it would be almost impossible to find him, what is his last name?'

'Not sure, we don't have last names like you, we call him Gor-don Judge. Everyone knows him in Fiji.'

'Sorry, I can't help, but thanks for the drink, it was great meeting you.' I stood up, ready to leave. He looked at me disbelievingly.

'But he come from village too, you must know him. We know everyone in Fiji, we visit every island.'

I sighed, and reluctantly sat again. 'Tell me more about this man, what does he actually do?'

'I have story, make you laugh, listen?'

'Okay.' I nodded.

'We go Vanua Levu island village. No big hall. We set up tent. Gor-don sleep on small bed in tent. We put table, two chairs near bed for Gor-don. He sit on chair with big book. He hear people there. He say, "You go prison, you guilty". Or "You not go prison, you not guilty". Me and my two men put guilty people in van. All finished. Gor-don meet people, they give him much good food, all happy. They like Gor-don. He funny.' I couldn't believe how primitive it all sounded, but all I said was 'What is funny about that?'

'Well,' he continued, 'Gor-don very tired, he sleep deep. He not wake at eight o'clock for judging. My policeman not know that, so he open tent door and people go in and sit quietly on floor to wait for judge to wake. Very quiet, very respectful, lot of people wait. I go sit and wait on chair near bed.

'I get big book ready for judge to read about people there, but I drop it and make noise. Gor-don, he jump awake and jump out of bed, saying bad English word, two times and he angry he late. He sleep in buff he told me. I not know word then. 'Buff, buff,' he said again and grinned. 'But now I do!' And Ben's whole body started to shake at the memory and he laughed a huge laugh. 'He turn round, no clothes on, people stare... he very white.'

'Oh my goodness, what happened then?' I asked.

'Everyone clap and cheer as Gor-don fast took sheet from bed, put it round him then sat on judge chair. I put tea on desk ready. He drank. Then he judge.'

I pictured the scene, no wig, no robes, literally nothing. My mind started working. Gor-don – Gordon, ex-schoolteacher, called to the bar, friend...? Apparently all he did then was raise his hand, all went quiet and that morning's judgements were made by an upright British judge sitting naked on a chair wrapped in a sheet.

No disorder, all good humour with law breakers going to prison. Amazing. Unbelievable. Surely only the Gordon I knew could have done just that. As Ben was speaking, my memory was reaching back into my village bubble, back to the man I knew as Gordon Ward, whose birthday celebrations we'd had at our house, who told stories and jokes in his booming voice and whose big personality made him a popular member of our group of friends. Who'd become a stipendiary judge halfway across the world.

Could it be him Big Ben was talking about...?

'Do you by any chance have a photo of him?' I asked.

He brought out a crumpled news item from the *Fiji Times*, the photo was indistinct but it was definitely our Gordon. There he was in the local rag with details of pardons, names of not guilty and names of guilty. The photo showed a man older than I remembered but the same grin, same eye twinkle, lacking a shirt and tie though, apparently wrapped in an indistinguishable something. The nether part of the photo was mercifully somewhat blurred. I could hardly believe that I could meet someone in Middle Europe, from a tiny island in the North Sea coming from an even tinier island halfway across the world. It must have been a sixty million to one chance (given the population of the UK) he knew someone I knew from my village almost in the centre of that isle situated just off the enormous land mass we call 'the continent'. I looked in awe at this extremely large black man sitting in front of me, giving me news of my old friend living and working in *his* native land. Goosepimply weird.

The whole episode had released the ever present homesickness felt by all of us on that mission.

My large new friend had blinked rapidly as he described the sea round the islands of Fiji. 'I miss sea,' he said. 'I don't sleep with no wave sound.'

'What do you do in your free time, living so far away from home?' I asked. He smiled a smile of pure joy as he replied, 'We sing, we all sing together.'

'Wonderful, so do I, we're singing Mozart. What do you sing?'

'Moz-art,' he repeated, 'don't know that one. We sing of sea. Gor-don, he sing like Cor-ries.' 'Of course.' I smiled reminiscently. I remembered he and Meg, his wife, were great Irish song enthusiasts. 'He loves Irish music and I remember he had a really good voice.'

Eager to hear more tales of Judge Gordon, I said goodbye to Ben, saying, 'I work in the rectorat in Pristina, come to my office and I'll try and make tea like yours. And I'll be happy to talk with you some more, maybe we could sing together!'

He beamed at me. 'I tell Gor-don about you.' I smiled and we shook hands.

I often wonder if Big Ben ever got to visit our little village set at the foot of the Chiltern Hills, in Middle England. I never found out.

Afterthoughts

My travels showed me a world of stark contrasts. From the breathtaking beauty of the coast of Tanzania to the corpses of dead animals on my drive into Pristina, Kosovo. From the sheer delight in the faces of two urchins frying a quail's egg in an old tin can for breakfast on a busy Jakarta street, to the desperate need in the eyes of the mother offering me her tiny girl child for £10.

I had lived my life with my eyes wide shut, cocooned in the security of my family, friends, and my way of life at home – until my first foray abroad.

Visiting famous and historic places such as Paris and Rome became a new-found love. Would I meet Hugo's hunchback of Notre Dame or bump into Sydney Carton from *A Tale of Two Cities* on his way to the guillotine as I sip my café au lait? Is it possible I would really glimpse a solitary lion in the bowels of the Colosseum in Rome? Could I peer into the huge amphitheatre there and watch long-dead slaves fight their last battle?

As my travels expanded to places like Athens, Penang, Jakarta, Dallas, and Albuquerque, my fantasies faded. Numerous encounters with new cultures, languages and people gradually changed my expectations and attitudes. I learned respect for new religions and different ways of living. I made and kept friends from various cultures and felt enriched by the awe-inspiring achievements of other nations.

Some of these experiences, each stored deep in my memory, lent themselves to my tales in 'Nuns, Guns and Disappearing Suns', capturing the essence of my sometimes difficult journey from a sheltered youngster to a seasoned traveller, forever changed by the world I was lucky enough to explore.

The End

Contact details

Sue Mowforth: Facebook Messenger.

Jeannette Marion Ellwood: Facebook Messenger.

Acknowledgements

Sue and Jeannette would like to thank our impressive editor Ian Skewis, www.ianskewis.com for guiding us through the intricacies of producing such a professional finish to our book.

We'd also like to thank the combined young talent of Joss Mowforth and Annette Miller for their creativity in designing the cover and the hand-drawn maps.

I.T. savvy neighbours John Evans and Mike Dawkins have provided sterling help on some technical issues for which we are really grateful.

Sue would also like to thank her friend, the naturalist and author Zai Whitaker for providing some extra insights into the life of members of the Irula tribe in the chapter *Healing Herbs and Sacred Snakes*.

References

All photos and images used in this book belong to the authors with the exception of the following:

Maps from *Hitch-hike to the Gods* and *A Disappearing Sun* by Annette Miller.

Map from *Memories are Made of This* courtesy of a free vector from Wikipedia. Coat of arms from *A Judge in the Buff* also courtesy of a free vector from Wikipedia.

Photos from *Healing Herbs and Sacred Snakes* accredited to the Madras Crocodile Bank Archives, India.

Photos from *Sighs, Smiles and a Restless Heart, First Foray, A Different World, The Lone Star State, Memories are Made of This, One Surprise After Another, Blind Encounter, A Greek Soldier, A Right Royal Meeting* and *A Right Royal Reflection* are courtesy of free photos and vectors from Pixabay.

Photo from *One Surprise After Another* by Peter Ellwood.

Photo from *My Girl Daxi* courtesy of Tarcani Gundogs.

www.ingramcontent.com/pod-product-compliance
Ingram Content Group UK Ltd.
Pitfield, Milton Keynes, MK11 3LW, UK
UKHW052108170125
453711UK00015B/86

9 781787 920804